Andrew Linn

Hay- on- Wye

1996

ELEMENTS OF GENERAL PHONETICS

ELEMENTS OF
GENERAL PHONETICS

DAVID ABERCROMBIE

EDINBURGH
UNIVERSITY PRESS

© 1967
David Abercrombie
EDINBURGH UNIVERSITY PRESS
22 George Square, Edinburgh

By the same author
Problems and Principles in Language Study
Longmans 1956
English Phonetic Texts
Faber & Faber 1964
Studies in Phonetics and Linguistics
OUP 1965
Printed in Great Britain by
Lewis Reprints Ltd.,
(member of the Brown Knight & Truscott Group)
London and Tonbridge
Reprinted 1968, 1970, 1971, 1972, 1973, 1974, 1975
ISBN 0 85224 028 7

Foreword

This book, which is based on the teaching given in the Ordinary Course in Phonetics at Edinburgh University, is intended to provide an introduction to the subject as traditionally understood and practised in Britain: it deals, that is to say, with phonetics as part of general linguistics. I hope I have been able to show that it is possible to present the subject, or at least its elements, without disfiguring the text with the somewhat repulsive diagrams of the vocal organs and the exotic phonetic symbols which, for the general reader, are apt to make it seem unattractive. Although the book is on general phonetics, I have as far as possible taken my examples from English.

My debt to the great phoneticians of the English-speaking tradition—Alexander Melville Bell, Alexander J. Ellis, Henry Sweet, Daniel Jones, Kenneth Lee Pike—must be apparent on nearly every page. I am indebted for help of various sorts to many friends and colleagues as well. I owe especial thanks to Lindsay Criper and Peter Ladefoged, who persuaded me to write the book in the first place, and who provided constant advice and criticism while it was being written. Particularly useful were lengthy and detailed comments on a number of chapters from three colleagues—T. T. S. Ingram, John Sinclair and David West—working in fields other than phonetics, and I am most grateful to them for taking such pains. I have been able to avail myself of criticisms from K. H. Albrow, Trevor Hill, Mrs Wendy Hilling, L. A. Iles, W. E. Jones, Mrs Jean Petrie, Peter Strevens and Mrs Elizabeth Uldall. My wife read and criticized the manuscript in all its stages. I was most fortunate in being able to have the book indexed by L. A. Iles, and in having help with the diagrams from Mrs June Baker. Miss Mary Macintyre, Mrs Grace Stobie and Miss Alice Ainslie typed innumerable drafts of the book. To all of these I would like to offer my very best thanks.

David Abercrombie
Edinburgh, October 1966

Contents

I

Introduction

1. *Language and medium*

The best way of introducing the subject of phonetics, and of making clear what it deals with, is to draw a distinction between *language* and *medium*. This is a distinction which is not popularly made, and is not immediately obvious, but a concrete illustration should make it clear.

If we compare a piece of written English with a piece of spoken English, regarding them simply as physical objects or events and forgetting for the moment the fact that they convey meaning to us, it is apparent at once that they bear no resemblance to each other whatever. The piece of written English consists of groups of small black marks arranged on a white surface, while the piece of spoken English consists of a succession of constantly varying noises. It would hardly be possible for two things to be more different. However, we have only to recall the fact that both of them convey meaning, to be in no doubt that, utterly dissimilar as they may be, they are both equally English. As soon as we make explicit this identity lying behind the complete difference, we have in fact drawn the distinction in question: we have recognized, in effect, that the piece of spoken English and the piece of written English are the same *language* embodied in different *mediums*, one medium consisting of shapes, the other of noises.

It is possible for the same language to be conveyed by different mediums because the language itself lies in the *patterns* which the mediums form, and not in the physical objects or events, as such, of which the mediums consist. When we distinguish language from medium, what we are doing is to distinguish a pattern from its material embodiment, of which, in a sense, it is independent. Language, we could say, is *form*, while the medium is *substance*.

In addition to the property of being able to form patterns which can carry language, a medium has its own independent properties as well. A written word, in addition to being a word, is also a shape like any other shape, and a spoken word, in addition to being a word, is also a sound like any other sound; and the mediums have the properties which all shapes or all sounds have, including, for instance, aesthetic properties. Moreover a written word or a spoken word is a product of human activity, an artefact. It has further properties which derive from this: the mediums are not only created by human activity, but they bear on them the stamp of the personality which created them. Most institutionalized activity of human beings indirectly reveals such things as mood, social status, geographical origins, and so on, and language mediums also have the property of doing this.

A medium, therefore, is not in itself language; it is a vehicle for language. *Linguistics* is the discipline which occupies itself with the study of language. But a language-medium is itself a many-sided enough thing to deserve to be an object of study in its own right. Among the aspects of a medium which merit investigation are, for example, the way in which it is organized into patterns to act as a carrier of language; its physical and aesthetic properties; its relation to other mediums; its relation to the language it carries; the kind of bodily movements involved in its production; and the extent to which it acts as an index to characteristics of the person who makes the producing movements. The study of the medium of *spoken* language, in all its aspects and all its varieties, constitutes the subject of *Phonetics*. Phonetics is concerned with the medium as used in speaking all human languages (whether 'primitive' or 'civilized'), and as used in all styles of speech (whether supposed to be good or bad, normal or abnormal). Phonetics and Linguistics, it has been said, together constitute 'the linguistic sciences'.[1]

The reason why the medium of spoken language has a subject all to itself, when no one single subject has arisen which embraces every aspect at once of the medium of written language (though some subjects–typography, graphology, palaeography, and so on–deal with selected aspects of it)[2], is largely because of the exceptional importance of the former as a medium; not only is it used more than any other, but it is also ultimately the basis on which all other mediums are constructed. Both in the mechanism of its production and in the manner of its perception, moreover, it is extremely complex. Finally, it needs special attention because of the extent to which technological progress during the last century has supplemented the resources of the medium by means of various mechanical and electronic devices. Such things as the telephone, the radio, recording machines and deaf aids, raise many problems of communication that are primarily phonetic problems.

2. *Aural, visual, and other mediums*

One thing all mediums have in common is that they *mediate* between the producer and the receiver of language. Thus every medium has associated with it two sorts of human activity: a producing activity from which the medium results, and a receiving activity by which the medium is apprehended. The first involves acts of mobile organs, the second involves acts of a perceiving sense. When one person communicates with another by language, the activity of the former is not *directly* perceived by the latter. What is perceived, and what effects the communication, is the *product* of the activity, the artefact, either noises or shapes–the medium, that is to say. The contact is indirect.

So far two language mediums have been mentioned, one for language in its normal spoken mode, and one for language in its normal written mode. Each is produced by a different sort of muscular activity, and each is addressed to a different sense. The medium of language in its spoken mode is created by movements of lips, tongue, larynx, lungs, and other organs, and is addressed to the ear. The medium of language in its written mode is created by movements of hand, arm and fingers, and is addressed to the eye. These two mediums (which may be called the *aural* medium and the *visual* medium respectively, according to the sense to which each is addressed) are the best known and by far the most widely used; but other language-mediums are possible. Theoretically there could be a language-medium addressed to any one of the human senses, though it is not very likely that either the sense of taste or the sense of smell could be put to much practical use for this purpose–the problems of organizing a smell-medium or a taste-medium into sufficiently differentiated patterns would be very great.

One sense, however, is well adapted to provide another medium, and that is the sense of *touch*. Such a medium is, in fact, extensively used by the blind in the form of Braille, Moon and similar systems: shapes or dots are embossed in patterns on paper, and 'read' by running the finger-tips over them. This is a *tactile*, or *haptic*, medium.

Another possible sense to which a language-medium could be addressed is the sense of *pressure-variation*, and experiments are at present being carried on in various places in the use of such a medium. Some success has been had with what has been called (not very happily) the 'hearing glove', which is an apparatus by means of which rapid variations in pressure can be applied to the fingers, the variations forming patterns which can be made to convey language.

It is still not perfected, however.[3] (The producing activity of the medium, as we shall see later, may be, and sometimes–as in the present case–must be, carried out with the help of instruments, such as, to take the simplest example, a pen. The receiving activity may also be assisted by auxiliary devices.)

All mediums also have in common their capability of being organized into patterns. They do not necessarily have in common, however, the *mode* of organization of their patterns. The marks which carry written language are shaped and arranged in such a way that they form patterns in *space*, but the noises which carry spoken language are arranged in such a way that they form patterns in *time*. All mediums are either spatially organized, with patterns in space, or temporally organized, with patterns in time. The tactile medium, like the visual, is a spatial one; its patterns, however, must necessarily be three-dimensional, whereas the patterns of the visual medium are only two-dimensional. A medium addressed to the sense of pressure-variation would have to be a temporal medium.

Although mankind existed for a very long time with only a single language-medium, the aural one, the advantages of having two mediums at one's disposal are manifest. Language has many different functions to fulfil in society, especially in civilized society. There are some circumstances in which the visual medium, because it is spatially organized, conveys language to best advantage, and other circumstances in which the aural one, being temporal, does so. They complement each other. The visual medium is slow and relatively laborious to produce, but on the other hand it is long-lasting and can be transported anywhere; these are the characteristics to be expected of a spatial medium. The aural medium is ephemeral and limited in range, but on the other hand it can be produced rapidly and easily, which are characteristics one would expect a temporal medium to have. These properties make the visual medium ideally suited to official announcements, public notices, and record purposes in general, whereas the aural medium is ideally suited to the ordinary every-day mixing of human beings.

To be blind or to be deaf is therefore a serious linguistic handicap. A blind person is unable to be a recipient of the usual spatial medium, and a deaf person is similarly cut off from the usual temporal medium. This is why other mediums, addressed to other senses, have been sought: the point of a tactile medium is that, as a spatial medium, it has comparable properties to, and can act as a substitute for, the visual one lost to the blind; and it is hoped that a pressure-variation medium, being a temporal one, will similarly take the place of the aural medium lost to the deaf.

3. *Properties of the medium: indexical*

The most important property possessed by a medium, of course, is that it can be formed into patterns (in space or time) which are complex and varied enough to carry language. The complexity and variety of the patterns needed for this are very considerable. Nevertheless the pattern-forming potentialities of a medium are much greater than any one language requires to use, as is shown by the astonishing diversity in the way the possibilities of the mediums are exploited by different peoples. There are hundreds of sorts of scripts in existence in the world, and there are as many ways of pronouncing as there are languages. Each script, each way of pronouncing, represents a small selection of patterns from the medium's great total resources as a language vehicle. Even the tactile medium has developed quite a variety of forms, although it is only three and a half centuries since experiment with it first started, and no more than 150 years since the publication (in Edinburgh) of the first book produced in it.

Thus a medium is far from completely absorbed by being a vehicle for a specific language. There is always a certain amount of play, as it were, within the limits of the patterns; all that is necessary for linguistic communication is that the contrasts on which the patterns are based should not be obscured. Usually, therefore, many things about a medium which is being used as vehicle for a given language are not relevant to linguistic communication. Such 'extra-linguistic' properties of the medium, however, may fulfil other functions which may sometimes even be more important than linguistic communication, and which can never be completely ignored. These properties are best illustrated from the two most familiar, the aural and the visual, mediums, though what is said of them would be doubtless true of any other medium which may ever come into use.

A medium is not just a physical object; as has already been observed, it is an artefact – a physical object which is brought into being by human activity; and from this fact spring some of the medium's most interesting extra-linguistic properties, and ones which can play an influential part in human relations. When we first meet people, the opinions we form of them are based to quite a large extent on the sorts of movements they make when they are walking, eating, gesticulating, and so on; we interpret their habitual ways of making movements as clues to the kind of people they are (we may or may not be aware that we are doing this). The sorts of movements they make for the purposes of talking and writing also provide clues of the same kind, but in these cases we take the clues, not from observation of the actual movements themselves, but from the resulting artefact, the medium; its physical form preserves in it the characteristics of the movements, or *gestures* as they could fittingly be called, which create it. Handwriting, it has been said, is 'inscribed gesture',[4] and pronunciation may equally aptly be said to be 'audible gesture'; and as such both carry signs which reveal personal characteristics of the writer or speaker. The medium, not being completely taken up by carrying the patterns which convey language, is thus able at the same time to accommodate a quite separate complex system of non-linguistic signs.

A sign of this sort may be called an *index*, and the features of the medium which carry such indices may be called its *indexical* features, as distinct from its *linguistic* features.[5] Perhaps the most famous illustration of what an important part indexical features can play in human relations is provided by the well-known occasion when the Ephraimites were trying to get past the Gileadites and over the river Jordan without revealing their identity.

> And the Gileadites took the passages of Jordan before the Ephraimites: and it was so that when those Ephraimites which were escaped said, Let me go over, that the men of Gilead said unto him, Art thou an Ephraimite? If he said Nay: then said they unto him, Say now, Shibboleth: and he said Sibboleth: for he could not frame to pronounce it right. Then they took him, and slew him at the passages of Jordan: and there fell at that time of the Ephraimites, forty and two thousand.[6]

Both sides spoke Hebrew, but the Ephraimites unwittingly, and fatally, disclosed their geographical origins by an indexical feature of their speech–the distinctive consonant which they used at the beginning of the word 'shibboleth', and doubtless in many other words too. Since that time the word 'shibboleth', although it has taken on other meanings as well, has been used in many languages for any peculiarity of pronunciation which is an index to a person's origins.

Some of the indexical features present in any one person's speech or handwriting will have been learnt from, and hence must be shared with, other people; while some are not learnt and are therefore individual and personal. Of the features which are shared with others, some will be shared with a few people, some with sizeable groups, and some with whole nations, or even groupings bigger than national ones. Nobody speaks always in the same way, moreover, and therefore while some indexical features are always present in a person's pronunciation or handwriting, others appear only from time to time.

There is a recognized name, 'graphology', for the study of the indexical properties of the visual medium and their interpretation. It has received the serious attention of psychologists,[7] and some people are quite expert at it: they can make very accurate judgements about sex, age, and character from handwriting. Graphologists have mostly been interested in indices which are individual and personal, rather than in those shared with (and therefore indicating membership of) groups of people, though the latter also are undoubtedly present in handwriting: nationality, for instance, is usually clearly revealed.

There is no accepted name for the study and interpretation of the indexical properties of the aural medium, probably because, while not many people practise graphology, everybody practises this latter; experts in this field do not need to be singled out. It is hardly possible to misinterpret the clues to sex and age which are contained in pronunciation, and nearly everyone is a passable expert at finding clues to personality and temper there. The indexical properties of the aural medium which arouse the greatest interest, in contrast to the visual medium, are probably those that indicate social rather than individual characteristics. However, the aural medium probably functions indexically more subtly and in a more pervasive way than any other kind of human behaviour. When we are with people whom we know, we constantly adjust ourselves to their moods by interpreting (unconsciously perhaps) variations in their manner of speaking, and we make immediate judgements on strangers, when we meet them, based far more on the way they talk than on what they talk about.

It is possible to make a rough division of the indices which are present in pronunciation into three classes, according to the kinds of things to which they refer:

(*a*) those that indicate membership of a group;
(*b*) those that characterize the individual;
(*c*) those that reveal changing states of the speaker.

As a few illustrations will show, this classification could be considerably elaborated; however, it is sufficient for our present purposes.[8] A similar division can also be made of the indices present in handwriting. Some examples follow.

(*a*) Almost all speakers of all languages have, as the Ephraimites had, *regional indices* in their pronunciation. These indices are shared by members of a community living in a particular locality, and in some parts of the world they give very precise indications of whereabouts a person was brought up; this is the case, for example, among speakers of Scots Gaelic. Other parts of the world, however, such as the Middle West of America, show very little regional differentiation in pronunciation over large areas. The word 'accent', in its popular sense, is usually used to refer to these regional indices. Professor Henry Higgins, the hero of *Pygmalion* and of *My Fair Lady*, was an expert at placing people by their accents, and most phoneticians are fairly good at it. But many non-phoneticians are good at identifying regional indices too.

Not all groups which have indices associated with them are based on locality. There are some communities in which pronunciation carries indices of social standing as well as of geographical origins. It certainly does so in England, and is reported to do so in other places–Israel, for example.[9] In other communities, however, such *status indices* appear to be entirely lacking; they are not found in the Gaelic-speaking parts of Scotland, nor in the Middle West of America. There are, in addition to social classes, other kinds of groups, not based on locality, which may–less commonly perhaps–have indices associated with them. In certain communities, for example, women have a different pronunciation from men, and in other communities indexical features accompany certain occupations.

All these indices to social characteristics, of course, are learnt from others, and are relatively permanent features of a person's pronunciation. It is perhaps more useful to use the word 'accent' to refer to all of them together, rather than to regional indices alone, and we will adopt the word as a technical term in that sense. Accent, then, could be defined as that aspect of a person's pronunciation which excludes, on the one hand, everything he has in common with all other speakers of the language, and on the other hand everything that comes under the two other classes of indices, (*b*) and (*c*). No two people speak alike, but many people speak with the same accent. Those who do so may be said to form an 'accent community'. The members of an accent community are bound together by the feeling that indices of class (*a*) unite rather than separate them.

(*b*) Indices that characterize the individual may be called *idiosyncratic*. Idiosyncratic indices enable us to recognize someone by voice alone–over the telephone, for instance, or in the dark. They are not usually learnt from other people; many of them, as a matter of fact, arise directly from physical causes, and so are outside the speaker's control. Signs in speech of sex and of age are indices of this sort, and so are the effects of abnormalities such as a cleft palate. There are other idiosyncratic indices which are often supposed to be outside the speaker's control, but which in reality really are not so: lisps, for example. These, and similar 'speech defects', are usually infantile habits which have persisted into adult life, and which can theoretically be changed at any time (if the speaker really desires to do so). However, idiosyncratic indices are seldom as obvious and as easily identified as the above instances. They are usually far more difficult to make explicit–and much more potent in their expression of individuality. A lot of research is still to be done on their identification and description.

An idiosyncratic feature must be judged to be such in relation to the speech of the community to which the speaker belongs. Thus in most parts of England a 'burr' (a 'voiced uvular fricative'; see ch. 4) for an *r* is idiosyncratic; but in the neighbourhood of Durham it is a normal feature of the speech of the community (and therefore a regional index in relation to the country as a whole).

(*c*) We can tell if someone is talking with his mouth full without looking at him. This is an extreme example of those indexical features which are not present all the time in a person's pronunciation, but come and go according to his physical or mental state. Other such indices accompany conditions such as fatigue, excitement, catarrh, grief, over-consumption of alcohol, nervousness. Physical states which directly affect the operation of the vocal organs naturally produce indices automatically; on the whole, however, these are not of very much interest, largely because other indications are often available of the states in question. More interesting are those indices that do not have a direct physical cause, those from which we infer feelings such as amusement, anger, contempt, sympathy, suspicion, and everything else that may be included under 'tone of voice'. Indices of this kind are probably more commonly learnt from other people than is generally believed: they are for the most part conventional rather than instinctive expressions of mood and emotion. They are particularly interesting, both to the linguist and to the man in the street, because on occasion they may convey, wittingly or unwittingly, an impression entirely different from that conveyed by the actual words which they accompany.

We usually interpret these *affective indices* very accurately when we hear them from people belonging to our own culture; from people belonging to other cultures, however, we can sometimes be disconcertingly wrong.

It is the business of Phonetics to identify and to describe these various indexical features which are present in pronunciation, but it is of course the business of other disciplines to investigate the part they play in human relationships.

4. *Properties of the medium: aesthetic*

Many attributes of a language-medium play little or no part in forming linguistic patterns or in carrying indexical features. The *scale* of the medium–the size of the shapes or the degree of loudness of the sounds–is an example. All that is needed for communication is that the shapes should be large enough to be recognizable and the sounds loud enough to be audible; beyond that, scale is free to be governed by whatever other considerations may seem important. Similarly, if linguistic patterns are to be apparent, the shapes of the visual medium must be distinct from their background; but the way in which this is brought about does not matter. Written language was described above as 'black marks on a white surface', but the marks do not, of course, really have to be black, nor the background white; white marks on black, or marks of any other colour on a suitably contrasting background, will do just as well. There may, indeed, be no contrast of colour at all; the shapes may be incised, or they may equally well be embossed. The manner in which shapes are distinguished from background will not affect the medium as a language vehicle, and can therefore be allowed to depend on the convenience of the moment or on what is most effective for decorative or other aesthetic purposes.

Although a medium's aesthetic aspects are in general more or less independent of its linguistic and indexical functions, people have always found them of the greatest interest and have often carefully cultivated them, particularly the musical properties possessed by the aural medium and the properties of design possessed by the visual medium. All literate peoples have a tradition of calligraphy, for instance. Chinese writing is probably the outstanding example of a script whose aesthetic possibilities have been exploited to the full, and Egyptian hieroglyphs also are obviously consciously decorative. Sometimes indeed the aesthetic aspect of a script comes to be valued more highly than its capability of communicating: some types of Arabic writing, for example, are very beautiful, but very difficult to read. In any case, it is not always a good thing for communication to be too easy. It can certainly be annoying to find, in something which it is important to read, that the letter-shapes have been so distorted for decorative purposes that the language patterns are almost submerged; but at the same time it has been pointed out that 'if all the lettering visible in our streets were immediately and compellingly legible, it would create a nightmare'.[10] With architectural lettering, at least, the first consideration must be design rather than legibility.

The aural medium consists of a good deal of sheer noise, but it has considerable musical properties also, notably *rhythm*, and also pitch variation or *melody*. It contains in addition constant fluctuations in sound quality or *tamber* (or *timbre*: also known as *tone-colour*[11]) which can be put to use for various aesthetic effects, such as rhyme, assonance, and alliteration. These musical properties of the medium have been exploited by poets in all languages, and they are nowadays also the object of attention of advertising copywriters and composers of political slogans. Some verse, and most political slogans and advertising catch-phrases, depend for their effectiveness as much on the 'incantatory' aspects of the medium as on the meaning which it carries. Notice the use of rhythm and alliteration in, for example:

'One man, one vote'
'Players please'
'Builds bonny babies'
'Workers of the world unite'
'Guinness is good for you'
'Du bo du bon Dubonnet'.

Poets, orators, calligraphers may make use of a medium in such a way that the results are generally admitted to be more beautiful than those produced by the ordinary person; but whether the ordinary everyday use of a medium for one particular language or dialect can be said to be more beautiful (or more ugly) than its use for another is a matter of almost universal dispute; and so even is whether one word, in its visual or in its aural form, can be more beautiful than other words within the same language. Discussion is easier, and some measure of common agreement more likely, when it is the visual medium that is concerned, though even here it is clear that what is considered beautiful at any one time is largely a matter of taste and fashion, as shown by the changes which scripts undergo. It is more difficult for us to discuss the aural medium dispassionately, for this is to an even greater extent a matter of taste, fashion and association, though it is the subject of endless, if inconclusive, argument. Is the sound of French inherently more beautiful than the sound of Zulu? Is a Cockney accent more ugly than that of a Guards officer, or of a Cornish fisherman? Is the sound of the word 'ermine' more beautiful than the sound of the word 'vermin', and if so why? These and similar questions are often disputed passionately, but objectivity on such points is not easy to attain, and they must nearly always remain a matter of opinion. The Danish for 'pretty girls' is 'smukke piger'. Many English speakers would feel that this is hardly a worthy way of referring to them, though the Danes doubtless feel it quite a suitable one. There is no doubt that apparent aesthetic judgements on the use of a medium are often in fact quite unconnected with sound or appearance as such, and are often based on chance associations, or on what we are used to.[12]

It has often been pointed out that language signs are *arbitrary*, in the sense that there is no reason why the mediums in which they are embodied should give them any one shape or sound rather than any other.[13] This is the same thing as saying that there is no necessary connexion between medium and meaning. It is true that when we are as thoroughly familiar with a language as we are with our mother tongue, it is difficult to bring ourselves really to believe that its words are arbitrary; they seem somehow inherently suited to their meanings, either in shape or sound or both. Most English-speaking people feel a sneaking sympathy, although they know they are meant to laugh at him, with the farmer in the well-known story who, looking over the wall of his sty, observed 'rightly is they called pigs' (just as pretty girls, they feel, are wrongly called 'smukke piger'). The feeling of the inherent aptness of the words of one's own language is deeply en-grained in most people – it accounts, for example, for some of the widespread popular hostility to spelling reform, which seems to be bound to have the result of making the shapes of words less suited to their meanings and thus depriving them of part of their effectiveness. Nevertheless it is not very difficult to demonstrate that this feeling, strong as it is, is almost entirely an illusion: 'cheval', 'pferd' and 'horse' can hardly all equally be inherently apt ways of referring to the same animal. The arbitrariness of language signs has to be ac-cepted as a general principle in linguistics.

Nevertheless, it has also to be admitted that there are times when the physical properties of the medium do make language signs appear to be not entirely arbitrary. In the aural medium this is shown, for instance, by Tennyson's lines, often quoted in this connexion,

> The moan of doves in immemorial elms,
> And murmuring of innumerable bees,

where the choice and arrangement of words is such that they produce when they are spoken, sounds reminiscent of the actual sounds to which the words refer; there seems here to be a direct and immediate link, rather than an arbitrary relation between the medium carrying the language signs and the things which the language signs stand for. In the visual medium something of the same kind can be found in the Mouse's Tale in *Alice in Wonderland*, where the words are arranged on the page in such a way that the shape they produce looks like a mouse's tail – the medium makes a sort of pun on the subject matter.

The direct link between medium and meaning, in these two last examples, lies in the *cumulative* effect of the look or sound of the words. Taken in isolation, the words fail, for the most part, to provide any such connexion: the sound of the word 'immemorial', for exam-ple, though it contributes to the total effect of these particular lines, bears no resemblance to the word's meaning. As a separate linguistic sign it is still arbitrary, and so are most of the other words in the couplet. Not all, however: the sound of 'murmuring' is in itself reminiscent of the sound to which the word refers (and, with some imagination and good will, we might feel the same thing to be true of 'moan'). Here there *is* a connexion between medium and meaning when the word is taken in isolation, and this relationship is what is meant by onomatopoeia. Onomatopes, or words whose sound has some association with their meaning, and which are therefore not arbitrary as language signs, occur in all languages. Examples from English are 'sizzle', 'clang', 'whack', 'cuckoo', 'bobolink', and many more names for types of noises or for things which make noises. The similarity between medium and meaning, it must be admitted, is mostly fairly tenuous, and if we did not already know the meaning of the word it would certainly not be obvious. Onomatopes with the same meaning in different languages do not sound very much like each other.

No recognized term exists for what might be called 'visual onomatopoeia'–a direct connexion between the *look* of a word and its meaning; but it is not difficult to see that such a relationship can exist. If we were to print the lines from Macbeth:

The multitudinous seas incarnadine,
Making the green one red.

with the word *green* in green ink and the word *red* in red ink, this would provide a direct link between visual medium and meaning which would be parallel to the link between aural medium and meaning provided by onomatopoeia.[14] Illustrations of the *shape* of a word providing such a link are not easy to produce from alphabetic writing systems (such as Roman, Cyrillic, or Greek), though there may occasionally be a word like 'zigzag' to be found which has something appropriate in the form of its letters. In other systems of writing, however, the design and structure of the shapes that compose the medium are quite often evocative of some aspect of whatever the words refer to. Chinese characters and Egyptian hieroglyphs are particularly good examples.

The aural medium may sometimes be evocative in ways that are more subtle than by simply providing an echo of a noise. Parts of words, even single sounds, may sometimes appear to have a symbolic value, though it is not always easy to explain why. A sixteenth-century Cambridge man claimed that the difference between a pretty girl and a plain one could be appropriately expressed by a change of vowel: 'si pulchra est *virgo*, sin turpis *vurgo* vocetur', or as translated by a later writer, 'let handsome girls be called *virgins*, plain ones *vurgins*'.[15] It has often been remarked that in many languages adjectives meaning 'small' have an *i*-like vowel, while adjectives meaning 'big' have an *a*- or *o*-like vowel: Greek 'mikros' and 'makros' are well-known examples (and English 'big' and 'small' well-known exceptions). We often find, moreover, pairs of words such as, in English, 'clink' and 'clank', 'slit' and 'slot', which have something in common in their meaning and their sound, but where a difference of size or intensity in the former is accompanied by this same opposition of vowel quality. It has been suggested that the effectiveness of this 'vowel antiphony', as it has been called, derives probably from the sensation produced by the bodily movements that produce the sound of the medium rather than from the actual sound itself: the tongue leaves a very small space in the mouth for 'i', but a large one for 'a'.[16]

If it really has a basis in articulatory movements, then the symbolism of this vowel antiphony could be expected to be universally valid. Examples of it, certainly, have been found in a large number of languages. However that may be, other instances of the properties of the aural medium seeming to possess symbolic power are almost certainly valid only within a given language. George Dalgarno, writing in the seventeenth century, said that 'there is something Symbolizing, and Analogous to the notions of the things' in the spoken form of words such as 'grumble', 'tumble', 'crumble', 'jumble', 'fumble', 'stumble', 'bumble', 'mumble'.[17] It would probably be agreed that all, or most, of these words have in common not only an element of sound but also something in their meaning, or perhaps we should rather say in the contexts of experience and situation in which they are used, which it is not easy to make explicit. There is nothing intrinsic in the common element of sound to connect it with the shared meaning, and it would be rash to suppose that we have here an instance of inherent sound symbolism, or synaesthesia (the linking of sensations from one sense with those from another). The common element of sound provides an echo, not of the objects of discourse, but of other words. Whenever a word containing, for instance, '-umble' is used it is supported or reinforced by the presence, in the 'unconscious background', of all the other words which contain the same sound sequence and occur in similar contexts. The whole group of words has a 'cumulative suggestive value'. Another illustration of a group of this sort is the series of words 'slouch', 'slack', 'slink', 'sloppy', 'sluggard', 'slut', 'sloth', 'slur', and others, all of which begin with *sl-*, and share a rather vague pejorative meaning. A word may belong to two groups simultaneously: 'flare' is associated, on the one hand, with 'flame', 'flash', 'flicker', and on the other with 'blare', 'glare', 'stare'.[18] Such groups of mutually reinforcing words probably exist in all languages. In all languages also we can find examples of *occasional* reinforcement of meaning, when a particular context links a word with other phonetically similar words which could be appropriate to the occasion, and which therefore form an unspoken background. The line,

Crossing the stripling Thames at Bablockhithe,

has more than once been quoted as one in which sound is especially suited to sense, this being attributed to the effect of the repeated *s*'s and *l*'s which are said to echo the sound of a running brook. It is much more likely, however, that the effectiveness of the line is due to the reminiscences of 'rippling' and 'babble' in stripling and Bablockhithe. All these various *phonaesthetic* aspects of the medium have been written about by many people, and have probably been best dealt with by J. R. Firth.[19]

5. *Auxiliary devices*

We have seen that the medium always has associated with it a producing activity and a receiving activity, and it has already been remarked that the first of these activities may, and indeed sometimes must, be carried out with the help of instruments. It *is* possible to write with the finger in, say, sand; but some sort of implement—brush, stylus, pencil, pen–has nearly always been used in its production throughout the whole history of the visual medium. Occasionally adjuncts to the aural medium too have been used, though only in special circumstances: a megaphone, for example, or a speaking tube, or an ear-trumpet. Subsequent invention has brought about various improvements in these auxiliary devices, as the fountain-pen and the electrically amplified loud-hailer show. But even in their most modern developments such things are still *tools*, extensions of the human body: a pen or a pencil is an extension of the hand, a megaphone an extension of the mouth. The producing movements of the body are still immediately connected with the production of the medium.

The technological developments of the Machine Age have had their influence on language mediums as on everything else. The last five centuries have seen the invention and introduction into the communication process of auxiliary devices of a different sort–not tools, but machines; they have complicated the simple and original form of the process, but have augmented very considerably its potentialities. These auxiliary devices are either mechanical in the strict sense of the word or, more recently, electronic. Their introduction into the process is radically different from the introduction of a tool–they are not simple extensions of the human body, but directly intervene between the medium and the bodily activities associated with it. An obvious example of technological progress in this field is the invention of printing from movable types, and another is the discovery of sound-recording. As can be seen from these examples, there are two ways in which such a machine can be introduced into the communication process. Either the auxiliary device may be interposed between the producing activity and the medium itself, as it is in printing, and in this case the medium is no longer directly created, or the auxiliary device may be interposed between the medium and the receiving activity, as it is in sound-recording, and in this case the medium is no longer directly perceived.

In the first case the usual producing activity is replaced by movements which do not create an artefact but operate a machine. The machine itself then creates the medium so that the latter is no longer 'hand-made', so to speak. The operation of Linotype, Monotype or Teletype machines, or of typewriters, or setting print from movable types, illustrates this. These machines all require bodily movements of a very different sort from those required by writing by hand with an implement. With some of them the producing activity becomes somewhat laborious, and it may lack that unconscious and 'automatic' nature which a medium-producing activity usually has (though this characteristic is certainly present in the movements of a skilled Linotype operator, for example, or a typist). The act of perception of the medium, however, is unaffected by this, and is in no way different from the perception of the visual medium when directly created.

In the second case both the producing and the receiving activities remain unchanged, but although the producing activity creates the medium as usual, the interposed device has the effect of recreating the medium in one way or another for the perceiver. Sound-recording, the telephone, the radio, hearing-aids, are all examples of this, and they are all relatively recent inventions.

It is interesting to note that, until not very long ago, auxiliary devices of the first sort, placed immediately after the producing activity, were always associated with the visual medium; while those of the second sort, placed immediately before the receiving activity, were all associated with the aural medium. Since the war, however, auxiliary devices have become possible which are placed immediately after the producing activity and yet are concerned with the aural medium, and bring about its 'indirect' creation. The result is *synthetic* speech, and its production is analogous to the indirect creation of the visual medium by printing. The construction of machines which will make synthetic speech is the object of research in several places at the present moment, and considerable progress has been made in it.

Some of these machines are able to simulate human speech with remarkable accuracy. The machine at Edinburgh University, known as PAT,[20] can be made to speak continuously for as long as a minute, and it has produced utterances in half-a-dozen different languages. Machines of this kind are used as instruments of research into various aspects of speech, and they also have important applications to the problems of telecommunications.

The next important advance in auxiliary devices will probably lie in a rather unexpected development of the second sort, those interposed between the medium and the perceiving activity. Devices are beginning to be worked out that will automatically convert one medium into another: they will make the aural medium visible, for instance, so that it can be read, or the visual medium audible, so that it can be listened to. One such machine, if perfected, would type out what you said when you spoke at it; another, when a printed page was put before it, would produce intelligible sounds. Some progress has already been made with such machines, though the difficulties still to be overcome are considerable. Enough, however, has already been done to show that they are well within the bounds of possibility. The device described above and called the 'hearing glove' will ultimately also be a device of this sort, for its greatest usefulness would lie in automatically converting the aural medium into a pressure-variation medium. The benefits to the deaf and the blind of all these devices, if they can be made to work successfully, are obvious.

6. *Medium and language*

Up to this point we have spoken as if the mediums were in all respects equal. There is one respect, however, in which this is not quite true. All known writing systems were created by first making an analysis of the aural medium and then allotting the visual signs to the units that result from this analysis. From the historical point of view, therefore, the visual medium has to be considered secondary to, because it is based on, the aural medium. It seems to be the case, in fact, that every medium except the aural must necessarily be derivative in this way, and a medium may sometimes be derivative at two removes: the haptic medium, as exemplified by Braille, for instance, is itself based on the visual medium.

Thus the aural medium came first, and in this genetic sense it is primary compared to all other mediums, including potential ones which do not yet exist. Can it be said that the aural medium is primary in any other than a genetic sense? Probably not. Once another medium, a visual one for example, has been created, it will assume full autonomy as a vehicle for language. A written sentence needs no translation into spoken language in order to be understood by those who are fully literate, and it does not first have to be spoken before it can be written down. Although it is true to say that the visual medium is a reflection of the aural medium, written language need not be in any way a reflection of spoken language.

Nevertheless, this priority of the aural medium has seemed to some students of linguistics good grounds for denying the validity of a distinction between medium and language at all. They would take the view that speech is the only true manifestation of language, writing being really only a 'language substitute'. The sound of speech would then actually be a part of language, rather than a medium for language, and the basic distinction would be, not between *language* and *medium*, but between *language* and *writing*. Since this would involve one in believing that the function of writing is simply to record true language, i.e. spoken utterances, and even in believing that all forms of writing are outside the domain of linguistics, it is a view which is unacceptable to many.[21]

It is true, of course, that medium and language are indissolubly united. Language can have no existence without a medium to carry it; disembodied language is inconceivable. We cannot even think in words without mentally clothing them in shapes or in noises. Because they are physically inseparable, language and medium naturally seem to us, most of the time that we are talking, reading, or otherwise using language in the course of our everyday lives, to be not two things but one. Under normal conditions it is the language which the medium carries, not the medium itself, which claims our attention: we are not conscious of the medium (whichever one it may be) *as* a medium. This, of course, must necessarily be the case if language is to be used efficiently. So little conscious of the medium are we, that it is sometimes difficult to recall whether a recently acquired piece of information came to us by reading or by hearing, even though sometimes we can even bring to mind the actual sequence of words in which it was contained. Because the medium, most of the time, is a mere vehicle it would hardly occur to us, unprompted, to distinguish medium from language.

The distinction, we have seen, is nevertheless a useful one; it is one, moreover, which sometimes is almost forced on us. Although we cannot conceive of language without medium, it is possible on occasion to experience medium without language: as a matter of fact this happens every time we listen to, or look at, a foreign language we have never learnt. Damage to the brain may result in a more dramatic divorce between medium and language. The disorder called *alexia*, or word-blindness, is one in which the medium of written language, although present and perfectly visible to the sufferer, no longer acts as a vehicle of meaning to him (though he may be able to make some use of language in all other ways). It is usual to distinguish *alexia*, and similar disorders such as *agraphia* and *anarthria* in which the medium, visual or aural respectively, cannot be produced, from *aphasia*, a disorder in which language rather than the medium is affected. There are other distinctions which have the difference between language and medium implicit in them. *Accent* and *dialect* are words which are often used vaguely, but which can be given more precision by taking the first to refer to characteristics of the medium only, while the second refers to characteristics of language as well.[22] A distinction which has long been made between *verse* and *poetry* can be conveniently reformulated in similar terms: verse may be said to depend on effects of the medium of spoken language only, whereas poetry depends on the use of language as well as (usually) both mediums.[23]

Phonetics, as was said above (p. 2), has as its object of study the aural medium in all its aspects. A broader subject, which would study language mediums in general – all aspects of all existing and potential mediums, and the relations between them – does not at present exist, but it seems clear that there is a growing need for such a subject. Phonetics as we know it today would be only a part of this new subject, but also its ancestor, for it is already showing signs of broadening its scope and of developing in this direction.

2

The Production of Speech

1. *The organs of speech*

The paradox is often quoted that there *are* no organs of speech. In other words, there is no part of a human being which is specifically designed for talking. The parts of the body which produce the sounds of language are incidentally useful for this purpose, but they all have other duties to perform which from the biological point of view are older and more important–duties connected, for instance, with breathing, chewing, swallowing, smelling, and other such activities. These duties are the *primary* functions of the organs used for speech (which engage also in more recently developed and less biologically useful activities such as smoking). 'Physiologically, speech is an over-laid function, or, to be more precise, a group of overlaid functions. It gets what service it can out of organs and functions, nervous and muscular, that have come into being and are maintained for very different ends than its own' (Sapir[1]).

The organs which we use for talking are basically the same, and work in the same way, in all human beings. No racial differences in their structure or in their manner of acting have ever been established (though the possibility of the existence of such differences has at times been suggested[2]). It follows from this that everybody who is free from abnormalities is capable of pronouncing anything. The 'unpronounceable sounds' (unpronounceable for everyone except natives) which some languages are alleged to possess are myths.

We can go further, and say that everybody is capable of pronouncing anything with no difficulty–though this is true only up to a certain age. A child, provided it has sufficient incentive, can attain effortless perfection in the pronunciation of any language with which it may come into contact. When we grow older, however, and have a foreign language to learn, a level of performance comparable to that reached by the child is something for which we have to work very hard. The exact age at which children lose their remarkable aptitude for copying speech sounds is not known, and much research on the subject remains to be done; but it is clear that the facility has left most people not long after they have entered their 'teens. Certainly, fully-grown adults must be prepared to devote a great deal of labour and time to acquiring the pronunciation of a foreign language, even if they want it to be no better than merely intelligible.

It seems probable that a child is not only capable of pronouncing all the sounds of the world's languages, it *does* in fact pronounce a very large number of them, as it passes through what is called the 'babbling' stage of its linguistic development.[3] In the course of this stage it runs through more or less the whole gamut of human speech-producing movements, and when people say that the child, in learning to talk, is 'imitating' the speech-sounds of the adults who surround it, they should probably rather say that the child is simply selecting appropriate sounds from the very wide repertoire which it already possesses.

More than half of a human body, from the head to the abdomen, is needed for the production of spoken language. There are three groups, or systems, of bodily organs which are brought into co-operation for this purpose: one group lies in the trunk, one in the throat, and one in the head, and they are usually known, respectively, as the respiratory system, the phonatory system, and the articulatory system (they can be thought of, on the analogy of a musical instrument, as bellows, reed, and resonator, though in fact no musical instrument exists which produces sounds in exactly the same way as the human speech apparatus does). The way in which these three diverse groups of organs, with very different primary functions, are made to work together as a unified whole to produce speech is very remarkable.[4]

The *respiratory system* comprises the lungs, the muscles by means of which they are compressed or dilated, the bronchial tubes, and the windpipe or trachea. As its name implies, breathing, and thereby assuring the supply of oxygen to the blood, is the primary function of this system. The *phonatory system* is formed by the larynx (or 'voice-box'), the front part of which is evident externally in adult males as the 'Adam's apple'. The primary function of the larynx is to act as a valve which can close off the lungs, partly for their protection, and partly so that the rib-cage can be made rigid while muscular efforts are exerted by the arms.[5] The larynx is in addition a source of sound in very many animals, including, of course, man. The *articulatory system* consists of the nose, the lips, and the mouth and its contents, including especially the teeth and tongue. This system of organs has a number of primary functions, such as sucking, biting and chewing, tasting, smelling, and swallowing – all of them closely connected with eating.

These various organs take part in a variety of sound-producing, but non-linguistic, acts, such as coughs, sneezes, sighs, yawns, sobs, laughs, and hiccups. All of these acts must have preceded speech in the history of the human race, and it is noteworthy that some of them possess communicative value: they convey information of various sorts about the person performing them. Perhaps here is to be found the connecting link between the more primitive functions of all these organs and their conditioning for human speech.[6]

Although it is not part of the *producing* mechanism of speech, we must include the *ear* among the vocal organs. Speech is not much use unless it is received as well as produced, and the main organ of reception is the ear (a minor one being the eye, for watching people while they talk undoubtedly contributes to understanding them; and of course the eye becomes the main, indeed the only, organ of reception of speech for the deaf person who lip-reads).

We do not, however, listen to speech in the same way as we do to other sounds – music, for instance. This is because speech is *meaningful* sound. We do not listen to the sound for its own sake, but because it is a *medium* for language. Usually the meaning receives our whole attention, and we are not conscious of the sound as such. This is a very different situation from listening to music, which may also be said to be meaningful: but here the sounds *are* the meaning and receive the whole of our attention. Only occasionally does the sound itself of speech come into conscious awareness – when the language is one we do not understand, for instance, or when the speaker has an unfamiliar accent or a speech defect or stammer. The rest of the time we are hardly aware, when we are listening to people talking, of the actual *noise* they make, and we will find that if, by an effort, we make ourselves conscious of the noise of speech, the meaning it carries begins to be difficult to grasp.

The ear is important to the speaker as well as to the listener. Any activity involving a succession of skilled movements has to be carefully controlled while the movements are being executed, and for this we need a continual stream of information about the progress, at every moment, of the activity. This information is provided by what has come to be called *feedback*: almost instantaneous reports from various senses, to that part of the brain responsible for initiating the movements, on how successfully the latter are being carried out. Probably there are no movements more skilled than those we make for talking, and we regulate many aspects of these movements by what is called 'auditory feedback'–we listen to their effects in the form of sound, and judge their success by that. Hearing is not the only sense concerned in monitoring the movements of speech, however, for an important part is played by the sense of touch, and a still more important one by the muscular or kinesthetic sense (the 'sixth' sense). If feedback information from any of the above sources is cut off for some reason (when part of the mouth is anaesthetized, for example, or when a person becomes completely deaf), it is difficult to talk properly. If an infant is so deaf that it cannot hear the people around it talking, it will be dumb as well as deaf when it grows up.[7]

The sound of speech, on the one hand, and the movements producing the sound, on the other, are in fact closely linked both for the speaker and for the hearer. Speaker and hearer are usually looked on as two distinct and separate roles in conversation, but in fact each partakes somewhat of the activities of the other. The speaker, as we have just seen, is simultaneously also hearer (he must be, for the normal conduct of speech); but the hearer is, in a way, simultaneously also speaker (at least when listening to his mother tongue) in so far as he 'empathetically' enters into the speaker's sound-producing movements, sometimes even making tentative movements of a similar nature himself. Recognition of this 'identity of speaker and hearer', or 'phonetic empathy', is important in understanding various problems in the perception of speech, particularly in connexion with its rhythmic features; and it provides an additional reason why speech is not listened to as other sounds are.[8]

Everything to do with the mechanics of talking has, with normal people, become quite unconscious through long habit, and indeed it is necessary for the efficient functioning of spoken language that this should be so. We are not conscious of making the producing movements, nor of monitoring our own speech for the purpose of controlling it. If the production of the sound of speech were not automatic it would cease to be a satisfactory medium for language, because its production would monopolize thought instead of conveying it. We need, as speakers, all our attention for *what* we are saying, and we have none to spare for *how* we say it. In the same way we need all our attention, as hearers, for what is being said, and we ignore the mechanics of its production.[9] (The trained phonetician, however, has learnt to be able, when he wishes, to listen to the sound of speech in a quite 'unnatural' way–his listening could be called *analytic* listening, and it is listening which is consciously in terms of the mechanics of speech production.)

Detailed anatomical and physiological descriptions of the various

organs used for the production of speech are available in many
publications for those who wish to study their structure and function
further, and there is no need to discuss this aspect of them at any
length here.[10]

2. *The pulmonic air-stream mechanism*

Speech may be said to consist of *movements made audible*. An air-
stream or moving current of air, provided by the action of some of
the organs of speech, makes audible the movements of other organs.
There are a few noises which the speech organs can produce without
an air-stream–gnashing or grinding the teeth, flapping the tongue
down on the floor of the mouth, making the teeth chatter; but none
of these sounds have been reported to occur in any existing language.
An air-stream, as far as we know, is the basis of the whole of the
sound, in all its variety, of human speech. An air-stream is produced
by an *air-stream mechanism*.[11]

An air-stream mechanism can be compared to a fruit-spray, a Flit
gun, a syringe, or a child's pop-gun. In all of these an enclosed, or
almost enclosed, body of air or liquid is set in motion by movements
of one part of the apparatus, usually a plunger. When the plunger is
moved in one direction air or liquid is pushed out in front of it, and
when it is moved in the other direction air or liquid is pulled in
behind it. In the human speech-producing apparatus the equivalent
of the plunger is called the *initiator*. The initiator sets an air-stream
in motion, and it is the most important part of an air-stream
mechanism.

Three main types of air-stream mechanism are used in human
speech, and each mechanism has a different initiator. (A few other
air-stream mechanisms are possible; one of these is described later in
this chapter.) All three mechanisms may be used to push air out
(when the air-stream is called *egressive*), or to pull it in (when the
air-stream is called *ingressive*).

The *pulmonic* air-stream mechanism is the one which must be
considered first; it consists of the lungs and the respiratory muscles.
The latter move the walls of the lungs, which form the initiator, so
that air is either drawn into the lungs or pushed out of them. It is
this air-stream mechanism which is the basis of almost all human
speech; an egressive pulmonic air-stream is the normal way of talking
or singing.

An ingressive pulmonic air-stream can be observed to occur in
various non-linguistic acts of the organs of speech, such as a yawn,
or most kinds of snoring. Linguistic use of an ingressive pulmonic
air-stream is certainly not common, but it can nevertheless be found

in many parts of the world in a variety of circumstances. Thus in English the first part of the word *yes*, spoken in a somewhat off-hand manner, is often pronounced by many people with an ingressive pulmonic air-stream, the final *-s* being egressive. Convulsive sobs occurring during speech will result in parts of it being pulmonic-ingressively produced. The quality of the voice is considerably changed when this air-stream is used, as a moment's trial will show, and in a number of communities an ingressive air-stream is used as a disguise when the speaker cannot be seen and does not wish to be recognized. Thus in some parts of the world it effectively conceals the identity of a suitor, courting his girl-friend at night outside the latter's house, from her parents.[12]

The pulmonic air-stream mechanism is, of course, the mechanism used for ordinary normal breathing, though it is not used for this purpose in exactly the same way as it is for speech. 'Speaking', it has been said, 'is modified breathing'. Under normal circumstances, the rhythmic movements which the lungs make for breathing are un-conscious (though they can be brought under conscious control), and only those movements needed for breathing *in* form an active process; breathing *out* is merely a mechanical consequence of having breathed in, and it requires no muscular effort. When a pulmonic egressive air-stream is used for purposes of speaking, however, breathing out or expiration must become an active process and must be brought under muscular control; this is part of what is meant by saying that speaking is *modified* breathing. (When an *ingressive* pulmonic mechanism is used for speaking, it does not appear to differ greatly from the ordinary process of breathing in.) Because we have been speaking for so much of our lives, from such an early age, muscular control of expiration for this purpose is, most of the time, just as much an unconscious process as the control of ordinary breathing (although special circumstances, such as an attack of nerves when speaking in public or when singing, may bring it back into awareness again).

3. *The glottis*

The pulmonic air-stream on its way into or out from the lungs has to pass through the wind-pipe or trachea, at the top of which is the complicated organ called the larynx, to which we have already re-ferred. The larynx plays an important role in the production of speech. It is not necessary to enter into the details of its structure; the most important parts of it for our immediate purposes are the *vocal cords* (the spelling *chords*, once common, is now little used). They are also known (less commonly, but perhaps preferably, since they are not in any way like either cords or chords) as vocal bands, lips, ligaments, folds or ledges. They are best thought of as a pair of lips placed from front to back horizontally across the top of the windpipe, joined in front but movable in such a way that they can either be brought together into contact, or pulled wide apart to form a V-shaped opening from the wind-pipe into the throat or pharynx. The best way of making clear the appearance of the vocal cords and their mode of action is by means of high-speed cinematography, so that their movements can be observed in slow motion; it is not easy to explain in words exactly how they work.[13]

The space between the vocal cords, the opening from the wind-pipe into the throat, is called the *glottis*. The vocal cords can by their action bring about a number of different states of the glottis, and the state of the glottis at any given moment during the speech produced by the pulmonic air-stream mechanism is of the greatest importance. It is enough at this point to distinguish *four* states (always bearing in mind that other states are possible both during speech and in non-speech acts). These four states of the glottis are:

(*a*) open glottis ('breath state');
(*b*) glottis in vibration ('voice state');
(*c*) narrowed glottis ('whisper state');
(*d*) closed glottis.

They may be described in detail as follows.

(*a*) The glottis may be *open*. The vocal cords are then drawn wide apart, so that an air-stream can pass through them quite freely. This is the state of the glottis for normal breathing, and it produces no sound, or at best a gentle rustling noise. It is in addition a state which the glottis commonly assumes in speech, and when it does so it is said to be the state or position for 'breath'. Any segment of speech which is produced with the glottis open is said to be produced 'with breath', or to be 'breathed' or (more commonly) to be *voiceless* (for reasons which will become apparent at once).

(*b*) The glottis may be *in vibration*: the vocal cords are alternately brought into contact and blown apart by the force of the pulmonic air-stream (ingressive or egressive) flowing through the glottis. The force of the air-stream and the tension of the vocal cords are adjusted so that the latter flap open and shut many times a second, allowing the air-stream to pass through in a series of rapid tiny puffs.[14] This flapping open and shut, or 'vibration', of the vocal cords constitutes the process called *phonation* (hence the name 'phonatory system' for the larynx), and it produces a buzzing noise known by the technical term *voice*. This second state of the glottis therefore is known as the *voice state.* The production of voice is rather similar to the manner in which a musical note is produced by a bugler or a trumpeter, who uses his lips in somewhat the same way as the vocal cords are used for phonation. When the glottis is in vibration the effect can be clearly felt (especially if the vibration is produced with vigour) on the surface of the front of the throat by resting the fingers there. If the ears are stopped by the fingers while voice is being produced, it can be heard as a quite distinctive buzzing noise inside the head.

In normal speaking with a pulmonic egressive air-stream, it is voice in the technical sense which is responsible for most of the noise that is made, and for the carrying power of what we say. However voice is not continuous during speech: part of the time the glottis is in vibration, part of the time it is not. When the English word *fever* is uttered, for example, it can be seen that both at the beginning and in the middle of the word there is a movement of the lower lip towards the upper teeth. No difference can be observed between the first occasion on which the lip moves and the second. Nevertheless the sound is not the same on the two occasions, and this is because the glottis is open for the first but in vibration for the second.

Any segment of an utterance which is produced while the glottis is in vibration is said to be produced 'with voice', or to be *voiced*, as distinct from *voiceless* segments which are produced 'with breath', i.e. with the glottis in the open state. So *f* is a voiceless part of the utterance *fever*, while *v* is a voiced part. The distinction between *voiced* and *voiceless* (there are many synonyms for both terms)[15] is very important in the description of speech, and will be discussed at greater length later.

The opening and shutting of the vocal cords can take place at varying speeds, the frequency at which they open and shut being governed by their tension and by the force of the air-stream brought to bear on them. It is the frequency of their vibration that determines the *pitch* of the voice: the more rapidly they vibrate, the higher the note. The pitch of the voice is in constant fluctuation while we are talking.

Surgical removal of the larynx ('laryngectomy') results of course in an inability to produce voice, and consequently to produce audible speech in the normal manner. It also renders a pulmonic air-stream impossible, and breathing takes place through a tube inserted in the neck. It is still possible to communicate by speech with other people, however, by means of an 'artificial larynx', or vibrator, which simulates noise produced by the vocal cords in vibration. The vibrator may be held against the neck, or it may be inserted in the mouth (incorporated in a dental plate, for example).

(*c*) The glottis may be *narrowed*: the vocal cords are brought close together, but not so close that they are set into vibration. The air-stream, however, is impeded by this narrowing as it passes through the glottis, and this cuts down the force of the air-stream and also produces a soft hissing noise, to which the technical name *whisper* is given. Any segment of an utterance which is produced with the glottis in this state is said to be *whispered*, and the state itself is known as the *whisper state* of the glottis.

In its popular sense, the word 'whisper' means to utter speech in which there are no voiced stretches at all. When people whisper, in this sense, any parts of the utterance which would normally be voiceless remain as they are, but those parts of the utterance which would normally be voiced are replaced by parts which are *whispered* in the technical phonetic sense, as defined above. It is important to avoid confusion between these two uses, the popular and the technical, of the term.

The whisper state of the glottis occurs not only in the course of 'whispering' in the popular sense, but also in a wide variety of other circumstances in the pronunciation of many languages (including English).

(*d*) The glottis may be entirely *closed*: the vocal cords are brought together with sufficient firmness to prevent the air-stream from forcing them apart. The air-stream is then completely interrupted, and the lungs are for the duration of the closure cut off from the outside air. To provide a closure of this sort was the original function of the vocal cords (p. 21). The glottis momentarily assumes this position for coughs, hiccups, and other non-linguistic acts, and also for the 'glottal stop' (a technical phonetic term that has attained considerable popular currency) of Glasgow dialect, and of many other urban, and some rural, British forms of speech.

4. *The glottalic air-stream mechanism*

The fourth, or closed, state of the glottis, which has just been described, provides the basis for the second of the three air-stream mechanisms, which for this reason is called the *glottalic* air-stream mechanism.

The larynx itself, with the glottis firmly closed, is the initiator. The larynx is provided with muscles by means of which it can be moved up or down in the throat, and if this is done when the glottis is closed, the larynx will act exactly as a plunger in a syringe: when moved downwards it will draw air after it, and when moved upwards it will push air out. The air it sets in motion is the air in the pharynx and above (for this reason it is also known, especially in America, as the *pharyngeal* air-stream mechanism); the air below the larynx, in the trachea, bronchial tubes and lungs, is not affected and takes no part in the air-stream.

Sounds produced by an ingressive or egressive glottalic air-stream are found in many languages; they are interspersed, so to speak, in the stream of pulmonic-egressively produced speech. They occur particularly commonly in languages of the Caucasus, of Africa, and of Central and North America. They occur sporadically, moreover, in many other parts of the world; they can sometimes be observed, in certain circumstances, in English and in French, for example. They are often made by small children for fun. Their sound cannot be described in words (they have a quite distinctive tamber), and they need to be heard to be appreciated.

The volume of air controlled by the glottalic mechanism is not sufficiently large for more than a small fraction of speech to be uttered at one movement of the initiator. Moreover vowels pronounced with this mechanism are inaudible (see ch. 4). It is therefore not found as a mechanism for continuous talking, although a close approach to such a use of it may be observed with some speakers who have undergone a laryngectomy (see p. 27), and who use an artificial larynx. The latter provides the carrying power for the speech and makes the vowels audible, and a glottalic egressive air-stream (if the speaker is capable of producing one) serves to reinforce the consonants.

It might be mentioned at this point that some laryngectomized speakers have been able, after practice, to bring another, somewhat unexpected, air-stream mechanism under sufficient control for it to be used as a basis for speaking. This is the mechanism constituted by belching, and its use produces what is known as *oesophageal* speech.

5. *The velum*

The egressive pulmonic or glottalic air-stream has two exits to the outer air: at the nostrils and at the lips. The paths to the two exits diverge in the throat above the larynx, one path leading to the outer air through the nose, and the other leading to the outer air through the mouth. Both paths, of course, can also serve as entrances for an ingressive air-stream, as well as outlets for an egressive one.

The outlet through the nose may be opened or shut at will by means of a valve which is placed at the point where the two paths diverge. The roof of the mouth, or palate, can be felt (with the tongue or finger) to be hard and bony immediately behind the upper front teeth, and for some distance further back. It then abruptly becomes quite soft, and continues so all the way back until it ends in the uvula. The hard part of the roof of the mouth, or hard palate, is quite fixed and immovable, but the soft part can be moved up and down by the action of muscles attached to it. It is this soft part of the palate, or *velum*,[16] which is the valve controlling the outlet through the nose. When the velum is lowered, the way through the nose is open. When it is fully raised it makes contact with the back wall of the pharynx, and the outlet through the nose is thus shut off. This movement of the velum can be clearly seen in a looking-glass.

If the velum is raised, the only escape for an air-stream is through the mouth; but if it is lowered, it can escape by both mouth and nose. There are, as will be shown in chapter 4, various means by which the outlet through the mouth can be closed, and if one of these is brought into play while the velum is raised, the air-stream cannot escape at all but will be dammed up until one of the obstructions is removed. If an obstruction in the mouth is brought into play while the velum is lowered, the air-stream will escape through the nose alone. Thus in *humming*, for example, the lips are together so that no exit for the air-stream is available through the mouth, but the velum is lowered so that it can escape through the nose.

When the velum is raised, there is said to be a *velic closure*; when the velum is lowered, there is no velic closure. Any part of an utterance produced *without* a velic closure is said to be *nasal* or *nasalized* (for the difference between these terms see ch. 4); a part which is made *with* a velic closure is said to be *oral*. During normal speech the velum is constantly being raised and lowered, often as frequently as several times a second; that is to say that normal speech consists of alternating nasal and oral stretches.

It was said above that the passage through the nose can be opened or shut at will, which is not wholly true: for although with practice and training the movements of the velum can be brought under conscious control, we are normally unconscious of its actions and unaware of which muscles control its movement. A phonetician has to learn awareness of the automatic velum movements which in his natural speech he executes without thought, and to make himself able to raise and lower the velum 'at will' in the full sense.

A 'nasal twang' is the result of keeping the velum lowered almost all the time one is speaking, which gives a characteristic tamber to the voice. A quite different effect, on the other hand, results from having the velum constantly raised, which can be the consequence of inflammation of the soft palate or pharynx because of, for example, a cold or infected adenoids. It is popularly said that a cold makes us 'talk through the nose', but its effect is really just the opposite: it actually *stops* us from talking through the nose, with the result that all nasal stretches of speech are replaced by oral stretches.

Smokers can very easily test whether the velum is raised or lowered if they are in the habit of inhaling the smoke, for this makes the egressive air-stream visible. An absence of velic closure will be clearly revealed by the appearance of smoke at the nostrils when the smoker exhales.

6. *The velaric air-stream mechanism*

We can now consider the third, and last, of the air-stream mechanisms. Its initiator is constituted by the back part of the tongue lifted up so that it comes firmly into contact with the velum (it assumes, that is to say, approximately the same position as it does for making the beginning and end of the English word *kick*), and it is then pushed forward in the mouth (still keeping it in contact with the velum) to make an egressive air-stream, or pulled back to make an ingressive air-stream. Because the initiator is this closure of the tongue against the velum, the mechanism is called the *velaric* air-stream mechanism. It sets in motion only the air in the mouth (and so is also known, especially in America, as the *oral* air-stream mechanism), and the air in the rest of the vocal tract takes no part in the air-stream.

Segments produced by an ingressive velaric air-stream are found, interspersed in the stream of pulmonic-egressively produced speech (just as sounds made by a glottalic air-stream are sometimes so interspersed) in certain languages in Africa, the best known of which are perhaps Zulu, Hottentot, and Bushman. These segments are known as 'clicks'. They have not been reported from anywhere else in the world, and an egressive velaric mechanism does not seem to be used to produce any part of human speech. 'Clicks' occur commonly in many parts of the world, however, as interjections. The sound that English-speakers use to express annoyance, and represent in writing as *tut tut* or *tsk tsk*, is made by an ingressive velaric air-stream, and so also is the sound made to encourage horses (the 'gee-up' click). One variety of the vulgar sound known as a 'raspberry' is produced by a velaric egressive air-stream.

The velaric is an important air-stream mechanism for smoking, and the phonetician can learn much from the way it is so used. Regular cigarette smokers inhale in two stages: they draw the smoke from the cigarette into their mouths by means of an ingressive velaric mechanism; and then, after the mouth has been filled with smoke, they take it into the lungs by means of an ingressive pulmonic mechanism. (The subsequent exhalation is made by an ordinary pulmonic egressive mechanism.) Occasional smokers—those who do not inhale—use a velaric mechanism both for extracting the smoke from the cigarette and for expelling it again–first an ingressive, then an egressive, velaric mechanism. For such smokers the smoke never gets further into the body than the mouth.

Inexperienced smokers can sometimes be observed to attempt to draw the smoke from the cigarette directly into the lungs by means of an ingressive pulmonic mechanism; they nearly always are made to cough violently as a result. There is probably a very good reason why the seasoned smoker inhales in two stages: the smoke, when it enters the mouth from the cigarette, is fairly hot, and the vocal cords are very sensitive to heat and easily damaged by it. By drawing the smoke no further than the mouth as a first step, the smoker is able, when he then brings the pulmonic ingressive mechanism into play, to mix the hot smoke with cool air and so prevent harm coming to the vocal cords. It is interesting that the normal practice when smoking a hubble-bubble (or hookah, or nargileh), in which the smoke is bubbled through water and thereby cooled, is to use a pulmonic ingressive mechanism and draw the smoke direct into the lungs, with no preliminary stage.

A velaric ingressive mechanism–which is in fact nothing more than an ordinary sucking movement–is the normal way of taking liquids into the mouth, though if a liquid is too hot for comfort it will usually be taken in by a pulmonic ingressive movement, accompanied by cool air (and noise).

The entire velaric mechanism is confined to the mouth, and it makes therefore no difference to its functioning whether the velum is at the time making a velic closure or not. If it is not, a pulmonic or glottalic air-stream is free to pass through the nose at the same time as a velaric mechanism is in action. Various combinations of air-stream mechanisms are thus not only possible, but are in fact used in certain circumstances, both linguistic and other. Some smokers are able to perform the trick (known, for some reason, as 'French inhaling') of letting smoke trickle out of the mouth and up into the nostrils, whence it is drawn into the lungs. This is done by the simultaneous use of a velaric egressive mechanism (to push the smoke out of the mouth) and a pulmonic ingressive mechanism (to draw it back into the lungs through the nose).

This same combination of two mechanisms is used by some players of the chanter, and other wind instruments, such as the oboe, which require only a small volume of air, in order to play continuously without apparent pauses for breath. The player uses a pulmonic egressive mechanism most of the time for playing, but when he wishes to re-plenish the air in his lungs he changes over to a velaric egressive mechanism for a short while, simultaneously takes a breath through the nose, and is then able to return to his pulmonic egressive mechanism once more.

It can be seen, therefore, that a number of different processes may be involved in the production of speech: there are the processes which produce the six different air streams (alone or in combination); there is the breath-, voice- or whisper-producing process for which the state of the glottis is responsible; and there is the nasalization process, for which the valve-action of the velum is responsible. There are in addition the articulatory processes, and these will be discussed in the next two chapters.

3

The Analysis of Speech

1. *The syllable*

In order to be able to describe and compare the pronunciation of different languages, we have to *analyse* speech: to split up into units the unbroken stream of movements, and of resulting sound, that constitute an utterance.[1] These units can then be classified into various categories, and used as a basis for description of the style of speech as a whole in which the utterance was made.

One unit seems an obvious starting point for this purpose, and that is the syllable. Most people seem to be able to say, without much difficulty, how many syllables are contained in a given word or utterance; and, with perhaps somewhat more difficulty, to say where each syllable begins and ends. Writing has to be based on an analysis of speech, and the majority of the systems of writing which mankind has from time to time invented are syllabic systems (though our system is not)–that is to say, systems in which each written sign represents a single syllable. The syllable would appear to be an intuitively recognizable unit even for primitive peoples.

Writers on linguistics have nevertheless not found it at all easy to say *what* a syllable is, and there have been many arguments about how it should be defined. No really satisfactory theory of how the syllable is produced or how it is perceived has so far been put forward. The theory which will be given in this chapter is probably the best in so far as it accounts for most of the facts; but it has not been fully substantiated by experimental evidence. It is a theory which explains the syllable in terms of the pulmonic air-stream mechanism. The saying that 'speaking is modified breathing' has already been quoted (p. 25), and we have seen that the modification in question lies partly in the fact that expiration is brought under muscular control when it is for speaking. The modification lies also, however, in the rather unexpected way in which the control is exercised, and this is where, according to the theory adopted here, the explanation of the syllable is to be found.

This theory maintains that when the pulmonic air-stream mechanism is in action, the air is not (as one might think) expelled from the lungs by a constant, regular muscular pressure, producing an even and continuous flow of air. What happens, rather, is that the respiratory muscles alternately contract and relax at a rate of roughly five times per second, so that the air is expelled in a succession of small puffs. Each contraction, together with the resulting puff of air, constitutes the basis of a syllable. In the view of those who hold this theory, therefore, the syllable is essentially a *movement* of the speech organs, and not a characteristic of the *sound* of speech, though in any given language the sound will contain clues, of the most varied kind, to the occurrence of the syllable-producing movement.

This syllable-producing movement of the respiratory muscles has been called a chest-pulse (because the intercostal muscles in the chest are responsible for it), or breath-pulse, or syllable-pulse (the term 'pulse' being used because of its recurrent and periodic nature). At least one such movement must be involved in whatever we may say: a syllable is the minimum utterance, and nothing less than a syllable can be pronounced. *Sh!*, *ah!*, *hmm!*, are each one of them syllables.

The syllable, then, is essentially a movement, and one which, in most cases, is an *audible* movement. It is not necessarily always accompanied by sound, however, and it is possible for a chest-pulse to take place quite silently, producing an inaudible syllable. Such a chest-pulse occurs, for example, in the speech of many English-speaking people when they pronounce a rather perfunctory *thank you*, so that nothing can be heard except *'kyou*. The movement of the respiratory muscles for the first syllable, which is auditorily missing, persists, however, as the speaker will often admit when his attention is drawn to the possibility.

A chest-pulse may be produced by exceptionally great muscular action: it is then a *reinforced* chest-pulse, and it gives an extra powerful push to the lung walls. As a result a stronger puff than usual of air is expelled from the lungs, and this very often causes, among other things, a louder noise. A syllable produced by a reinforced chest-pulse is called a *stressed* syllable, and the extra strong muscular movement itself is called a *stress-pulse*. A speaker of English can, for example, easily make himself aware of the extra effort he makes when he reaches the stressed syllable in the word *university*, especially when the word is pronounced vigorously.

Although a stress-pulse usually has the effect of producing a louder-sounding syllable, it does not follow that it will always do so. In *thank you* the first of the two syllables is a stressed syllable, and it persists as a stressed syllable in the perfunctory pronunciation '*kyou*–a silent stressed syllable.[2] The presence of this silent stress (and other similar ones) is often revealed by a 'synkinetic' nod, or other gesture, preceding the audible syllable. Silent stresses play an important part in the structure of English verse.

There are circumstances in which all syllables are stressed syllables: when shouting, for example, or declaiming slowly, every chest-pulse is a reinforced one. In speech at normal speed, however, most syllables are 'unstressed'.

The pulmonic air-stream mechanism, therefore, is seen to be a complicated one. It consists of the periodic syllable-producing movements, recurring at a rate of about five a second, and at intervals a reinforcement of these movements, producing the stressed syllables. These two processes–the syllable process and the stress process–together make up the pulmonic mechanism, and they are the basis on which the whole of the rest of speech is built.

Different languages co-ordinate the two processes in different ways, and the manner in which they are combined, that is to say the manner in which stressed and unstressed syllables succeed each other, is what produces the *rhythm* of a language. Something will be said later about the kind of rhythmic differences that can be found between languages. It is probable that the rhythm of a language is one of the most fundamental things about it, in the sense that it is among the earliest things learnt by the infant, and perhaps the most difficult thing for the adult speaker to modify, when he wants to learn to pronounce a foreign language. There are types of aphasia in which brain damage has caused every feature of the production of speech to be lost except the pulse systems of the pulmonic air-stream mechanism, as if these were the most resistant to damage to the speech-centres of the brain.[3] Rhythm is a much neglected factor in language teaching, though intelligibility undoubtedly depends on it to a considerable extent.

The weak point of the syllable theory presented here is that it seems very likely that words such as the English *better* which all are agreed must be considered to consist of two syllables, can be uttered with only one chest-pulse. Undoubtedly much further research remains to be done on the subject.[4] The present theory owes a great deal to R. H. Stetson, an American psychologist, and it is usually associated with his name, though in its essentials the theory is a great deal older.[5] A number of other syllable theories have been put forward from time to time, and these will be discussed briefly and compared with Stetson's theory in a later chapter.

2. *Analysis of the syllable*

The essential basis of a syllable, therefore, is a chest-pulse, which may or may not be accompanied by the muscular reinforcement which makes it a stress-pulse. The pulse may–and usually will, in normal speech–have associated with it movements of the vocal cords and of the velum, and also *articulatory movements*–movements, principally, of the tongue and lips. (The term 'articulatory' is used by some writers to include the valve-action of the velum in opening or closing the nasal cavity, and by other writers to exclude this action. The latter usage is preferred here.) All these movements, combined together, are superimposed on the fundamental syllable- and stress-producing processes of the pulmonic mechanism, and they are felt by both speaker and hearer to constitute one single speech-producing act. The syllable has an essential unity. It is a *complex* act, certainly, with numerous different organs taking part in it, but it is nevertheless an integrated whole, and in this respect it is comparable with many other complex but essentially unitary actions, of which a golf swing would be a typical example. A golf swing involves movements of fingers, wrists, arms, trunk, legs, and so on, all working closely together and co-ordinated to produce one single effect, so much so that the different ingredients of the total movement, and their sequence in time, are not at all easy to disentangle. The movements of a syllable are on a much smaller scale than the movements of a golf swing, and are consequently all the more difficult to sort out.

However, although a syllable is in this sense one single act, it is too large and complex a unit to serve the purposes of general phonetic description adequately. There are certain languages, perhaps, for which it might be a possible unit of description–those which have a relatively simple syllable structure, such as Japanese; but for the description of many, perhaps most, languages it is certainly necessary to analyse speech beyond the syllable: to divide the syllable, that is to say, into constituent *segments*–just as the golf professional must analyse a golf swing for purposes of teaching.

Analysis of the syllable means primarily analysis of the associated articulatory, voicing, and nasalizing movements, which 'shape' the chest-pulses into articulate speech. This complex of movements is split into *successive* elements or segments. Each segment therefore is itself complex, with various organs of speech contributing to its production.

Such an analysis is a far from easy task, and although the man-in-the-street can with fair success divide speech up into syllables, it is only with great difficulty that he can split it up any further into smaller units. Before describing how segments resulting from analysis of the syllable are obtained, it might be as well to say something about the difficulties involved in the analysis. Four of these difficulties should especially be noted.

(*a*) The movements to be analysed are very *complex*: lips, jaw, tongue, velum, vocal cords, lung muscles, all take part in them. A great deal is going on at once.

(*b*) The movements are very *rapid*, even when the resulting speech would be considered slow speech. When we are talking at normal speed, for instance, the tongue alone may make as many as *twelve* adjustments of shape and position *per second*.

(*c*) The movements are very *small*. The human ear is sensitive to the effects of tiny adjustments of the tongue, lips, and other organs. The adjustments may be so small that they can be measured only with difficulty, though the differences of sound that they produce are apparent enough.

(*d*) The movements are *continuous*; seldom are the organs maintained, even for a fraction of a second, in anything that could be called a *posture*.

These difficulties are increased by the fact that any actions which are normally performed unconsciously are difficult for the performer to analyse, as the old story of the centipede illustrates: when asked to explain how it managed its hundred legs when it walked, it was not only unable to explain, but unable any longer to walk. We have already seen that the normal functioning of speech movements demands that their execution should be unconscious. To focus attention on them gives them a feeling of instability, even of unreality.

However, though analysis of the syllable is a difficult thing to carry out, it is certainly not impossible. Most systems of writing invented by man have been syllabic systems, but not all. The invention of a system of writing based on *segments* of the syllable has taken place once, but only once: it was the brilliant discovery of the Greeks, and it gave us *alphabetic*, as distinct from syllabic, writing. All contemporary systems of alphabetic writing (and there are many) are derived from the Greek system.[6] For most languages an alphabetic system of writing is much the most economical and practical system which can be devised, but the analysis on which it is based has proved too difficult for most peoples to reach independently.

3. *Vowel and consonant*

Analysis of the syllable yields segments of the syllable, which are successive points in the complex sequence of movements of which the syllable consists. (The segments are also known by the technical term *speech-sounds*, but this term is best avoided for the present, because although the segments of the syllable are *identified* by their sound, they are analysed and described in terms of the processes which produce the sound, rather than the sound itself.) These segments fall naturally into two classes, *vowels* and *consonants*.

Vowel and *consonant* are traditional categories deriving ultimately from the Greek grammarians. They have by now become fairly ambiguous (for example they are often applied to letters of the written alphabet, not units of the spoken language at all). The terms are used here in what is probably very close to their original sense, that is to say for two different sorts of syllable-segment distinguished from each other by the part they play in the syllable. The other ambiguities of the terms will be discussed later, but until this is done no precise definition of them will be attempted. What is said below is intended to do no more than give a rough indication of how the terms can be used for the time being.

The basis of the syllable is a sudden brief contraction of the respiratory muscles, and this contraction expels a small amount of air from the lungs. The air so expelled needs for its escape to the outer air a relatively free and unrestricted passage through the vocal tract, and it is this moment of least restriction in the sequence of movements that make up the syllable that is the *vowel*. The vowel 'carries' the chest-pulse; during it the speech organs in the vocal tract are shaped so that a distinctive quality of sound is produced, but not so that the passage of the air is hindered. A vowel is the nucleus or central part of the syllable; as we shall see, a consonant on the other hand is a marginal part, associated with the beginning and ending of the movement of air engendered by the chest-pulse. In a syllable such as the one that makes up the English word *cease*, for example, it can readily be perceived that the middle part of it provides a fairly free passage for the air (whereas it does not have such a free passage either at the beginning or at the end of the syllable).

The stream of air expelled by the chest-pulse can be both released and arrested by accessory articulatory movements. These movements produce the *consonants* of the syllable.

A consonant at the end of a syllable is a movement of the articulatory organs which so constricts the vocal tract that the passage of air is cut down or stopped. It thus brings the syllable to an end: it is an arresting or closing movement. Thus in the word *cease* the *-se* constricts the vocal tract, and cuts down the passage through it of the air stream. This *-se* part of the syllable is called an *arresting consonant*.

A consonant at the beginning of a syllable releases the movement of air engendered by the chest-pulse. It constricts the vocal tract, as an arresting consonant does, and it constricts it at the moment when the initiator makes the sudden movement of the chest-pulse, so that the air is momentarily compressed behind the constriction. It 'triggers' the syllable off: it is a releasing or opening movement. Thus in the word *cease*, the *c-* acts in this manner, and is therefore called a *releasing consonant*.

In this word *cease* the same constricting articulatory movement (we must not be misled by the difference in the spelling) is used in both the arresting and the releasing functions in a syllable. It is usual to say, in a case like this, that there is the *same* consonant at the beginning and at the end. Similarly in the word *bib* there is a *b* at the beginning and a *b* at the end, but the first is a releasing *b*, the second an arresting *b*.

Considered as a product, or aspect, of the pulmonic air-stream, then, a syllable has three phases:

(*a*) the starting, by a chest-pulse, of a small amount of air on its way out from the lungs;

(*b*) the passage of this air through the vocal tract;

(*c*) the conclusion of the movement of this air (coinciding, often, with the beginning of another chest-pulse).

These phases, or factors as they are sometimes called, of the syllable are known as the release, the vowel, and the arrest, respectively.

Thus a syllable such as *cease*, or *bib*, is divided articulatorily into three segments: a vowel, the central part; and two consonants which are marginal, one flanking the vowel on each side. These segments are co-ordinated with the three phases or factors of the syllable mentioned above. Using the symbol V for vowel and C for consonant, both syllables can be represented in a generalized formula as CVC.

People are apt, at times, to look on segments as being something like bricks from which a syllable is built up. But it is important to remember that they do not form a succession of things which are equal in size and in function to each other, as bricks are. The three segments of *cease* or of *bib* not only have very different functions as associated articulatory movements with the factors of the chest-pulse, but they also extend over very different lengths of time–they are of different sizes. Releasing consonants are very short in duration indeed, and the vowel takes up most of the time occupied by the syllable as a whole. The arresting consonant, while often shorter than the vowel, is seldom anything like as short as the releasing consonant.

The words *cease* and *bib* are typical syllables of English, but many other syllables are different from them in various ways. For instance the arresting or releasing articulatory movements may be quite complex, as in the English single-syllable word *streets*, or the word *clutch*. On the other hand there may be no releasing or arresting consonants at all. If there is no releasing consonant, then the movement of air is started solely by the initiator movement; if there is no arresting consonant, then the movement of air either dies away, to merge in the stream of ordinary breathing, or is renewed by a fresh chest-pulse. In the English syllables formed by the exclamations *ah!*, *oh!*, there is only a vowel, and neither releasing nor arresting consonants. If we use O to mean absence of a consonant, then syllables such as these can be represented by O V O. In a word such as *seeing*, no consonant arrests the syllable *see*, and none releases the syllable *ing*; these syllables can be represented by C V O, and O V C, respectively.

A syllable which is arrested by a consonant is said to be a *closed syllable*, and one which has no arresting consonant is said to be an *open syllable*. The distinction is an important one for various reasons. In the history of the Romance languages, for example, considerable differences are found between the development of open and of closed syllables. *Cease* or *bib* are closed syllables, whereas *bee* is an open syllable.

It happens at times that a syllable does not contain anything that would traditionally be considered a vowel. An exclamation such as *sh!* is a syllable, yet it consists solely of something that we usually think of as a consonant; it would undoubtedly be functioning as a consonant in the word *she*, for instance. In *sh* the air-stream from the chest-pulse is, exceptionally, emitted during an articulation which considerably constricts the vocal canal.

It will be gathered that we have so far given *vowel* and *consonant* no precise definition. In the following chapter the types of articulatory movements which are *usually* used for the consonant and vowel elements of syllables will be described; but, as *sh!* shows, what will here be called a consonant or a vowel does not necessarily *always* have that function in the syllable. It is best to have a rather rough-and-ready division into the two types of segment at this stage, and no misunderstandings should result. A later Chapter will show how more rigorous definitions can be obtained by introducing some more technical terms.

4

Segments

1. *Description of consonants*

A consonant is a segment of a syllable. Strictly speaking, it is a *point* in the constantly changing stream of speech, but we treat this point, for purposes of description, as if it were frozen in time. Although the organs of speech are in continuous movement all the while we are talking, we describe syllable-segments as if they were produced by *postures* of the organs. Speech is not really a succession of discrete postures, but the only practicable way to describe it is as if it were.

We can arrive at a description of a consonant segment adequate enough for most practical purposes by answering *seven* questions about it (though we must remember that the answers to these questions will certainly not tell us *everything* about the segment in question). These questions are as follows:

Q1   What is the air-stream mechanism?
Q2   Is the air-stream ingressive or egressive?
Q3   What is the state of the glottis?
Q4   What is the position of the velum?
Q5   What is the active articulator?
Q6   What is the passive articulator?
Q7   What is the degree and nature of the stricture?

Questions (1) and (2) need no further clarification after what has been said in chapter 1. Together they give us six different air-streams to select from: pulmonic ingressive, pulmonic egressive, glottalic ingressive, glottalic egressive, velaric ingressive, velaric egressive. Most consonant segments, of course, will be (1) pulmonic, (2) egressive; but the phonetician must always be prepared to come across a segment that is neither: such segments are by no means confined to 'exotic' languages. He must also be prepared to meet segments in which two air-streams are involved simultaneously.

Question (3) will usually have one of three answers: either vocal cords apart, or vocal cords in vibration, or vocal cords in whisper position. The segment will then be described as being, respectively, voiceless, or voiced, or whispered.

Question (4) has, for practical purposes, only two answers – there either is, or is not, a velic closure. The segment is said to be oral, in the one case; nasal or nasalized, in the other. (It is theoretically possible, however, to distinguish various degrees of lowering of the velum, and therefore of size of opening into the nasal cavity.)

There can be a wide variety of answers to questions (5) and (6). The *articulators* are those vocal organs which are situated along the vocal tract above the glottis. The articulators are responsible for the accessory movements of the syllable (see ch. 3). They either, for its arrest and release, act so as to restrict the vocal tract to varying degrees; or they shape the vocal tract for the production of the vowel. In either case one of the articulators is moved towards another one, in such a way that the configuration of the vocal tract, through which the air-stream has to pass, is changed. The movable articulator is called the *active* one, and it is moved towards a *passive* articulator, which remains motionless. Most of the passive articulators are attached to the immovable upper jaw; most of the active articulators lie on the lower side, or floor, of the vocal tract. Articulatory movements, therefore, are nearly all *upward* movements.

The passive articulators are the upper lip, the upper teeth, the roof of the mouth, and the back wall of the throat or pharynx. The roof of the mouth is (relatively) a large area, and we need to refer to different parts of it for purposes of phonetic description. It can be divided into: the ridge which lies immediately behind the teeth, or 'teeth-ridge', as it is called; the hard palate, which is the bony part of the roof of the mouth; and the soft palate or velum, which is the fleshy part of the roof of the mouth further back than the hard palate, and which also has the function, as we have seen (p. 29), of acting as a valve to the nasal cavity (in this function it may be said to be an *active* organ of speech, which does not prevent it from being simultaneously a passive articulator). (Since the term 'velum' is commonly used instead of 'soft palate', the adjective 'hard' can usually be omitted from 'hard palate' without ambiguity.)

The active articulators are principally the lower lip, and the tongue. It is the upper surface of the tongue which is mostly concerned with articulation, and since it also is relatively large we need to impose arbitrary divisions on it (since there are no natural ones) in order to obtain accurate phonetic descriptions of segments. It can be divided into: the tip or 'point'; the blade[1] (which is just behind the point, and lies, when the tongue is at rest, immediately under the teeth-ridge); the front (which lies below the hard palate, and perhaps would be better referred to as the 'middle', though we shall here continue to use the traditional term 'front'); the back (which lies below the velum); and the root (which faces the back wall of the pharynx, and is more or less out of sight even when the mouth is wide open). The uvula also is usually included among the active articulators, because it is occasionally, in some languages, made to vibrate rapidly against the back of the tongue (which then becomes the passive articulator in the production of that particular segment).

Finally there is question (7). The *stricture*[2] is the technical term for the position taken up by the active articulator in relation to the passive one; it tells us how and to what degree the passage of the air-stream through the vocal tract is restricted at that point.

First we must distinguish the most extreme type of stricture, which is *complete closure*, the articulators making air-tight contact with each other. It can clearly be seen that this is what the two lips are doing at the beginning and end of the word *bib*. Such a stricture will completely prevent the air-stream from passing through the mouth.

Secondly there is a type of stricture which is characterized by intermittent passage of the air-stream through the mouth: it involves the rapid beating, or vibration, of the active articulator against the passive, and therefore the alternate opening and closing of the vocal tract at that point. It could be called a stricture of *intermittent closure*. A stricture like this would hardly seem at first sight to involve a *posture* of the organs of speech. The beating or vibration, however, is not produced by muscular action (it would be too rapid for that). What happens is that the active articulator (which must be a sufficiently elastic one for the purpose) is held in such a position that the air-stream, in passing by it, causes it to vibrate and to make a series of taps in quick succession against the passive articulator. Thus the vibration is a mechanical consequence of a certain posture being assumed. The typical stage Scotsman's *r* is produced by this type of stricture, and so is the vibration of the uvula against the back of the tongue which was referred to above.

In some cases the posture for 'intermittent closure' may be maintained for such a short time that it produces only one single tap of the active articulator against the passive one (English people often pronounce the word *very* with, in the middle, a segment made thus). A third type of stricture (the only one which cannot really be described in terms of a posture) is in effect very similar to this. It involves a 'ballistic'[3] movement of an active articulator made in such a way that the articulator strikes in passing against a passive articulator. Segments made thus are rather uncommon, and do not occur in normal English. Examples can be found in many languages in India, however, in certain Norwegian dialects, and elsewhere.

All other types of stricture are less extreme and allow the air-stream to pass continuously through the mouth, some with more, some with less, difficulty. They may entail contact of articulators at the *sides* of the vocal tract, through the centre of which the air-stream then passes (*central* passage of the air-stream); or they may entail contact of articulators in the *centre* of the vocal tract, the air-stream then passing round one or both sides of the contact (*lateral* passage of the air-stream). In the case both of central and of lateral passage of the air-stream, the stricture may impede it sufficiently to cause audible friction at the point of articulation (this is then called *close approximation* of the articulators); or it may allow the air-stream to pass through without audible friction at the point of articulation (*open approximation* of the articulators). Not all these types of stricture can be illustrated from English, but in *sh!* we have central passage of the air-stream with close approximation of the articulators; in the consonant segment at the beginning of *you* we have central passage of the air-stream with open approximation of the articulators (a similar stricture, moreover, is used for all vowels); and in the consonant segments at the beginning and end of *lull* we have lateral passage of the air-stream with open approximation of the articulators. Lateral passage of the air-stream with close approximation of the articulators produces the consonant at the beginning of the Welsh word *llan*, 'church', which begins so many place-names in Wales.

It should finally be mentioned that during the type of stricture of intermittent closure mentioned above there may be, in the intervals between the taps, open approximation of the articulators, in which case the only noise is that of the vibrating active articulator; or there may be close approximation of the articulators, in which case audible friction will be produced as well.

We can now see how the seven questions given on p. 42 would be answered if asked about a few typical consonant segments. Let us consider those segments at the beginning of the three English words *fat, mat, pat*, and the one which, twice repeated, constitutes the common exclamation of annoyance *tut tut* (or *tsk tsk* – both are very inadequate ways of spelling it). The movements of the articulators are clearly visible in the case of the first three, though not in the fourth.

(*a*) The *f* of *fat*

(1) The air-stream mechanism is pulmonic.
(2) The air-stream is egressive.
(3) The vocal cords are apart.
(4) There is a velic closure.
(5) The active articulator is the lower lip.
(6) The passive articulator, or rather articulators, are the upper front teeth.
(7) There is close approximation of the articulators, with central passage of the air-stream. (The consonant is made by some speakers with lateral passage of the air-stream. The resulting difference in sound, if any, is small.)

(*b*) The *m* of *mat*

(1) The air-stream mechanism is pulmonic.
(2) The air-stream is egressive.
(3) The vocal cords are in vibration.
(4) There is no velic closure.
(5) The active articulator is the lower lip.
(6) The passive articulator is the upper lip. (It is never entirely 'passive' as an articulator, but can be seen to make a small movement downwards as the lower lip is raised towards it.)
(7) There is a stricture of complete closure.

(*c*) The *p* of *pat*

(1) The air-stream mechanism is pulmonic.
(2) The air-stream is egressive.
(3) The vocal cords are apart.
(4) There is a velic closure.
(5) The active articulator is the lower lip.
(6) The passive articulator is the upper lip.
(7) There is a stricture of complete closure.

(*d*) '*Tut*'

(1) The air-stream mechanism is velaric.
(2) The air-stream is ingressive.
(3) The vocal cords are apart. (With a velaric air-stream mechanism, the state of the glottis does not matter unless another air-stream mechanism is

brought into play simultaneously; this is because the air-stream is initiated above the glottis, as explained on p. 31. In the present case there *is* another air-stream; see the answer to the following question.)

(4) There is no velic closure. (A velaric air-stream is initiated in front of the opening into the nasal cavity; whether there is a velic closure does not matter, therefore, unless another air-stream mechanism is brought into play simultaneously. The exclamation, as uttered by English people, is usually pronounced while breathing at the same time through the nose, and with the glottis open; there is therefore a simultaneous pulmonic mechanism, either ingressive or egressive, in play, and hence there is no velic closure.)

(5) The active articulator is the blade of the tongue.

(6) The passive articulator is the teeth-ridge.

(7) There is a stricture of complete closure.

2. *Place and manner*

A simple system of classification of consonant segments, based on the foregoing scheme of description, has been in use for a long time, and is known as *classification by place and manner*. It embodies in summary form the greater part of the information given by the answers to the seven questions. 'Place', short for 'place of production', means the point of articulation of the segment (i.e. the active and the passive articulators as elicited by questions (5) and (6) above). 'Manner' short for 'manner of production', means primarily the type of stricture which the articulators are making to produce the segment (i.e. the answer to question (7) above), but it may in addition include reference to the position of the velum (question (4)) and to the air-stream (questions (1) and (2)). Both the category of 'place' and the category of 'manner' yield a number of different classes of consonant segments, and any given consonant segment can be fitted simultaneously into one of the classes of place and one of the classes of manner. The different classes arising from *place* of production need no special attention after what has been said with reference to questions (5) and (6) in the preceding section. The usually recognized classes arising from *manner* of production are seven in number, and are as follows.

(1) A *stop* is a type of consonant segment produced by a stricture of complete closure, accompanied simultaneously by a velic closure. Because of these two closures the air-stream, if egressive, is momentarily completely dammed up, and unable to get through the vocal tract at all. The air is, therefore, compressed behind the point of articulation, and will escape with a small explosion when the active articulator is removed from contact with the passive one. If the air-stream is ingressive, on the other hand, the air behind the point of articulation is rarefied, and there will be a sudden rush of air inwards, instead of outwards, when the active articulator is removed. In both cases some sort of a popping noise will result. Typical examples of stops made with an egressive pulmonic air-stream may be found at the beginning and end of the English words *pick*, *top*, *bag*, *did*. The exclamation *tut tut* is a stop, twice repeated, made with an ingressive velaric air-stream.

It is convenient sometimes to have special names for stops made with different air-streams. It has never been felt necessary to coin a term for a stop made with a pulmonic ingressive air-stream, nor for one made with a velaric egressive air-stream, but the four other possibilities have the following names ('click' has already been mentioned on p. 31):

	ingressive	*egressive*
pulmonic	—	plosive
glottalic	implosive	ejective
velaric	click	—

These four names, therefore, give information about the air-stream as well as about the stricture. 'Stop' is a more general name which does not specify the air-stream.

(2) A *nasal* is a type of consonant segment which, like a stop, is produced by a stricture of complete closure; a nasal, however, unlike a stop, has no simultaneous velic closure. The air-stream, therefore, though prevented from passing through the mouth, is not dammed up; it is entirely diverted through the nose. Examples of nasals made with an egressive pulmonic air-stream may be found at the beginning and end of the English words *man*, *name*, and (in the pronunciation of most–though not all–English speakers) at the end of the word *sing*.

(3) The stricture which produces the type of consonant segment

called a *fricative* is one of close approximation of the articulators, with central passage of the air-stream. Close approximation of the articulators, as we saw above, produces audible friction as the air is forced through the partially obstructed vocal tract: hence the name of this class of consonant. There are probably, in the languages of the world, more different kinds of fricatives than of any other type of consonant. Typical examples may be found at the beginning and end of the English words *cease, thief*.

For this class of consonant (and for all the subsequent ones) there may or may not be a simultaneous velic closure. It is customary to take it for granted that there *is* one unless a specific statement is made to the contrary (see section 7); but in any case some at least of the air-stream will pass through the mouth (if there is not a velic closure, some will pass through the nose as well).

(4) A *trill* is a type of consonant segment resulting from a stricture of intermittent closure. (Trills are also sometimes called *rolled* consonants.) The stage Scotsman's *r* is a trill in which the vibrating organ is the point of the tongue. Another kind of trill occurs if the two lips are made to vibrate against each other (in which case it becomes pointless to distinguish an active from a passive articulator); a sound made thus may still occasionally be heard from a groom as he is rubbing down a horse. The uvula can make a trill by vibrating in a groove formed in the back of the tongue, and a consonant made thus can be heard in Portuguese, and occasionally in German and French. Trills are one type of *r*-sound.

If there is close approximation of the articulators while a trill is being made, the result is a *fricative-trill*, in which the noise of friction, as well as the noise of vibration, can be heard. A segment made thus is found in Czech; it occurs in the middle of the composer's name *Dvořák* (as pronounced, of course, by a native). Segments of this type are somewhat uncommon.

A trill in which the active articulator strikes only once against the passive articulator is called a *one-tap-trill*. As well as being sometimes heard from English people in the middle of the word *very*, a one-tap-trill occurs in the Spanish *pero* 'but' (as distinct from *perro* 'dog'); and also in the middle of the word *pity* as pronounced by many Americans (when it would not popularly be thought to be a kind of *r*-sound). One-tap-trills closely resemble the type of consonant segment described next.

(5) A *flap* [4] is the appropriate name for the type of consonant segment produced when an active articulator, during a 'ballistic' movement, strikes in passing against a passive one. Such a segment occurs when the point of the tongue, after being curled upwards and back,

falls forward on to the floor of the mouth, hitting the teeth-ridge on its way; this consonant is found in many of the languages of India. The lower lip can also be drawn inwards over the lower teeth and then thrown forward so that it hits the upper teeth in passing; consonant segments made thus are found in certain languages of the Sudan.[5] Because of the similarity of a 'ballistic' movement of this kind to the movement involved in a one-tap trill, the term *flapped r* is sometimes used for the latter.

(6) A *lateral* is a type of consonant segment produced by a stricture of complete closure in the centre of the vocal tract, so that there is lateral passage of the air-stream, round the side or sides of the obstruction. A segment of this kind, with open approximation of the articulators, is found in the English word *lull*, or the Italian word *gli*. When there is close approximation of the articulators, as in the beginning segment of the Welsh *llan*, and audible friction results, the segment is called a *fricative-lateral*.

If the air-stream passes round one side only of the central obstruction we can, if we wish, use a more exact term: *unilateral*; and we can use *bilateral* if the air-stream passes round both sides. The sound in Welsh *llan* is usually of the former kind, that in English *lull* the latter. The difference to the ear, however, is small, and the more general term *lateral* suffices for most purposes.

(7) Finally there are segments made with central passage of the air-stream and open approximation of the articulators, so that no noise of friction is produced. All vowel segments are made by this type of stricture (sometimes without any actual contact of the articulators at all), and so are various segments often called consonants, for example the segment at the beginning of the word *run* as pronounced by most people in England and America, and the segments at the beginning of the words *we* and *you*. The rather unsatisfactory names *semivowel* and *frictionless continuant* have usually in the past been given to such segments, but, following a recent suggestion by P. Ladefoged, we shall here adopt the term *approximant* for them.

3. *Naming of consonants*

Classification by place and manner enables us to give brief descriptive names to typical consonant segments (or rather to the posture we take to represent them), so that we can talk about them conveniently and economically. According to this system of naming, a *noun* identifying the *manner* (such as plosive, click, implosive, nasal, trill, flap, lateral, fricative, and so on) is preceded by an *adjective* identifying the *place*. The adjectives referring to place are taken from the Latin names for the articulators (which gives them a certain international currency). In nearly all cases it is the *passive* articulator which provides the adjective: thus the adjective *labial* is used when the passive articulator is the upper lip; *dental* is used when the passive articulator is the upper teeth; *alveolar* is used when the passive articulator is the teeth-ridge; *palatal* is used when the passive articulator is the hard palate; *velar* is used when the passive articulator is the velum; *pharyngal* is used when the passive articulator is the back wall of the pharynx.

Since the adjective usually refers to the passive articulator, it is taken for granted that the *active* articulator is the one which lies immediately opposite it when the vocal organs are at rest. Thus the adjective *velar* means that the stricture takes place between the velum or soft palate and the back of the tongue; *palatal*, between the hard palate and the front of the tongue; *pharyngal*, between the back wall of the pharynx and the root of the tongue; and so on.

In certain types of stricture, the active and passive articulators are organs which do *not* lie, when they are at rest, immediately opposite each other; the stricture is then said to result from a 'displaced' articulation, and some adjective which is more specific than one indicating only the passive articulator must be used to refer to it. An example of a 'displaced' articulation is when the lower lip approaches the upper teeth, and a consonant made by these articulators, such as English *f* or *v*, is described as *labio-dental*, which is an adjective identifying both articulators at once. (When it is necessary to make quite clear that, as distinct from a consonant of this sort, the lower lip is articulating against the upper *lip*, i.e. the articulation is not 'displaced', the adjective *bi-labial*, also identifying both articulators at once, may be used.)

Another example of a displaced articulation is when the point of the tongue is raised towards the hard palate, which means it must be *curled back* as well. The adjective *retroflex* is used for this class of consonants, and although it does not directly identify the two articulators concerned, it is nevertheless descriptive of what takes place. Segments so made are common in the languages of India, and in many other parts of the world also.

When during the production of a segment the uvula is made to vibrate against the back of the tongue, the adjective *uvular* is used to identify the place of production. The same adjective is usually also used for consonants in the production of which the root of the tongue is the active articulator, and the very back of the velum, including the uvula, the passive. One such segment is the consonant in Classical Arabic which is usually transliterated into the roman alphabet as *q*.

The combination of adjective, referring to 'place', and noun, referring to 'manner', must be preceded, in order to make a brief descriptive name of this sort adequate, by a further adjective giving the
answer to question (4) above, and making clear the state of the
glottis. Thus we can say that the word *theme* begins with a *voiceless
dental fricative* and ends with a *voiced (bi-) labial nasal*; *light* begins
with a *voiced alveolar lateral* and ends with a *voiceless alveolar
plosive*; and so on.

Each of these brief descriptive names therefore consists of three
terms, two adjectives and a noun, corresponding to three 'dimensions' of classification, and such three-term labels are sufficient to
identify most consonant segments for many, perhaps most, purposes;
but they do not, of course, provide anything like a complete description of how the vocal organs form the consonant in question. More
precise descriptions can be obtained, when they are needed, by adding
to the number of 'dimensions' of classification. Thus, in addition to
the dimensions of place, manner, and voicing, it may sometimes be
important to specify the *shape* of the active articulator, which gives
us a fourth dimension of classification. The shape of the articulator
is often the chief difference between the initial consonant of the
English word *sip* and that of the English word *ship*. With many
speakers both can fairly be described as voiceless alveolar fricatives,
but the former is made with a groove, from front to back, in the
articulator. The two can then be distinguished from each other by
calling the former a voiceless *grooved* alveolar fricative. Alternatively,
since many speakers pronounce the latter consonant further back in
the mouth than the former, namely at the junction of the teeth-ridge
and the hard palate, a more specific adjective for the place of its production, *palato-alveolar*, may be used to distinguish it. Thus while
the *s* of *sip* could be called a voiceless alveolar fricative, the *sh* of *ship*
could be called a voiceless palato-alveolar fricative.

It is also sometimes necessary, when discussing dental and alveolar
consonant segments, to specify explicitly the active articulator, which
as we have seen is usually implicit in the adjective for 'place' and
taken as understood. This is because both the point of the tongue and
the blade of the tongue may equally well be supposed to lie, when in a
position of rest, beneath the upper teeth and the teeth-ridge; therefore
a consonant described simply as *dental* may be made with either the
point or the blade articulating against the upper teeth, and similarly a
consonant described as *alveolar* may be made with either the point
or the blade against the teeth-ridge. Very often we do not need to say
specifically which of the two is the case. However *s*-sounds and *sh*-
sounds, which are both alveolar, can be made in either way, and

sometimes it is an advantage to be able to draw special attention to whether it is the point or the blade that is being used. We can do this by employing the adjective *apical* to mean that the point of the tongue is the active articulator, and the adjective *laminal* to mean that the blade of the tongue is the active articulator (the adjective *dorsal* is also used in the same sense by many writers).[6] The following convenient compound adjectives, identifying both articulators at once, may be used in three-term labels instead of the simple *dental* and *alveolar* when necessary: *apico-dental, lamino-dental, apico-alveolar, lamino-alveolar*. Some English speakers use apico-alveolar *t* and *d* sounds, while others use lamino-alveolar ones. The *t* and *d* sounds of most French speakers are lamino-dental.

Another dimension of classification ('secondary articulations') of which we need sometimes to take account is explained later, in section 7 (p. 60).

Mention must here be made of what is known as a *glottal stop* (it was referred to briefly on p. 28). This sound is commonly found in languages all over the world. In English dialects, for example, it often takes the place of *t*, and sometimes of other consonants, between two vowels or at the end of a word. It is popularly supposed to be characteristic of Cockney and of Glasgow dialect, but as a matter of fact it can be heard in nearly all large towns in Britain and, in certain positions in the word, in the speech of many educated people. When novelists imitating dialect write, for instance, something like 'be'er bu'er', they mean the words *better butter* pronounced with glottal stops instead of *t*'s. Although it is sometimes alleged that the use of a glottal stop in speech is harmful to the vocal cords, it is nevertheless an important sound in the standard form of many languages, such as German, Arabic, and Danish.

No articulators are used in making this sound, but the vocal cords act very much in the same way as articulators to produce a complete but brief closure in the path of the air-stream, with resulting momentary compression of the air behind the closure if the air-stream is egressive, or rarefaction if it is ingressive, as with any other stop. It can only be produced with a pulmonic air-stream mechanism, and since the vocal cords themselves are concerned in making the sound, it is meaningless to describe it as either voiced or voiceless or whispered – all three are states of the glottis incompatible with the use of the vocal cords to make a glottal stop. A two-term label is therefore sufficient in this case to identify the sound; and we have to add, for its sake, the category *glottal* to the other categories of place.

The following are examples of how three-term labels are applied to various consonant segments.

f in English *fat* is a voiceless labio-dental fricative.
m in English *mat* is a voiced labial nasal.
p in English *pat* is a voiceless labial plosive.
'*tut*' is a voiceless alveolar click.
ll in Welsh *llan* is a voiceless alveolar fricative-lateral.
gn in French *montagne* is a voiced palatal nasal.
ng in English *sing* is a voiced velar nasal
ř in the Czech name *Dvořák* is a voiced alveolar fricative-trill.
g in English *go* is a voiced velar plosive.
ch in Scottish *loch* is a voiceless velar fricative.
h in the Arabic name *Mohammad* is a voiceless pharyngal
fricative.

Classification by place and manner can be exhibited in convenient
synoptic form by means of what is known as a 'consonant chart'.
This is a table constructed by arranging the categories of place along
the top, and the categories of manner down the left-hand side. The
categories of place are usually set out, starting from the right, in the
order in which an egressive air-stream would meet them, i.e. starting
with pharyngal (or glottal, if that is included), and finishing with
labial. (Consonant charts of over fifty years ago used to reverse this
order.) The categories of manner are usually set out with those involving a stricture of complete closure at the top, and those involving
a stricture of open approximation at the bottom, with the other categories arranged in between. Lines ruled horizontally and vertically so
that they separate the categories from each other will produce a number of 'pigeon-holes', and if a sufficient number of categories has
been used in the chart, any given consonant segment in any language
can be fitted into its appropriate 'pigeon-hole', though voiced and
voiceless segments will not be distinguished. It is possible to give a
quick view of the consonants of any language or group of languages
by means of a consonant chart of this sort.

Some of the pigeon-holes, however, must remain permanently
empty, whatever language is being dealt with, because it would not
be physically possible to make the articulatory movement necessary
to fill them. The front of the tongue, for example, is not, with most
people, elastic enough to produce a *palatal* trill; and many people
would be unable to produce a *labio*-dental stop because an air-tight
closure between their lower lip and upper teeth would not be possible
–the interstices between the teeth would allow the air-stream to
escape through them, and the result would be a fricative.

4. *Description and naming of vowels*

Vowel segments are a great deal more difficult to describe and classify than consonant segments. Nearly all consonant segments, as we have seen, are made with a stricture involving contact of relatively large areas of both active and passive articulators. Since the contacts involved in the production of any given consonant can be ascertained fairly easily, such contacts provide a convenient and obvious basis for consonant description, and one which has been made use of for a very long time.

Vowel segments, on the other hand, being made with 'open approximation' of the articulators, involve little contact and sometimes none at all. They are thus, literally, less 'tangible' than consonants, and early investigators, not having the sense of touch to reinforce kinesthetic sensations, found great difficulty in producing any coherent system for description of vowels. It is true that sometimes the sense of sight will help us (the mouth, in several vowels, is wide open enough to make a good deal of the tongue visible, and the lips can always be seen), but much speculation and discussion was required before what is essentially the system of classification put forward here was evolved in the first half of the nineteenth century.[7] Even now, x-ray photography has shown itself to be the only really satisfactory way of revealing the action of the articulators in pronouncing a vowel segment. The categories of description of vowels, because of these difficulties, are less obvious and simple than those of consonants, and more difficult for the beginner to apply in practice. Another difficulty which arises when explaining vowel classification in writing, as distinct from explaining it by word of mouth, is the great diversity of different types of English in the matter of vowel sounds. Words given as examples to illustrate a particular kind of vowel segment under discussion may contain, for some readers, a vowel of quite a different kind. It is not possible to guard completely against misunderstandings which may arise for this reason.

The distinctive quality of sound of any vowel segment results from the general shape given to the mouth and throat during its production. The mouth and throat together form a tube-shaped cavity which starts at the larynx and ends at the lips, and the configuration of this tube, which we may call *the vocal tract*, is moulded by the action of the articulators: it depends partly on the position which the tongue takes up in the mouth and throat, and partly on how the lips shape the exit from the cavity. We will consider these two articulatory factors—the action of the tongue and the action of the lips—in turn, and see how they are taken into account in describing vowel segments.

The tongue assumes a large number of very varied postures and shapes in order to produce different vowel segments, but in all these positions the upper surface of its main body is always found to be convex; the tongue, that is to say, always makes a 'hump' in the mouth. If, for any given vowel segment, we can state the whereabouts during its production of the *highest point* in the mouth of the hump of the tongue, then that will be enough to specify with fair accuracy the position the tongue as a whole occupies in the vocal tract. This is because the tongue must be looked on as a flexible mass of muscle which, although it can assume many different shapes, does not in doing so change its total volume. Location of the highest point of its curved upper surface is therefore a means of describing simply and briefly what effect its total mass, for any given vowel, has on the shape of the vocal tract. We can infer where the tube of which this consists is narrowest and where it is widest, and what the degree of curvature of the tongue's upper surface must be. We can thus account for an important part of the distinctive quality of sound of the vowel segment (the action of the lips accounting for most of the rest).

In order to say whereabouts this highest point of the tongue lies in the mouth, we must locate it simultaneously on two axes: one horizontal, from front to back of the mouth, and the other vertical, from the floor of the mouth to its roof. We need to distinguish a series of points along each axis. Since our choice of points must be arbitrary, their number will be dictated purely by convenience. The points along each axis must be taken to be equidistant from each other.

Theoretically a large number of points along both axes could be distinguished, all resulting in vowel qualities that the trained ear is capable of discriminating. However, it is usually found sufficient to have *four* points on the vertical axis, and *three* on the horizontal. The four vertical points, starting with the tongue at the greatest distance from the floor of the mouth and descending from there, are called:

> close
> half-close
> half-open
> open

('close' because the tongue is close to the roof of the mouth).[8] An example of a close vowel is the one in the English word *see*; an example of an open vowel is the one in the English word *far*. In a close vowel there is contact of the sides of the tongue with the upper back teeth and the sides of the roof of the mouth, though the stricture is 'open approximation' and there is no audible friction. In an open vowel there is no contact of articulators.

The three horizontal points are called:

front
central
back

(On this axis, 'front' lies beneath the hard palate, 'back' beneath the soft palate, and 'central' lies below where they meet.) The vowel in *see* is a front vowel; that in *far* is a back vowel (at least in the pronunciation of a very large number of English speakers); the first vowel in *again* is a central vowel, and another example of a central vowel is the one in *bird* as pronounced by most people in England.

If, then, we call the vowel in *see* a *close front* vowel, we have located it simultaneously on the two axes. So also if we call the vowel in *far* an *open back* vowel, and the one in *bird* a *half-open central* vowel.

These two axes, the vertical and the horizontal, give us two dimensions of classification for vowels. (It can be seen that these two dimensions are somewhat similar to the dimensions of 'manner' and 'place' which are used for classifying consonants.) The four points on the vertical axis and the three on the horizontal axis yield, when combined together, twelve different locations in the mouth for the highest point of the tongue.

We need more than these two dimensions, however, for adequate description of a vowel. They tell us how the tongue is modifying the shape of the vocal tract, but we still need to know what sort of an exit from the vocal tract the lips are providing. Experiment with a mirror will show that it is possible to produce a variety of positions of the lips (whose movements are quite independent of those of the tongue), from one extreme when the corners are drawn back as for a smile, to the other when they are pushed forward to make a small round opening as for blowing out a candle. If we compare, in a mirror, the posture of the lips for the vowel in *see* with that for the vowel in *too*, the two can be seen to be markedly different.

The posture of the lips provides a third 'dimension' of classification for vowel segments. It would be possible to have several categories in this dimension, and if necessary, since we can see what is going on, we could be very exact in describing lip position. For most practical purposes, however, two categories are enough: *rounded*, when the corners of the lips are brought forward, and *unrounded*, when the corners of the lips are pulled back. The vowel in *too* is a rounded vowel, that in *see* an unrounded vowel. (The term 'spread' is sometimes used instead of unrounded.)

5

It is usually the case that, when a vowel is rounded, the degree of rounding (i.e. the extent to which the lips are pursed) is linked to the height of the highest point of the tongue: the higher the tongue, the greater the rounding. The term *rounded* may therefore be taken, in any particular case, as implying that degree of rounding appropriate to the height of the tongue. The two things are not always linked, however, and the terms *over-rounded* and *under-rounded*, which are self-explanatory, may be used when necessary. (It is probably the amount of jaw-opening, correlated with the height of the tongue, that influences the degree of rounding.)

These three dimensions, therefore, give us a system of three-term labels for identifying vowel segments, just as for consonant segments. The vowel in *too* is a *close back rounded* vowel; that in *see* is a *close front unrounded* vowel; that in French *lune* is a *close front rounded* vowel. It can be seen that the order of terms in these labels is: (*a*) highest point of tongue, vertical axis; (*b*) highest point of tongue, horizontal axis; (*c*) lip posture.

The two categories of lip position, when combined with the twelve different locations in the mouth of the highest point of the tongue, give us twenty-four different three-term labels for vowels. These labels, however, do not specify a vowel segment exactly, for it is a fact that the ear, after some training, can distinguish many more than twenty-four different vowel qualities. The twenty-four labels, or rather a selection from them, are usually enough if we are dealing with any single language, but for some purposes, such as when comparing languages, we may wish to be more exact in the specification of vowel segments than they make possible. If we wish to be more exact, we must either enlarge the number of categories in some or all of the dimensions of classification, or add to the number of dimensions (by, for instance, taking the *muscular tension* of the tongue into account; variations in tension are supposed by some to affect the total volume of the tongue, and so to be responsible for small variations in vowel quality).[9] Alternatively, we can base the description of vowels on quite different principles from those set out in this Chapter (see ch. 10). But the twenty-four (relatively) approximtae labels should be mastered in use before anything more ambitious is tried.

5. *Voiceless vowels*

Vowels are usually thought of as being essentially voiced, and the etymology of the word (ultimately derived from the Latin *vox*, 'voice') might lead us to believe this must be so. It will have been noticed that in the three-term labels for vowels explained in the previous section, the state of the glottis is not specified. Nevertheless, although a vowel may be taken to be voiced if nothing is said to the contrary, voiceless vowels may be heard in many languages. In English, for example, the first vowel in the word *potato*, or the vowel of the word *to* in *come to tea*, or *I'm going to town*, are often pronounced without vibration of the vocal cords in normal conversational speech. In French also the final vowels of *entendu, tant pis,* or *c'est tout*, when they occur in conversation before a pause, are usually voiceless.[10] Voiceless vowels are even more common in other languages, for instance in Portuguese, and in a number of American Indian languages.

A vowel may also, of course, be *whispered* (in the technical phonetic sense; see p. 28). In ordinary whispering, using the word in its popular sense, all vowels are whispered in the technical sense. They are also reported to occur in normal speech in some languages.

The so-called aspirate, the sound which in English and many other languages corresponds to the letter *h*, is in fact a voiceless vowel. That *h*, which is popularly called a consonant, is from the phonetic point of view a voiceless vowel segment, illustrates the ambiguous nature of the traditional terms 'vowel' and 'consonant' (the ambiguities are discussed in the next chapter). It is nevertheless the case that in a word like *hat*, the articulatory position of the vowel is more or less assumed at the very beginning of the word, but the glottis is open briefly, at the start of the chest-pulse, before it assumes the position for voice: in other words, *hat* starts with a voiceless vowel, immediately followed by a voiced one. In fact the letter *h*, where it is pronounced in English, represents a voiceless version of the vowel which follows it, as in *who, hit, heat, heart, hurt*, and so on.[11]

Direct inspection of the glottis of English speakers by means of instruments reveals that on occasion there is some approximation of the vocal cords during the pronunciation of an initial *h*. It is probable that the vocal cords may even, especially when the *h* occurs between two vowel segments as in *behind*, assume the position for whisper. Very often also, for an *h* between two vowel segments, the whisper position of the glottis is combined with that for voice, the vocal cords vibrating along part of their length and being merely brought close together along the rest. In this case the resulting segment is usually called (not very happily perhaps) a *voiced h*. This sound occurs in all positions, initial and other, in words, in Czech, Egyptian colloquial Arabic, and other languages.

In some languages voiceless vowels occur *following* a corresponding voiced vowel. Scots Gaelic, except in its eastern dialects; Icelandic; and some American Indian languages, provide good examples of this.

All the vowel segments which we have so far discussed are made with a pulmonic mechanism, though they can be made equally well whether the air-stream is ingressive or egressive. If the articulators are in the position for a vowel when a glottalic or velaric mechanism is brought into play, the result is inaudible.

6. *Diphthongs*

In many languages there are vowel segments whose quality is not *constant*: it changes continually while the vowel is being uttered. English has a number of such vowels. If the vowels of the two words *gnaw* and *now*, as pronounced by nearly all English speakers, are compared, it can be observed that the first has a vowel of unchanging quality, which can be prolonged at will, whereas in the course of pronouncing the second a change takes place which is obvious to both the ear and the eye: the quality of sound is not the same at the end as it was at the beginning, and the lips can be seen to have moved (the tongue has moved also, though this cannot be seen; however a movement of the lower jaw, reflecting the tongue movement, may be observable). Similarly in the word *eye* a change of sound is accompanied by a change in the position of the tongue (as revealed by the accompanying jaw movement). In both cases the change in sound, and the movement of the tongue or lips or both, are continuous throughout the vowel.

The technical term for a vowel of continually changing quality is a *diphthong*; vowels that do not change are called *monophthongs*. In the pronunciation of very many English people the vowels in the words *day* and *no* are diphthongs, whereas in the pronunciation of most Scots they are monophthongs.

A diphthong may be described and identified in terms of its beginning and ending points, using the categories for monophthongs discussed above in section 4, with the assumption that the articulators, in their movement, take the shortest path between these points. Thus the diphthong in the word *noise* starts in a *half-open back rounded* position, and the tongue and lips then move immediately to a *half-close front unrounded* position.

It should be noted that although monophthongs are often referred to as 'pure' vowels, no special virtue attaches to them.

No harm is done by thinking of a diphthong as a sequence of two vowels, provided it is remembered that they occupy only one syllable. A sequence of two vowels which occupy two syllables, as in *gnawing* or *ruin*, is not a diphthong.

7. *Secondary and double articulations*

Although the description of a vowel segment appears to concentrate attention on the lip posture and on the position of one particular part of the tongue, we have made it clear above that in fact it is the configuration of the tube-shaped vocal tract as a whole that gives a vowel its characteristic sound. This is true, though less obviously so, of consonant segments as well: the sound that is produced depends on the entire vocal tract. But while the location of the highest point of the tongue on two axes, together with the lip posture, provide a fair indication of the configuration of the whole vocal tract in the case of a vowel (with the exception to be mentioned later on in this section), in the case of a consonant the total configuration can hardly at all be inferred from the place and manner of the stricture. The terms of place and manner inform us about the state of affairs at one particular point in the vocal tract, but what goes on elsewhere is usually ignored, and we do not refer to it when assigning a consonant segment a three-term label. Nevertheless there are occasions when it is necessary to draw attention to aspects of the vocal tract other than place and manner of the stricture, and when this is so, we do it in terms of *secondary articulations—secondary*, because the stricture referred to by place and manner in the classification of a segment is regarded as its *primary* articulation. We have here, therefore, another dimension of classification for segments, though one which may often be conveniently ignored.

An illustration will best make clear how and when this extra dimension is used in classification. The primary articulation of a *voiced labial nasal*, the first segment of the English word *me* for example, is a stricture of complete closure between the two lips. Behind this primary articulation lies the whole of the rest of the vocal tract, in which the tongue is free to assume any shape since it is not involved in the primary articulation. The variety of shapes assumed by the tongue in English voiced labial nasals is probably not very great. There is undoubtedly a difference between the *m* of *me* and the *m* of *move* in tongue position (though it needs training to observe this), but it is a small one, and we usually neglect it and give the two segments the same label without causing any confusion. (We could not ignore the difference, of course, if we were trying to give an *exhaustive* description, including as many details as possible, of the pronunciation of the two words.) However in certain other languages segments which are also labelled *voiced labial nasals* are accompanied by more extreme modification by the tongue of the vocal tract behind the lips. In Russian, for example, it is possible to have a voiced labial nasal in which the tongue is raised high in the front of the mouth, in the same position as for a close front vowel. In Egyptian colloquial Arabic it is possible to have a voiced labial nasal in which the tongue is low in the mouth and retracted towards the back wall of the pharynx. In both languages there are other voiced labial nasal segments in which the shape of the vocal tract is not modified by such extreme tongue action, and there is a noticeable difference of sound between these and the others. The raising of the front of the tongue, in the one case, and its retraction towards the back wall of the pharynx, in the other, are therefore regarded as articulations which, though secondary to the primary labial one, at the same time should not be ignored: they must find a place in the classification of the segments, and a fourth term must be added to their labels. If the tongue is raised to the close front position, that is to say close to the hard palate, the secondary articulation is one of *palatalization*, and the Russian segment referred to is classified as a voiced *palatalized* labial nasal. If the tongue is low in the mouth and retracted towards the back wall of the pharynx, the secondary articulation is one of *pharyngalization*, and the Egyptian Arabic segment referred to is classified as a voiced *pharyngalized* labial nasal.

Many different secondary articulations can be distinguished, but only a few—those most commonly encountered—will be mentioned here. It should be remembered that when we include a secondary articulation in the label of a segment, we are drawing attention to some posture of the articulators *other* than those concerned in the primary articulation; hence it would be meaningless to describe, for example, a *palatal* consonant as being at the same time *palatalized*. The terms used to refer to secondary articulations of consonant segments are all coined on the same pattern; the commonest are:

> *labialization* (adjective *labialized*)
> *palatalization* (adjective *palatalized*)
> *velarization* (adjective *velarized*)
> *pharyngalization* (adjective *pharyngalized*).

In all these, the secondary articulation is a stricture of *open approximation* of the articulators, and as such involves less constriction of the vocal tract than the primary articulation does, whatever it may be. The secondary articulation may be either in front of, or behind, the primary articulation. Other terms for secondary articulations can be coined on these models as the need arises. It is possible for there to be two simultaneous secondary articulations, if the articulators involved in the primary articulation allow of this.

Labialization consists of rounding the lips during the production of the segment, just as for a rounded vowel. (This same action of the lips is not regarded as a secondary articulation in the case of vowels, because both the tongue-action and the lip-action are of equal importance: the one cannot be said to be secondary to the other.) The segment represented by the letters *sh* in the word *shall* is a voiceless palato-alveolar fricative; but as most speakers of English pronounce it (as can easily be confirmed by observation), the corners of the lips are brought forward somewhat, and it is therefore labialized. There is generally no need to refer to this in the classification of the segment, but the fact must not be forgotten in a detailed description of it: the sound would be different if the labialization were not there. A similar (though not identical) lip action can be observed with many English speakers in the segment *r* beginning the word *run*. Labialization may accompany any segment in which some part of the tongue is responsible for the primary articulation.

Palatalization has already been described. Palatalized segments are important in many languages, notably in Russian and Gaelic, and in those languages this secondary articulation must find a place in the labels attached to the appropriate segments. English speakers, especially in England and in Ireland, pronounce the *l* at the beginning of the word *little* with some, although not very marked, palatalization (i.e. the tongue is in the position not for a close front vowel, but a half-close one).

Velarization consists of raising the back of the tongue to the same position as for a close back vowel. Russian contains both a palatalized and a *velarized l*, and the difference in sound between them is very noticeable. Velarized segments are also important in Gaelic.

Pharyngalization has already been described. Arabic contains a number of pharyngalized segments in addition to the voiced labial nasal mentioned above; the *l* in the middle of the word *Allah* 'God' is an example of one of these. A less markedly pharyngalized segment is found in the second *l* in the word *little*, as pronounced in the south of England (though not, this time, in Ireland).

The adjectives *clear* and *dark* are often used to refer to a not very marked degree of palatalization and of pharyngalization respectively. Thus the first *l* in the word *little* is often described as a *clear l*, and the second as a *dark l*, in the pronunciation of people from the south of England. The adjective *dark* is used of segments with a not very marked degree of velarization also, such as the second *l* in *little* in some kinds of Cockney.

Nasalization is something which is often, and conveniently, classed among secondary articulations, though it is of a rather different nature. We have seen that the answer to question (4) on p. 42 ('What is the position of the velum?') is incorporated in some of the categories of *manner* used in consonant classification, but not in others. The position of the velum forms part of the definitions of *stop* and of *nasal*. In the remaining five categories, it is taken for granted that there *is* a velic closure during the production of the segment 'unless a specific statement is made to the contrary' (p. 49). If there is *not* a velic closure, then a fourth term must be added to the classificatory label, and the segment is called *nasalized*. A voiced nasalized labio-dental fricative may be heard from some people in the word *emphatic* for the sound written *m*; other people would use a voiced labial nasal here. Nasalized consonants (which must not be confused with *nasal* consonants; see p. 48) are not very common.

Vowel segments, as well as consonant segments, may be nasalized, that is to say pronounced without a velic closure, and unlike the latter they occur commonly in many languages. French is an example of a language which distinguishes nasalized vowels from non-nasalized ones, and in the phrase *un bon vin blanc* four different nasalized vowels are to be found.

Nasalization is not, strictly speaking, a secondary *articulation*, either in the case of vowels or consonants. A genuine secondary articulation, however, is needed for the description of certain vowel segments commonly found in a number of languages; in these segments the total configuration of the vocal tract is *not* adequately specified simply by location of the highest point of the tongue and statement of the lip posture. In most vowel segments, it is true, the blade and point do not act separately from the rest of the tongue; they are an indistinguishable part of its total mass. However, the blade and point are extremely mobile; they are perfectly capable of independent movement, and in some vowel segments they introduce modifications into the general configuration of the vocal tract which are additional to, and independent of, the way it is shaped by the main body of the tongue. Only one modification of this sort need be noticed here: it results from the point of the tongue being curled up and back towards the hard palate. This is a secondary articulation, *retroflexion*, and the vowel is said to be *retroflexed* (cf. the category *retroflex*, used of consonants, described on p. 51). Retroflexed vowels occur in the speech of many people in the west of England in such words as *far, more, burr*. The vowel in the last word, for instance, would be classified as a half-open central retroflexed unrounded vowel. Such segments are found in many other languages.

A *double articulation* is a different thing from a primary articulation accompanied by a secondary articulation, where the latter is subordinate to the former. A double articulation consists of two strictures of equal importance, and in such a case the descriptive label has to contain *two* terms of place (joined by a hyphen). For example, a voiceless *alveolar-velar* fricative is found in some dialects of

Swedish: it is as if the *ch* of Scottish *loch* and the *sh* of *shall* were said at the same time. Stop consonants made with two simultaneous closures are very common in languages of West Africa. Both voiced and voiceless *labial-velar* stops are found, some made with a pulmonic air-stream mechanism and others with a glottalic mechanism. *Labial-alveolar* stops are more rare,[12] but can also be found. Rounded vowels, strictly speaking, are examples of double articulations.

8. *Isolation*

Considerable experience with living speech is needed before one can apply the above categories in practice to the description and classification of segments. It is certainly not possible to learn to apply them simply by reading this chapter, the object of which is only to try to make clear the principles on which description and classification are based.

The beginner in phonetics who wants to attain practical familiarity with these categories must start with their application to his own speech, and as a preliminary step to this he needs to acquire facility in *isolation*–the separation of any given segment from its environment in natural speech. Various electronic devices exist by means of which any piece, however small, of a recorded utterance can be separated from the rest of the utterance, and reproduced by itself. Isolation is something like this, though it is done with the living, and not a recorded, voice; furthermore we must prolong the isolated piece, which electronic devices cannot as yet do, so that we can study it at leisure. To isolate a piece of one's own speech is to hold the speech organs static in a position which is normally rapidly passed through, thus turning a point in the continuum of movements into a sustained posture. With the organs of speech artificially arrested, the posture is available for examination by the senses of touch, sight, and kinesthetic awareness, and if necessary also by instrumental means. We can learn what it is that makes the posture characteristic of the segment, and we can compare it with other similarly isolated postures.

Isolation involves four successive steps, and they are all difficult for the beginner. The first step is to say the word or utterance, from which the segment is to be isolated, in a natural manner. When one's own speech is brought under introspective scrutiny in this way, it immediately takes on an air of unreality. It is an artificial situation, and only after experience does one gain confidence that an approximation to a natural utterance is being produced. The second step is to arrest the continuum of movement at the desired point, and at first this will probably have to be done by successive reductions of what is on either side of this point. The third step is to prolong this point *ad libitum*, after it is isolated, without changing in any way its quality or posture. The fourth step, which requires a lot of practice with the preceding three, consists of hitting on this artificially-isolated posture from memory, without having to refer back first to the utterance from which it was isolated.

When an isolated segment can thus be obtained with confidence, and when it can be said *long, loud,* and (if voiced) *level* in pitch, the posture of the organs of speech during its production can be examined and classified according to the principles set out above. We should, however, take to heart what Abraham Tucker, a 'prolix but pleasing philosopher' and an observant and accurate pioneer phonetician,[13] had noted as early as the eighteenth century: 'It were endless, and indeed impossible, to describe the exact posture of our organs in making the vocal sounds.' We should not try to do so. We should only select such aspects of the posture as are important for the purpose of the moment, and for which we are equipped with descriptive terms.[14]

When taxonomic familiarity has been obtained with segments of one's own speech, segments of other languages can similarly be brought under scrutiny. But the ascription to segments of categories of phonetic classification should always be based on first-hand experience. The phonetician is trained to avoid an attitude too commonly 'seen in the writings of some Learned men', as another early student of phonetics, William Holder, put it: when they discuss speech sounds, they 'speak of them by Tradition, as of some remote exotick thing, whereof we had no knowledge, but by uncertain and fabulous relations.'[15] It requires skill and practice to discuss them in taxonomic terms; but they are not remote and exotic: the phonetician is constantly surrounded by the material of his study, and it is available for immediate examination.

We may conclude this chapter by summarizing the speech-producing processes that have so far been dealt with:

process		*responsible for*
pulmonic	chest-pulse	syllable
air-stream		
mechanism	stress-pulse	stress
adjustment of glottis		voice, whisper, voicelessness
movement of velum		nasality
movements of tongue	(articulatory movements)	vowel and consonant characteristics, i.e. primary and secondary articulations
movements of lips		

9. *Taxonomic terms*

It may be useful at this point to provide an alphabetical list, with a brief indication of their meanings, of the more important taxonomic categories, or terms of segment classification, that are used in connexion with three-term labels. The similarity of some of these terms to each other (e.g. *velar*, *velaric*, *velarized*, in addition to the terms *velum* and *velic* which are not used in segment classification) is unfortunate and at first confusing.

ALVEOLAR. The teeth-ridge is passive articulator, and either the point or blade of the tongue is active articulator

ALVEOLAR-VELAR. The teeth ridge and the soft palate are simultaneously passive articulators, and the point or blade of the tongue and the back of the tongue are simultaneously active articulators. (A double articulation.)

APICAL. The point of the tongue is active articulator

APICO-ALVEOLAR. The point of the tongue is active articulator, and the teeth-ridge is passive articulator

APICO-DENTAL. The point of the tongue is active articulator, and the upper front teeth are passive articulator

APPROXIMANT. With open approximation of the articulators, and central passage of the air-stream

BACK (vowel). The highest point of the tongue lies beneath the soft palate

BI-LABIAL. The lower lip and the upper lip are articulators

BILATERAL. A LATERAL in which the air-stream escapes round both sides of the central obstruction

CENTRAL (vowel). The highest point of the tongue lies beneath the junction of hard and soft palates

CLEAR. Moderately PALATALIZED

CLICK. A STOP made with a velaric ingressive air-stream

CLOSE (vowel). The highest point of the tongue is close to the roof of the mouth

DARK. Moderately VELARIZED or PHARYNGALIZED

DENTAL. The upper front teeth are passive articulator, and either the point or blade of the tongue is active articulator

DIPHTHONG. A vowel of continually changing quality

EGRESSIVE. The air-stream moves outwards

EJECTIVE. A STOP made with a GLOTTALIC EGRESSIVE air-stream

FLAP. The active articulator strikes in passing against a passive one

FRICATIVE. With close approximation of the articulators, and central passage of the air-stream

FRICATIVE-LATERAL. With close approximation of the articulators, and lateral passage of the air-stream

FRICATIVE-TRILL. A TRILL with close approximation of the articulators

FRONT (vowel). The highest point of the tongue lies beneath the hard palate

GLOTTAL. Produced by the action of the vocal cords

GLOTTALIC. An air-stream initiated by movement of the larynx, with the glottis closed

GROOVED. The active articulator has a central groove from front to back

HALF-CLOSE (vowel). The highest point of the tongue is higher than half-way between its position for a CLOSE vowel and its position for an OPEN vowel

HALF-OPEN (vowel). The highest point of the tongue is lower than half-way between its position for a CLOSE vowel and its position for an OPEN vowel

IMPLOSIVE. A STOP made with a GLOTTALIC INGRESSIVE air-stream

INGRESSIVE. The air-stream moves inwards

LABIAL. The lower lip and the upper lip are the articulators

LABIALIZED. With a secondary articulation made by the lips

LABIAL-ALVEOLAR. The upper lip and the teeth-ridge are simultaneously passive articulators, and the lower lip and the point or blade of the tongue are simultaneously active articulators. (A double articulation.)

LABIAL-VELAR. The upper lip and the soft palate are simultaneously passive articulators, and the lower lip and the back of the tongue are simultaneously active articulators. (A double articulation.)

LABIO-DENTAL. The lower lip is active articulator, and the upper front teeth are passive articulator

LAMINAL. The blade of the tongue is active articulator

LAMINO-ALVEOLAR. The blade of the tongue is active articulator, and the teeth-ridge is passive articulator

LAMINO-DENTAL. The blade of the tongue is active articulator and the upper teeth are passive articulator

LATERAL. The air-stream is obstructed in the centre of the vocal tract, but escapes round one or both sides of the obstruction

MONOPHTHONG. A vowel of constant quality

NASAL. With complete closure in the mouth and no velic closure; the air-stream escapes through the nose

NASALIZED. With no velic closure, but the air-stream escaping partly through the mouth as well as the nose

ONE-TAP-TRILL. A TRILL in which the active articulator strikes only once against the passive articulator

OPEN (vowel). The highest point of the tongue is as far as possible from the roof of the mouth

ORAL. Made with a velic closure

OVER-ROUNDED (vowel). More rounding than usually goes with the height of the tongue

PALATAL. The hard palate is passive articulator, and the front of the tongue is active articulator

PALATALIZED. With a secondary articulation made by raising the front of the tongue towards the hard palate

PALATO-ALVEOLAR. The junction of teeth-ridge and hard palate is passive articulator, and the blade of the tongue is active articulator

PHARYNGAL. The back wall of the pharynx is passive articulator, and the root of the tongue is active articulator

PHARYNGALIZED. With a secondary articulation made by retracting the root of the tongue towards the back wall of the pharynx

PLOSIVE. A STOP made with a PULMONIC EGRESSIVE air-stream

PULMONIC. An air-stream initiated by movement of the respiratory muscles

RETROFLEX. The hard palate is passive articulator, and the point of the tongue is active articulator

RETROFLEXED. With a secondary articulation made by raising the point of the tongue towards the hard palate

ROUNDED (vowel). With the corners of the lips brought forward

STOP. With the articulators forming a stricture of complete closure

TRILL. The active articulator vibrates so that it strikes repeatedly against the passive articulator

UNDER-ROUNDED. Less rounding than usually goes with the height of the tongue

UNILATERAL. A LATERAL in which the air-stream escapes round one side only of the central obstruction

UNROUNDED (vowel). With the corners of the lips pulled back

UVULAR. The end of the soft palate, with the uvula, is passive articulator, and the root of the tongue is active articulator

VELAR. The soft palate is passive articulator, and the back of the tongue is active articulator

VELARIC. An air-stream initiated by movement of the tongue, the back of which is in close contact with the soft palate

VELARIZED. With a secondary articulation made by raising the back of the tongue towards the soft palate

VOICED. With vibration of the vocal cords

VOICELESS. With open glottis

WHISPERED. With narrowed glottis

5

Structure and System

1. *Phonology*

As was stated above (p. 5), the potentialities of a medium are always much greater than the use made of it by any one language, and this is conspicuously true of the aural medium. The full range of possible human phonetic performance is very wide. There are, in fact, innumerable different ways of performing the articulatory movements of tongue and lips; different ways of synchronizing the articulatory movements with the various states of the glottis, with the valve-action of the velum, with the air-stream mechanisms; different ways of combining the resulting movement-complexes into sequences. (The variety of processes involved in the production of speech is indicated in outline on p. 66.) Only a selection, however, from this full range is put to use by the speakers of any single language–a selection, moreover, which is not only limited, but different in very many (one might almost say nearly all) respects from the selection used by speakers of every other language. It is this selection from the full general human phonetic range which is formed into the patterns which carry the particular language. The selection, and the patterns into which it is formed, constitute the *phonology* of the language. The phonology of every language is peculiar to that language, and different from that of every other language.

In the three preceding chapters we have been examining the aural medium in general human terms. We have shown how the elements of any utterance can be identified and described by means of taxonomic categories which can be applied to them without regard to the particular language in which the utterance was spoken. This is a *general phonetic* approach to an utterance. By means of it we can describe the way in which each individual language is pronounced in the same terms as we can describe the way in which every other language is pronounced. A general phonetic approach, however, will not enable us to show how the medium is acting *as* a medium: why it is not just mere noise, but is capable of being a vehicle for a particular language. It will not reveal the phonology of a language, in short. A *phonological* approach to the medium is one that will bring out the pattern-forming capabilities of the elements of utterance as used in a particular language, rather than place them in relation to general human phonetic resources.

The general phonetic approach and the phonological approach to the aural medium complement each other, and both are needed to provide an adequate account of the medium as used for a given language. Both approaches deal with the same facts; they differ in the way the facts are 'selected and grouped in attention' (to use Angus Sinclair's phrase).[1] (The distinction between the two approaches is, perhaps, rather unfortunately expressed by means of the terms 'general phonetic' and 'phonological', though this is common usage. The terms might lead one to think that the latter approach is not part of the subject of phonetics, while the former obviously is. The study of the phonology of languages is, of course, of great importance in general linguistics also, in fact it provides common ground between the two 'linguistic sciences' (see p. 2); it is nevertheless an integral part of the subject of phonetics, and is not a separate subject, although the word 'phonology' is at times used as though it was a name for one.[2] It is seldom possible, indeed, to adopt one approach to the aural medium to the complete exclusion of the other–they are always to some extent intermingled.)

The patterns into which the aural medium is capable of being organized are not immediately obvious to inspection (however immediately intelligible, to those who know it, the language may be). They are embedded in the medium, and they have to be extracted from it. Their discovery, analysis and description is best done in terms of two concepts, that of *structure* and that of *system*. The patterns can be looked on as consisting of units, which are arranged in various ways. The concept of system deals with the units themselves, and the concept of structure deals with their arrangement.

To put it another way: the units of the aural medium that are used for building up the patterns which compose the linguistic entities of a language are not freely combinable in any order. Peculiar to each language is not only its own selection from the general human repertoire of possible phonetic units, but also the restrictions on the sorts of combinations into which they can be put. The concept of structure deals with *syntagmatic* relations, as they are called, between units– relations which hold between the units which are together present in an utterance; the concept of system deals with *paradigmatic* relations between units—relations which hold between units which are not present together in an utterance, but can be substituted for each other to produce different utterances.[3]

Thus in the spoken English sentence *look at the cat* there occurs a phonetic unit which we can identify as being represented by the letter *c* in the spelling; it forms part of the linguistic entity which is the word *cat*. *c* is in syntagmatic relation with the other units in the same linguistic entity, namely -*at* (less obviously, perhaps, it is in syntagmatic relation with everything else in the sentence). It is in paradigmatic relation with those other phonetic units which could also be found in English in the same place in a linguistic entity as *c* is: for example *r* (*look at the rat*), *b* (*look at the bat*), *m* (*look at the mat*), and so on. The two kinds of relations can be shown thus:

$$
(\text{look at the}) \left\{ \begin{array}{l} \overset{\frown}{c \quad at} \\ r \\ b \\ m \end{array} \right.
$$

where the horizontal link expresses the syntagmatic relations of *c*, and the vertical link the paradigmatic relations of *c*.

We can say, therefore, that *c* belongs to a *system* of elements which can occur in a certain place (in this case the initial position) of a *structure* of a certain type. The system is the complete inventory of the elements possible in that particular place (there are more, of course, than *c r b m*); and the structure in this particular case is a single syllable, which is also a word, which both begins and ends with a consonant.[4] (The same element, *c*, may enter into many other syntagmatic and paradigmatic relations, and therefore play a part in other structures and systems.)

The concepts of structure and system are based on generalizations which discard a certain amount (sometimes quite a lot) of general phonetic detail, since, as we have seen earlier (p. 5), the language-bearing patterns do not by any means completely exhaust the medium. In the analysis and description of phonological patterns and the elements that compose them, many things about the medium will inevitably appear irrelevant—everything to do with the indexical side, for instance, and everything that is idiosyncratic: such features do not enter into the language-bearing patterns. We are of course concerned, in dealing with phonology, both with the *form* of phonological elements, in the sense of their general phonetic nature, and also with their *function* in structures and systems; but function here takes precedence over form. (The study of the phonology of a language has been aptly termed 'functional phonetics'.[5]) Very great phonetic detail may at some points be important in describing the phonology of a language, but at other points it may be unnecessary. Items may be taken to be the same in a functional sense which are not the same in a formal, that is to say general phonetic, sense: contrasts and differences may be more important than resemblances. (Though it must be remembered that the kind of phonetic detail that is considered irrelevant in the phonology of one language may not be irrelevant in another.)

We shall see that there are considerable differences between languages both in respect of structure and of system. It will be easiest to explain the concept of structure first, and to see what sort of differences can be found there, and afterwards to go on to the concept of system. We will begin by examining the structure of syllables.

2. *Structure*

A syllable (see chapter 3) is a product of the way the pulmonic airstream mechanism works. Its basis is a chest-pulse, on which are superimposed the articulatory movements, and the allied movements of the vocal cords and velum, which produce segments. A syllable has three phases (p. 40), with which segments may coincide. If the syllable is audible at all, there must be a central segment associated with phase 2, the passage through the vocal tract of air set in motion by the chest-pulse; but there may or may not be marginal segments associated with the first, or releasing, phase and the third, or arresting, phase. The four English syllables *oh, go, oat, goat* (each of which, incidentally, is also a word) will illustrate this. Their segments are related to the phases of the syllable as follows:

1	2	3
	oh	
g	o	
	oa	t
g	oa	t

To each phase of the syllable corresponds a *place* in syllable structure, and different patterns of structure arise from the manner in which the three places are filled by segments, which represent the elements of syllable structure. There are two sorts of elements, and symbols have already been introduced for them (p. 40) by means of which the patterns can be expressed in formulas. The symbol V is used for the element in place 2 which is always present and which may be called the syllabic element; and C is used for the releasing and arresting marginal elements in places 1 and 3. O, or zero, indicates that place 1 or place 3 is empty, with no element of structure there. Thus the four syllables just quoted exemplify the following four different patterns:

	1	2	3
oh =	O	V	O
go =	C	V	O
oat =	O	V	C
goat =	C	V	C

The difference between these structural patterns lies only in whether the marginal places are filled or empty. They are four very simple patterns. Other, less simple, patterns are possible which arise from complex articulations occurring at the marginal places, resulting in several C elements there instead of just a single one. For example, the English syllable *streets* has CCC in place 1, and CC in place 3: its structural pattern is CCCVCC. Sequences of C elements of this sort are known as consonant *clusters*; by the *size* of a cluster is meant the number of C elements contained in it.

Different languages make use of different ranges of patterns of syllable structure. English, clearly, has a large number of different patterns. Some languages have an even larger number than English, while others have a more restricted range. There is no language known that allows only one pattern, though there are many which have only two. For example, Keresan (a language of the Rio Grande Valley) makes use of the patterns CVC and CVO only, and no others are permissible.[6] These two patterns of syllable structure can be expressed – or compressed – in a single generalized formula CV(C), where the brackets round the C indicate the optional presence of an element at that place–(C) is equivalent to 'either C or O'. This formula summarizes the possibilities of syllable structure in Keresan phonology.

The existence in a language of only these two particular syllable patterns, where C is obligatory in place 1, is not a common state of affairs. Quite a number of languages, however, make use of only the two patterns OVO and CVO, with place 3 always empty. Japanese is such a language, and so are many Polynesian languages. A generalized formula for these languages, constructed in the same way as the one for Keresan, would be (C)VO.

Some languages (Cantonese, for example) have all four of the simple patterns OVO, CVO, OVC, CVC, but none more complex. Like the languages already mentioned, they do not permit consonant clusters. The generalized formula for the syllable structure of these languages would be (C)V(C).

Among the languages which do permit consonant clusters, differences are found both in the size of the clusters, and in the structural place where they are permitted. For example, both Spanish and Arabic syllable patterns contain clusters, but of not more than two consonants. In Spanish, however, clusters are only permitted in place 1, while in Arabic they are only permitted in place 3. Other languages allow larger clusters. The largest possible cluster in place 1 in English is CCC, and the largest in place 3 is CCCC (though B. L. Whorf has pointed out[7] that CCCCC might conceivably occur if a person who habitually inserts, as some do, a *p* between *m* and *f* were to use the expression 'Thou triumphst!', in which we would find m-(p)-ph-s-t). Many languages have larger clusters still. In Georgian, clusters of up to six consonants can be found in place 1,[8] and so in other languages of the Caucasus. Some American Indian languages also allow clusters of this size.

A generalized formula for English syllable structure (ignoring the dubious *triumphst*), constructed in the same way as the preceding ones, would be $(C)(C)(C)V(C)(C)(C)(C)$. However, this is neither very elegant nor compact. There is a simpler way of generalizing syllable structure formulas for languages which have clusters. The formula for English, for example, would be $C_{0-3}VC_{0-4}$. The subscript figures here indicate the possibilities, in terms of number of elements for that place of syllable structure. Thus C_{0-3} means that there can be anything from no to three C elements in place 1.

Some languages have structural restrictions of various sorts which operate within the limitations imposed by the range of patterns of their syllable structure. Thus in English the consonant corresponding to the letters *ng* in the word *hang*, a voiced velar nasal, can represent a C element in place 3, but it cannot represent a C element in place 1. A voiced velar nasal is free from this structural restriction in many other languages—Maori, for example. (The first name of the well-known writer, Ngaio Marsh, is a Maori word, and it has a voiced velar nasal in place 1.) The converse restriction applies to the consonant *h* at the beginning of the word *hang*: this can represent a C element in place 1, but never in place 3. Other languages, such as Sanskrit or Arabic, do not have this restriction.

Among the languages that permit consonant clusters, some, such as many Caucasian languages, have no restrictions on the way the consonants are arranged within them; others, such as English, allow only severely restricted combinations. Thus, although there are the syllables *stay, tray, stray* in English, no syllable *sray* exists – *sr* is, for English, an inadmissible cluster. The syllable *spy* is possible, but not *psy* – *sp* is a permissible cluster in place 1, but *ps* is not (though a very few people make an effort to pronounce the *p* in *psychology*, and rather more do so in the neologism *psionic*). Both *sp* and *ps* are possible clusters in place 3, however, as shown by *asp* and *apse*. A further kind of restriction in English is that in releasing clusters of the type CCC, the first C can be represented only by *s* (*square*, *split*, *strong*); there is no other possibility.

(It is important not to confuse a consonant cluster with a sequence of consonants which extends over two syllables. Thus the sequence *tr* is a cluster in *tray*, but it is not in *hatrack*, where the *t* and the *r* belong to different syllables. In the latter case, the sequence is said to consist of *abutting* consonants.[9] The sequence *-xfr-* (i.e. *-ksfr-*) in *tax-free* consists of two abutting clusters, *ks* and *fr*).

Such structural regularities in the phonology of a language produce, in its speakers, deep-rooted habits of speech which are difficult to change. This is shown by the way new words introduced into a language–slang, trade names, borrowings from foreign languages– conform to the existing structural patterns. Recent examples from English are *blurb*, *snoop*, *grotty*, *derv*, *daz*, *blitz*. The nonsense words of Lewis Carroll and Edward Lear–*brillig*, *slithy*, *borogove*, *jumblies* –are not complete nonsense, as J. R. Firth has pointed out: they are English nonsense, conforming strictly to English patterns of structure.[10] Nobody would think of calling a new detergent *fnodr*, or *shnatk*, which violate the structural rules of English.

Impermissible clusters are difficult to pronounce, however familiar their constituent consonants may be. Thus in English the sequence *-pfl-* offers no difficulty when *p* is an abutting consonant and only *fl* is a cluster, as in *hipflask*. But most speakers of English found it difficult to pronounce the name of the French politician M. Pflimlin, when it was in the news, because of the unfamiliar releasing cluster *pfl*. Bernard Shaw, in his play *Caesar and Cleopatra*, makes a joke of Caesar's inability to pronounce the name of Cleopatra's nurse, Ftatateeta: *ft* is not an admissible cluster in Latin, and was therefore foreign to Caesar's phonetic habits.

We have taken most of the illustrations, in this account of syllable structure, from English, and the examples chosen have been not just syllables but single-syllable words, or *monosyllables*. In some languages it is sufficient to describe the structure patterns of monosyllables: they will be the structure patterns of all syllables, including those that go to make up *polysyllables*, or words of more than one syllable. This would be the case with French. There are other languages, on the other hand, in which monosyllables are not representative of all syllables, and English is one of these. There are various restrictions on the C and V elements of monosyllables which do not always apply to the constituent syllables of polysyllables. For instance, *tr* is not permissible as an arresting cluster in a monosyllable;

but it is an arresting cluster, in the pronunciation of many people, in the first syllable of the polysyllable *petrol*. (One of the symptoms of *tr* being a cluster here is that *r* is a voiceless fricative, instead of the voiced approximant which it would be if it was an abutting consonant, as for example in *hatrack*.) Similarly *tl* is not permissible in monosyllables as a releasing cluster in most types of English (see however, ch. 8, p. 139), but it is a releasing cluster, in some people's pronunciation, in the second syllable of the polysyllable *A-tlantic* (many other people, of course, would say *At-lantic*).

Restrictions which concern vowels in English monosyllables do not always apply in polysyllables. The vowels in the words *bit, but, book* can only represent the V element in a monosyllable if place 3 is filled, that is to say they cannot occur in a syllable pattern which ends in O. In polysyllables, however, they can be found in such patterns: for example in the final syllables of *pity* (in many accents of England), *china* (in Scotland), *follow* (again, in many accents of England).

On the other hand we find, in many languages, restrictions, in polysyllables, on what may fill *word-initial* places or *word-final* places, which override those which apply simply to syllable-initial or syllable-final places. Thus the consonant which is found in the middle of the word *measure* can never be word-initial in English, though it may be syllable-initial within the word, as in many people's pronunciation of *seizure*. In German in word-final position fricatives and stops are always voiceless. In Finnish[11] only five consonants, *l n r s t*, are permissible in word-final position, though others can be syllable-final within the word. In word-initial position in Finnish no clusters are allowed, though releasing clusters are found elsewhere within the word.

Consideration of polysyllables brings up some further points concerning structure. If, for example, there is a sequence -VCV- within a word, the C between the two Vs could, theoretically, belong to either of the two syllables: it could be arresting, in place 3, of the first syllable; or releasing, in place 1, of the second syllable, i.e. the sequence could be -VC OV-, or it could be -VO CV-. (These two alternatives can be expressed more concisely, and so in other cases when syllables follow each other, by putting a point in place of the O; the point then indicates the syllable division: -VC.V- or -V.CV-.) Both alternatives are possible in English, as can be seen by comparing the two words

    beekeeper
    beefeater

which are, respectively, V.CV (bee.keeper) and VC.V (beef.eater). But in some languages only one of the two alternatives is allowed. It is a structural rule of French, for instance, that -VCV- must always be -V.CV-, as in *ba.teau*, whereas in Keresan (the American Indian language mentioned above) -VCV- must always be -VC.V-.

Similarly a sequence -VCCV- may be variously divided. If we compare the two English words

> teatray
> heatray

we find the first is -V.CCV- (tea.tray), while the second is -VC.CV- (heat.ray): in the second case the consonants are abutting, in the first they form a releasing cluster. So with longer sequences:

> mousetrap
> toestrap

where we have -VC.CCV- in the first (mouse.trap) and -V.CCCV- in the second (toe.strap).[12] The syllable division in these cases follows the etymology, i.e. it reveals how the words are compounded. In other languages the division of consonant sequences follows strict rules, and the etymology is irrelevant.

However, syllable division in English does not by any means always go according to the etymology, and sometimes one finds quite unexpected divisions (in the sense that etymology would suggest they should be different), even when the consonant sequence extends over two words. There is a good deal of personal variation in this point, but the following examples of unexpected syllable division have been noted within words: *war.drobe, teas.poon, hemis.phere, ea.chother, aw.kward, mi.stake*, and between words: *Extre.me Unction* (from Catholics), *a.t least, not a.t all, a.t home, thi.s afternoon, Sain.t Andrews*. It is of interest, in view of the last example, that the word *tawdry* derives from *St. Audrey*.[13]

Another structural point arises, in English, in connexion with polysyllables. Usually the syllabic element, in the central place of a syllable, is represented by the kind of segment that up to now has been called a vowel (which is why it is symbolized by 'V'), in the sense given in chapter 4. It is not always a segment of this kind, however. It is always a vowel, in this sense, in monosyllables; but syllables occur in polysyllabic words in which it may not be. In the second syllable of the polysyllable *button*, for example, as pronounced by most English speakers, there is no vowel (the spelling should not mislead us here)–nothing intervenes between the *t* and the *n* (see below p. 142), and it is the latter, a segment of a kind that up to now we have been calling a consonant, that represents the syllabic element. The *n* of *button*, when the word is pronounced in this way, is called a *syllabic n.* In the same way, a syllabic *l*, following immediately on the *p*, occurs in the last syllable of the polysyllable *people*.

3. *Vowels, vocoids, etc.*

This is a good point at which to look more closely at the two kinds of elements of structure, C and V, that constitute syllables, and at the division of segments into the two categories *consonant* and *vowel*. As was briefly indicated in chapter 3, these terms are ambiguous (which is natural in words with such a long history behind them): they have sometimes been used in reference to the *form*, and sometimes in reference to the *function*, of a segment. The confusion which has resulted is demonstrated by the emergence of compromise terms such as semi-vowel, demi-vowel, semi-consonant, vocalic consonant, consonantal vowel, vowel-like, consonantoid, vocaloid, and others.

Most contemporary textbooks define 'vowel' and 'consonant' according to the general phonetic *form* of the segment, in terms such as 'vowels are modifications of the voice-sound that involve no closure, friction, or contact of the tongue or lips', all other segments being consonants.[14] Difficulties arise, however, when the same words 'vowel' and 'consonant' are used to refer to the phonological *function* of segments in the syllable, the term vowel being used for the syllabic element, and the term consonant being used for the marginal elements. In Greek, which is where the terms originated ultimately, the categories of 'general phonetic vowel' and 'phonological representative of V element' (and similarly the categories of 'general phonetic consonant' and 'phonological representative of C element') coincided more or less, and so they do in many languages today; but in many other languages in the world (including, as we have just seen, English) they do not. As another instance, C as well as V elements of structure in English can have a stricture of open approximation, involving 'no closure, friction, or contact of the tongue or lips'. Hence a term such as semi-vowel, a semi-vowel being a segment which defined by phonetic form is a vowel, but by phonological function is a C element in a syllable pattern–such as the *y* in English *yet*, or the *w* in English *wet*. The existence of the term is a symptom of the conflict between the general phonetic and the phonological uses.

The difficulty is one of which people have long been aware, and interesting discussions of the problem can be found by, for example, H.D. Darbishire, F. de Saussure, and L. Bloomfield. The obvious solution to the difficulty is to introduce new terms and to re-define the old ones, so that a conflict between application of a term according to form and application according to function is no longer possible. Darbishire, Saussure, and Bloomfield all did this, but their neologisms never caught on.[15] The simplest, and much the most successful, attempt to disambiguate the terms in this area is that of K. L. Pike, put forward in his *Phonetics* (1943).[16]

Pike introduced two new terms to replace the words vowel and consonant when used with reference to phonetic form, without regard to syllabic function: *vocoid*, and non-vocoid or *contoid*. The terms are very rigorously defined.[17] A vocoid is a segment with a stricture of open approximation, with or without a velic closure, and with central passage of the air-stream. All other segments are contoids. Pike then puts forward the term *syllabic* for a segment representing a V element of syllable structure, and *non-syllabic* for a segment representing a C element of syllable structure. The two sets of terms when used together give us, for any segment in a given utterance, its category in general phonetic terms and its place in structure. Thus we have, in English, a *syllabic vocoid* in *awe*, a *non-syllabic vocoid* at the beginning of *yet*, a *syllabic contoid* in the second syllable of *people*, and a *non-syllabic contoid* at the beginning of *pet*. The traditional terms vowel and consonant, Pike suggests, can be used as synonyms of syllabic vocoid, and non-syllabic contoid, respectively.

Syllabic vocoids (vowels) and non-syllabic contoids (consonants) are the most common of the four categories in the languages of the world. Non-syllabic vocoids and syllabic contoids are rarer, and are the two categories that have caused confusion in the past, because there was no accepted way of referring to them which was unequivocal. They are nevertheless quite common. Voiced non-syllabic vocoids, besides those at the beginning of English *yet* and *wet*, are found at the beginning of English *run* (in most accents of England and America), and at the beginning of French *huit*; and voiceless non-syllabic vocoids of various qualities are found at the beginning of English *he*, *who*, *half*, and many other words in many other languages. Syllabic contoids are often heard in interjections, such as English *sh!* or *h'mm!* Syllabic *l* and *n* are found in many languages besides English; syllabic *m* is found in many African languages; a syllabic trill *r* is found in Serbian. In English informal rapid speech many syllabic contoids can be detected; for instance in *never forget* a syllabic *v* sometimes makes up the whole of the second syllable of *never*; and two syllabic *s*'s can sometimes be detected in *solicitor*, one in the first syllable and one in the third.

4. *Quantity*

It is necessary, at this juncture, to say something about the relative *length*–the duration in time–of segments. From the point of view of general phonetic taxonomy, the length of a segment is quite irrelevant; but it may have phonological importance from the point of view of syllable structure.

In many languages a fixed and predictable relationship holds between the lengths of the segments in a syllable. This is true of most kinds of English. All monosyllables in English tend to be of the same length, under similar circumstances, but there is considerable variation in the way the total length of a monosyllable is made up by the lengths of the individual segments that constitute it. Releasing consonants contribute little: they are uniformly very short. The relative lengths of the remaining segments depend on two factors. The first factor is the pattern of structure in which they find themselves. Thus the vowel in a syllable of the pattern CVO is longer than the vowel in a CVC pattern, which in turn is longer than in a CVCC pattern. The three monosyllables *bee, beat, beast* illustrate this. The other factor is the phonetic nature of the segments themselves: a final voiced consonant is shorter than a final voiceless one, and therefore a vowel before a voiced consonant is longer than a vowel before a voiceless one. The overall length of the two monosyllables *bead, beat* is the same, but the vowel of the first has about twice the duration of that of the second. Another regularity, of a rather different kind, is illustrated by the fact that the vowel in *bead* has greater duration than the vowel in *bid*, and the vowel in *beat* than that in *bit*, and these two vowel sounds always have this difference of length when they occur in the same circumstances. They may not have it, though, if the circumstances are not the same; thus the vowel in *beat* is shorter than the vowel in *bid*—the rule about voiced and voiceless consonants has overridden the other.[18]

The rules for duration of segments in monosyllables in English are, as can be seen, fairly complicated, and for polysyllables they are even more so. Moreover the rules vary from one accent of English to another. Regular relations of duration between the segments of syllables hold in many other languages, though they will seldom be the same as English has. None of these regularities affect the patterns of structure of the syllable, however, but there are languages in which the duration of segments is not always fixed, but is sometimes independent of regularities of this sort. For example, if the two monosyllables *leek* and *leak*, as pronounced in educated Scots of the West of Scotland, are compared, no difference will appear between them in the quality of the segments. There will be a difference, however, in the lengths of the segments: the vowel in the first word is a short vowel, the vowel in the second word is a long vowel. This is a difference which cannot be covered by a general rule which applies automatically.

Although there is a difference in vowel duration between the two monosyllables *bit* and *beat*, they both exemplify the same pattern of syllable structure, namely CVC. The two monosyllables *leek* and *leak*, in this particular accent, however, must be regarded as exemplifying different patterns. The first is CVC, but the second is best formulated as CVVC, the long vowel being indicated by the two Vs. A difference of vowel length which makes a difference of syllable structure is called a difference of vowel *quantity*.

This particular type of Scottish accent is unusual; most accents of English do not have structural distinctions of either vowel or consonant quantity. Such distinctions, however, are found in many other languages. They are most common where vowels are concerned (Gaelic and Finnish are examples of languages which have distinctions of vowel quantity), less common where arresting consonants are concerned (Arabic and Hungarian are examples), and even less common where releasing consonants are concerned (an example of a language which makes distinctions of quantity there being Pame, spoken in central Mexico).[19]

There are occasions when a vowel posture is maintained for longer than it is in other circumstances in the language, but its duration extends over two syllables. The word *pitying*, in the pronunciation of many (not by any means all) English speakers, has the same vowel posture maintained from the *t* to the *ng*, but a chest-pulse occurs in the course of it, i.e. it represents V.V. The French word *créer*, similarly, has the structure CCV.V: it contains a single vowel posture, but two syllables. We have in both these cases what is known as a *double* vowel, which must be distinguished from a long one, such as VV in *leak*. Double consonants also must be distinguished from long consonants. A double consonant is one whose duration extends over two syllables, whereas the duration of a long consonant is confined to a single syllable. Double consonants are frequently found in English, especially at word junctions: *wholly* (as said by many), *unknown*, *book-case*, *this Sunday*. They occur in many other languages.

5. *System*

The other concept used for describing the phonology of a language, the one that deals with paradigmatic relations, is the concept of system. A system is an inventory of the items in a language that can represent one of the two elements of structure, C or V; there is thus a C-system and V-system. The two are often referred to together as the sound-system of a language. Languages can differ from each other in the matter of system, as well as in structure.

An immediately obvious difference between languages is in the size of their systems, that is to say in the number of items they contain. V-systems, for instance, may range from three items, as in Classical Arabic and some modern forms, through five (modern Greek, Spanish), seven (Italian), eight (Turkish), to much larger systems such as those used by educated speakers in Britain, which may comprise from thirteen to twenty-one items. C-systems, also, may be small (but never, as far as is known, as small as V-systems can be): Hawaiian has eight, English twenty-two, Scots Gaelic about thirty, some American Indian languages, such as Tlingit, spoken in Alaska, over forty.

There seems to be no necessary relation between the size of the V-system of a language and the size of its C-system; both may be large, or both small, or one small and the other large. An extreme example of the latter case is provided by Kabardian, a Caucasian language, which has forty-five items in its C-system, and three in the V-system.[20]

Another difference between languages concerning C- and V-systems lies in the way they use the general resources of the medium. There is nothing striking about English, for example, in this; but it is striking when we find a whole range of phonetic possibilities is missing from a system. Thus a C-system with no labial contoids at all (though with many labialized contoids, and a non-syllabic vocoid *w*) is found in Tlingit; and a C-system with no nasal consonants at all is found in Wichita, an American Indian language spoken in Oklahoma (it has no labial consonants either).[21] A similar general phonetic characteristic of a C-system is the presence of a very large number of items made with a glottalic egressive air-stream, such as in Kabardian, or of a large number of items made without voice, such as in Icelandic or Gaelic.

Systems can usually be set out according to general phonetic taxonomic categories so as to reveal symmetries of various sorts in the system; indeed there is a strong tendency towards symmetry in the phonology of languages. If, for example, a hitherto undescribed language is under investigation, and in its C-system voiced and voiceless velar stops, voiced and voiceless dental stops, and a voiced labial stop, are found, it would be fairly safe to assume that there was a voiceless labial stop also, waiting to be discovered. Such symmetrical pairing of voiced and voiceless stops, and also fricatives, is very widespread. However, it would not be entirely safe to make the assumption–it could turn out that there was, after all, no voiceless labial stop in the C-system, and it would so turn out if we were investigating Egyptian Arabic, for example. Such asymmetries–'holes in the pattern', as they are sometimes called–are quite common. In V-systems also the same kind of symmetry is found; thus a system of six items might consist of three front vowels and three back vowels, or it might consist of two front, two central, and two back. But Icelandic, for instance, is asymmetrical in its V-system in having six front vowels and only two back vowels.

There is a danger of over-doing the search for symmetry and regularity in a language, and of distorting facts to make them fit patterns. Language, after all, is human behaviour, which is always untidy in one way or another; a systematic analysis of it will always reveal loose ends. Moreover the problem is not only that human behaviour is never completely consistent, and that individuals never behave in exactly the same way; it is also that language, and the medium that carries it, are constantly in a state of change. New patterns of structure are always emerging, and old structures falling into desuetude; systems are contracting and expanding. Any moment when an analysis is made is likely to be a transitional stage in the language or the medium in one respect or another. One should beware, in linguistic descriptions, of a spurious appearance of perfect symmetry.

A system is not just a list of items, however. It is called a 'system' for good reason: J. R. Firth has said that it is 'a scale of interdependent qualities'.[22] Each item in a system has a place in relation to the other items, a place in a systemic pattern, just as an element of structure has a place in a structural pattern. This shows itself in many ways. In the history of sound-changes in a language, we find that if one vowel has altered its quality in the course of time, other vowels in the system will also have undergone change, so that the basic systemic pattern tends to be undisturbed. Very considerable changes can happen to individual vowels in a system, as in English over the last 500 years, without the system as such being greatly affected. Different speakers of the same language, using the same V-system, often have very different representations, from the general phonetic point of view, for the individual items in the system. When they listen to each other talking, they have learnt to translate phonetic quality into systemic place; if they did not do this, they would never understand each other. This is known as *conversion*: the listener converts a phonetic value into a phonological value.[23] The same applies, though less obviously, to consonant systems. The system is therefore, to this extent, a psychological reality.

6. *Phoneme theory*

The concept of system brings with it a problem, which an example from English will demonstrate. The monosyllables *kit* and *cat* exhibit the same pattern of syllable structure, CVC. They are different syllables, obviously, because in place 2 they have different terms of the

V-system, as the letters *i* and *a* in the spelling reflect. Equally obviously they have the same term of the C-system in place 3. But what about the releasing consonants, occupying place 1, in the two syllables? Are they the same or different? (We must, of course, take no notice of the difference between *k* and *c* in the spelling, which reflects nothing of phonological interest.) It can be said at once that the two segments would not receive the same general phonetic description: the stricture of complete closure is further forward in the mouth for *kit* than for *cat* (to different degrees in different accents of English), and their auditory quality is different. They are, in fact, different segments. Do they therefore represent different items in the C-system? Phoneme theory enables us to give the convenient answer 'no' to this: they represent the same systemic item.

Every language contains a very large number–hundreds, perhaps–of segments, both vocoids and contoids, which, from the point of view of general phonetic taxonomy, are different, and are auditorily distinguishable even without special training. There are many more such segments than it would be convenient to have as terms in the C- and V-systems. Phoneme theory relates a great deal of the variation in the phonetic quality of segments to their environment, and thereby reduces the amount of phonetic detail that is phonologically relevant. It thus reconciles the extensive variety of segments with a limited size of systems. The items in a system are phonemes, not segments, and there are very much fewer phonemes than segments in a language. It is possible, in any language, to formulate rules by which the phonetic quality of any given segment can be accounted for (*a*) by saying what phoneme it represents, and (*b*) by saying what its environment is.

By the environment of a segment, we mean the other segments which occur with it, particularly those immediately before and after; its place in a pattern of structure; and sometimes various accompanying features of voice dynamics (to be dealt with in the following chapter). (The environment of a segment is often called its 'phonetic context'. Context, however, is an overworked term in linguistics, and environment is therefore preferred here.)

Let us consider the environment of the consonant segment at the beginning of *kit*:

(*a*) it represents the releasing consonant in a syllable of the pattern C V C;
(*b*) the syllable containing it is a monosyllable;
(*c*) the V element of structure in the pattern is represented by a half-close front unrounded vowel.

Now let us consider the environment of the consonant segment at the beginning of *cat*:

(*a*) is the same as for *kit*;
(*b*) is the same as for *kit*;
(*c*) the V element of structure in the pattern is represented by an open front unrounded vowel.

We can call these two different environments env[1] and env[2], respectively. Many other segments occur in env[1], for example in *bit, pit, fit, sit, hit*; and many other segments occur in env[2], for example in *bat, pat, fat, sat, hat*. The segments represented in the spelling by *b, p, f, s, h* are in *parallel distribution* in the above examples, i.e. they are distributed among possible environments in the same way.

Let us call the two initial segments of *kit* and *cat* k[1] and k[2] respectively. An examination of the medium as used for English will show that k[1] occurs always, and only, in env[1]; whereas k[2] occurs always, and only, in env[2]. A segment having the phonetic characteristics of k[1] is never found in env[2]; and vice versa. When different segments are only found in different environments, and never occur in the same environment, they are said to be in *complementary distribution*. k[1] and k[2] are in complementary distribution.

A group of segments in complementary distribution constitutes a phoneme. Not only do k[1] and k[2] belong to the same phoneme, but so do many other segments of different phonetic qualities, for example segments to be found in the words *skit, scat, quid, squid*. (The reader may care to work out the general phonetic differences between these segments, and to try characterizing the environments they go with.) A phoneme therefore is a group of segments which are different from the point of view of general phonetic taxonomy, but have the same function phonologically. The segments which a phoneme comprises, or which represent it, are said to be members of that phoneme, or *allophones* of it.[24] Each allophone is *tied* to a certain kind of environment: it never occurs apart from certain features in the environment. In any language, every discriminable allophone has an environment that goes with it, and that can be clearly identified and described, sometimes in very general terms, sometimes necessarily in fairly exact ones.

There is a great deal more to be said about phoneme theory, and the reader is referred to the very extensive literature on the subject.[25] It may seem, at this point, to be a lot of fuss about very little. It seems obvious that there must be *something* that is the same about the initial consonants of *kit* and *cat*, even though in another sense they are different. (We have made it seem more obvious, and have, in a sense, begged the question, by using 'k[1]' and 'k[2]' when speaking of allophones of the phoneme, that is to say by identifying each allophone in advance as 'a kind of k.') But it is obvious only because they *are* allophones of the same phoneme in English; and it is obvious only to a native English speaker.

It is true that k^1 and k^2 are certainly very similar. However it is not true, as is sometimes claimed, that English speakers can hear no difference between them. They usually have no trouble in hearing the difference; the only thing is they feel the difference 'doesn't matter'. But it is only to English speakers that the difference 'doesn't matter'. The important part of phoneme theory is that two segments may be in complementary distribution in one language, but in parallel distribution in another. They will belong to the same phoneme in the former case, but to different phonemes in the latter. And the difference between them will certainly 'seem to matter' to speakers of the second language.

It often seems obvious why different allophones of a phoneme are tied to particular contexts. In the original examples *kit* and *cat*, for instance, the differing points of contact between tongue and roof of the mouth for the initial consonant—further forward in the former, further back in the latter—result in the tongue having to travel the minimum distance in order to reach the posture required for the following vowel. There is an economizing of effort. This accommodation of the articulation of one segment to the articulation of an adjacent segment is known as a *similitude* (which must be carefully distinguished from an *assimilation*, which will be the topic of chapter 8; assimilations concern changes in word forms, but similitudes do not involve changes of any sort).[26]

Although many allophones appear 'natural' in their environments in that they exhibit similitudes in this way, it must be remembered that there is nothing inevitable or necessary about this. Allophones are not grouped into phonemes by nature, but by the phonology of a particular language. Thus in French we find a difference between the consonant segments of *qui* and *cas* which is similar to (usually greater than) the difference between the consonant segments in English *key* and *car*. (This is a comparable difference to that found in *kit* and *cat*.) A similar difference is found between the final consonants in French *pique* and *Pâques*; but in most accents of English *peak* and *park* do not show the difference, though it would be just as 'natural' to make it here as in initial position. (There may be no similitude involved in the relation of an allophone to its environment. This is the case with the *l* in *leaf* and the *l* in *feel*, which are different allophones of the same phoneme.)

It is important to bear in mind that it is risky to compare segments of one person's speech with those of another's, when trying to establish the phonemes of a language. If the two speakers had identical accents there would be no difficulty; but if they had not, confusion might result, since there might be differences of system between them. In fact the term 'complementary distribution' is, strictly speaking, taken to mean distribution 'within the speech of a single individual, talking in a given style' (for everyone has more than one style of talking), or within a single *idiolect*, to use a convenient and recently introduced term.

We see, then, that the concepts both of structure and of system deal with abstractions. In the case of structure, the abstractions are the elements of the patterns, C and V; in the case of system, they are the terms in the system, the phonemes. An actual occurring segment in an utterance simultaneously represents an element of structure, and represents a term in a system; it is not identical with either, since both are generalizations from very many segments.

6

Voice Quality and Voice Dynamics

1. *Three strands of the medium*

We have up to now been occupied almost exclusively with the *articulatory* aspects of the aural medium, in other words with the features which give us segments of syllables, or vowels and consonants. These 'segmental' features, however, do not by any means account for the whole of the medium. We must now take a more general view of it and see what else, in addition to the segmental features, goes to make it up. We shall find we have to recognize the existence of a number of 'non-segmental' components or ingredients in the medium which up to now we have tacitly ignored. These other components are what would be left over, so to speak, if we took the vowels and consonants away. Non-segmental components of the medium fall into two groups, one of them consisting of the components which contribute to the general quality of the voice, and the other consisting of components which arise out of the way the voice is handled. Components of the first group concern *voice quality*, and those of the second group concern *voice dynamics*.

Thus we have three groups of components in the aural medium:

(*a*) segmental features;
(*b*) features of voice quality;
(*c*) features of voice dynamics.

They are like three strands, separable though closely woven together, all simultaneously and continuously present and together making up the totality of the medium.

These three strands may vary quite independently of each other from speaker to speaker; there do not seem to be any necessary correlations between them. And all three strands may show traits which range from the personal and idiosyncratic, through traits characteristic of various sizes of social groupings, to traits which are

7

universally human. If we want to give a full description of the way someone talks a given language, or to bring out clearly the points of difference between his pronunciation and that of someone else (whether
talking the same or a different language), we must take all three strands
into account.[1]

The strand consisting of the segmental features of an utterance is
made up of complex auditory qualities which are in fairly rapid
fluctuation, reflecting the rapid succession of movements of the articulators. The strand of voice dynamics also consists of features which
fluctuate in auditory quality, but considerably more slowly. Many of
them are linked to the syllable- and stress-producing processes (see
ch. 3), and they are closely related to those aspects of sound that
assume importance in music–things such as pitch, loudness, tempo
and rhythm. The strand consisting of features of voice quality, in contrast to the two preceding, has a quasi-permanent character: it remains constant over relatively long stretches of time, and fluctuation
here is much less apparent.

Although we, as phoneticians, are able to unravel the total complex of the aural medium into these three strands (and indeed are not
only able, but obliged to do so), this is not the case with the non-
phonetician, and the ordinary person's judgements on ways of speaking are usually made without explicit differentiation of the three
strands. There are, in fact, no terms in ordinary language by which
people can discriminate between them, and whenever the medium as
such is under discussion they usually fall back on the all-purpose
word 'voice', a word which sometimes refers to the medium as a
whole (as in, for example, 'I knew him by his voice'), but sometimes
to a part of it only.

Thus if someone is said to possess 'an educated voice', the word
refers to the strand of segmental features, since (in English, at least)
it is this strand that carries the indexical signs that give rise to such a
judgement; and it is also segmental features that are in question when
we say that someone has 'a clear voice' (this may not be immediately
apparent, but it is the way segmental features in English are treated
that makes for clarity of utterance); but 'a hoarse voice', more obviously, is connected with features of voice quality, and so usually
(though again this is perhaps less obvious) is 'a pleasant voice'; and
finally 'a loud voice' and 'a low voice' clearly refer to features of
voice dynamics (though the latter expression is itself ambiguous, since
it may mean either low in pitch or low in volume).

It is probable that all three strands carry indexical signs of social
affiliations in roughly equal degrees; and all three moreover have
aspects which are idiosyncratic and characterize the individual, so

that 'speaker recognition' (a technical term for the ability to identify a person from voice alone) depends equally on all of them.[2] From the linguistic point of view, that of the formation of language-bearing patterns, it is the segmental features that are the most important strand in the medium, which is why so much more attention has been paid to them by phoneticians and why we know more about them than about the features of voice quality and voice dynamics. These last two strands, however, also have a part to play—greater in some languages, smaller in others—in the formation of language-bearing patterns; and they also have a role in giving the medium as used for a particular language its own peculiar character, which is an additional reason why they are of linguistic interest. More should be known about them, and it is a pity that they have so far not been the object of very much research by phoneticians. Although in the present state of our knowledge there is not a great deal to be said about some of the features that compose these two strands, the rest of this chapter will be devoted to giving at least some outline of this neglected side of phonetics. We will take the strand of voice quality first, though it is the features of voice dynamics that will occupy most of the chapter.

2. *Features of voice quality*

'Voice quality', though it is a traditional term, is possibly a misleading one. It does not mean the quality of 'voice' in its well-defined technical phonetic sense ('sound resulting from phonation, i.e. vibration of the vocal cords'; see p. 26); it has a much more general meaning than that. Indeed, many of the components of the medium which come under the heading of 'features of voice quality' are present when we whisper, that is to say when 'voice' in the strict phonetic sense is entirely absent. Some of them are even present when we simply cough, or sigh, or clear the throat. The term 'voice quality' refers to those characteristics which are present more or less all the time that a person is talking: it is a quasi-permanent quality running through all the sound that issues from his mouth. These characteristics do, naturally, include some that have their origin in the anatomy of the larynx, and are therefore concerned with phonation, but as we shall see they also include many other characteristics which have their origin elsewhere. It is convenient to continue to use the traditional term 'voice quality', provided a warning is given that in this particular context 'voice' has a broader meaning than its technical phonetic sense (though, at the same time, not so broad as the all-embracing popular sense illustrated above in section 1). Voice quality is the least investigated of the three strands of the medium. Much about it is not understood, and the following account is necessarily no more than tentative.

The components of voice quality are of two different kinds, those which are outside the speaker's control, and those which are within it. The latter components can therefore be acquired by learning from other people, while the former can not.

Some of the components which are outside the speaker's control are innate: we are born with the physical characteristics that produce them. Among these anatomically-derived components are the effects of such things as the bone-structure of the head and chest, the length of the vocal tract from larynx to lips, the size of the tongue, the shape and height of the palate, the nature of the dentition, the size of the vocal cords, and so on. The strikingly obvious differences between the voice quality of a man, the voice quality of a woman, and the voice quality of a child are largely the consequences of such physical characteristics; and as a child grows, the changes in its physique are accompanied by changes in voice quality. Outside a speaker's control also is the effect on voice quality of a deformity of the vocal organs, such as for instance a cleft palate (which will have an influence on segmental features as well)–as long, at least, as it is not repaired surgically. A really great singing voice, as distinct from a merely well-trained one, probably results from innate characteristics of the singer's physique.

There are other components of voice quality which, though not innate, are nevertheless outside the speaker's control. Some of them may be quite temporary. They may arise, for example, from such causes as adenoids, tonsillitis, laryngitis, pharyngitis, or a common cold. These and other infections involve inflammation of the tissues of the vocal tract at various points, which will usually result in modifying the quality of the sound which the vocal tract conveys. A badly-fitting denture may also contribute to a speaker's voice quality (though its effect is more likely to be noticeable on segmental features).

Because the components of voice quality which are outside the speaker's control cannot be learnt, it follows that they cannot be used to carry language patterns, nor can they be characteristic of the way the medium is used for particular languages. They may be indexical, but only of groups of people who share physical characteristics–women, for instance. They cannot be indexical of membership of social groups. They naturally serve to characterize the individual, however.

The remaining components of voice quality are those which are within the speaker's voluntary control, and do not derive from his physique. They originate in various muscular tensions which are maintained by a speaker the whole time he is talking, and which keep certain of the organs of speech adjusted in a way which is not their relaxed position of rest. These adjustments give a kind of general 'set' or configuration of the vocal tract, which inevitably affects the quality of sound which issues from it.[3] (Though acquired by learning, the habit of such muscular tensions can, once acquired, be so deeply rooted as to seem as much an unalterable part of a person as his anatomical characteristics.)

For example, it is possible to maintain, the whole time one is talking, a posture of the vocal organs that is in effect a secondary articulation (see pp. 60 ff.), but one which is continually present instead of being confined to the duration of a segment or two. In such a case it is more convenient to consider the muscular adjustment responsible as a contributor to voice quality rather than to a segmental feature. Any one of the secondary articulations described in chapter 4, or any possible combination of them, may be found as a constant accompaniment of some people's speech. For example, the lips may be held in a slightly rounded position, giving a continuous over-all labialized quality to the resulting speech; or there may be palatalization, or velarization, or pharyngalization running all through it. Each one of these maintained secondary articulations gives an auditory effect which is difficult to put into words, but which is immediately recognized as familiar when demonstrated. The valve-action of the velum may also be affected by a continuing muscular adjustment: failure ever to make an adequate velic closure results in nasalized voice quality, while failure ever to relax a velic closure results in a very different quality, one which could be described as rather 'adenoidal' (cf. p. 94).

Other continuing muscular tensions affect the adjustment, and therefore the mode of vibration, of the vocal cords, producing different types of phonation (here is a point where 'voice', in the strict phonetic sense of the word, enters into voice quality): for example they may be adjusted so that a lot of air escapes through them while they are vibrating, resulting in 'breathy' phonation; or so that very little air does, resulting in 'tight' phonation. The process of phonation may be modified in other ways. Continuing muscular tensions can hold the larynx in a slightly raised, or a slightly lowered, position in the throat. Others may constrict the pharynx, producing what is sometimes called a 'pulpit' voice, a kind of voice quality that is also associated with some tenors. (Such adjustments of the vocal cords and larynx, when they are assumed only for short stretches of time, will have to be considered again below among features of voice dynamics, under the heading of 'register'. They are more fully described there.[4])

There are no adequate categories of description, and few technical terms, for the various components of voice quality which we have been discussing, and impressionistic descriptions, or 'imitation labels' as K. L. Pike has called them, have for the most part to be used for them. Very often all we can do is to borrow from popular speech, which for describing voice quality has a wide range of metaphorical adjectives drawn from various sensory fields. Thus a voice may be *cracked*, *dry*, *flat*, *hollow*, *husky*, *melodious*, *raucous*, *rough*, *thin*, or *tinny*–to take a representative selection. However, these afford no sort of basis for a scientific classification of voice qualities, and a lot of investigation is needed before we have categories and descriptive terms comparable in adequacy with those developed for segmental features.[5]

The relative importance of the learnt and the unlearnt in voice quality is difficult to assess. Voice quality was described above as a *quasi*-permanent strand in the medium because it can in fact be altered, and sometimes is. Probably most people are capable of making some change in their voice quality. It is even possible to neutralize, by means of muscular adjustments, the components in voice quality which are anatomically derived–at least to some extent, and perhaps even, given enough skill, entirely. There are many professional mimics on stage, radio and television who are able to give convincing imitations of their fellow actors and of public figures, imitations in which the performer's own voice-quality characteristics are effectively submerged. The ventriloquist, also, has to have command of several voice qualities. The extreme of virtuosity, probably, was reached by a certain music-hall performer, a large middle-aged man, who had learnt to produce, completely convincingly, the voice-quality of a seven-year-old girl, showing that it is possible to compensate, by muscular adjustments, for extreme anatomical differences.

Performances such as this show what the theoretical possibilities are in this direction. In practice it is sometimes hard to say how much of voice-quality is learnt, and is thus an institutionalized feature common to a group of speakers. There is no doubt that a special voice quality is recognizable as characteristic of certain languages or dialects, which means that in these cases the learnt components are predominating over the unlearnt. A striking example of this is afforded by some urban slum communities where adenoids, due doubtless to malnutrition and lack of sunlight, are prevalent, with their consequent effect on voice quality, but where people can be found with adenoidal voice quality who do not have adenoids–they have learnt the quality from the large number who do have them, so that they conform to what, for that community, has become the norm. (Continuing velic closure, together with velarization, are the principal components needed for counterfeiting adenoidal voice quality.) The accent of Liverpool seems to have had its origin in such circumstances.

3. *Features of voice dynamics*

The third of the three strands, the constituents of the medium grouped under the heading 'features of voice dynamics', must be dealt with next, and will occupy the greater part of the chapter. They are features that are under the speaker's control, and therefore can be acquired; consequently they tend to be copied from other people, and so are capable of characterizing social groups as well as individuals. Typical features of voice dynamics can be considered under the following heads:

> loudness
> tempo
> continuity
> rhythm
> tessitura
> register
> pitch fluctuation.

We will consider each of them in turn. They vary considerably in their linguistic importance; that of the first three is small, but some will require sections to themselves.

Loudness, or the *scale* of the medium (see p. 9), depends on the degree of force with which air is expelled from the lungs by the pulmonic air-stream mechanism while the vocal cords are in vibration – the greater the force, the greater the loudness. The range of loudness of which the human voice is capable is very considerable, but it is an easily controlled feature, and one which speakers of all languages adjust automatically and immediately to suit the conditions under which they are talking. The adjustments are very exact, and the 'feedback' (see p. 22) on which this fine control is based is almost entirely auditory. The control becomes much less exact if hearing is interfered with: ladies under a hair-drier often talk louder than they realize, or than they would wish to in public; and the hard-of-hearing have great difficulty in suiting their loudness to the changing circumstances under which they are talking.

Although everyone in talking covers, at different times, a wide range of loudness, individuals vary quite considerably in the loudness of their average normal speech. It seems possible, moreover, that degree of loudness may be one of the things that characterize the habitual speaking of certain languages (though no measurements which would prove this have so far been made). Thus Egyptian Arabic, for example, gives the impression of being spoken, under comparable conditions, more loudly than, say, Scots Gaelic.

That loudness has little linguistic importance is shown by the fact that a poor-quality loudspeaker does not reproduce contrasts of loudness with any fidelity, in fact it may nearly obliterate them. Yet when it is reproducing speech this defect passes unnoticed by most people.

By *tempo* is meant speed of speaking, which is best measured by rate of syllable-succession. It is a feature which, like loudness, is varied from time to time by the individual speaker. Some people employ more variation in tempo than others, but everyone has a norm which is characteristic of his usual conversational style. Tempo is like loudness also in that it may possibly be one of the things that characterize a language, though this would be a difficult thing to demonstrate. Everyone who starts learning a foreign language, incidentally, has the impression that its native speakers use an exceptionally rapid tempo.

Closely connected with tempo is *continuity*, which refers to the incidence of pauses in the stream of speech – where they come, how frequent they are, and how long they are. The incidence of pauses, whether they are hesitations or whether they are deliberate cessations of talking for the purpose of taking breath, seems to be a highly idiosyncratic matter, and there is a lot of variation from speaker to speaker. Under the conditions of ordinary conversation nobody's speech is fluent, and it is probably true to say that the more thought there is behind what one is saying, the less fluent will be the speech. Pauses, for the most part, pass unnoticed by both speaker and hearer; yet they frequently occur at apparently unpredictable places, as is revealed by conversations which have been recorded. Pauses bear little relation to syntax, in spite of popular belief to the contrary.[6]

4. *Rhythm*

Although hesitations and other pauses tend at times to disguise the fact, all human speech possesses *rhythm*. This emerges clearly during those moments when speech is fluent and uninterrupted. Rhythm, in speech as in other human activities, arises out of the periodic recurrence of some sort of movement, producing an expectation that the regularity of succession will continue. The movements concerned in the rhythm of speech are those of the syllable- and stress-producing processes, which together make up the pulmonic air-stream mechanism (p. 36). Speech rhythm is essentially a muscular rhythm, and the muscles concerned are the breathing muscles.

There are important implications for perception here. Speech-rhythm is experienced as a rhythm of movement. Obviously it is directly so experienced by the speaker, but what of the hearer? We can say that he, too, is vicariously experiencing a rhythm of movement–he, in a sense, is speaker also. As was pointed out above (p. 23), recognition of 'the identity of speaker and hearer' is essential to an understanding of many aspects of speech perception. We talk, for convenience, about 'hearing' rhythm, but in fact we *feel* it, entering empathetically into the movements of the speaker, to which the sounds we hear are clues. But in order to have this immediate and intuitive apprehension of speech rhythm it is necessary, of course, that speaker and hearer should have the same mother-tongue–otherwise 'phonetic empathy' will not work: the sounds will not be recognized as accurate clues to the movements that produce them.

It is the way in which the chest-pulses and the stress-pulses recur, their mode of succession and co-ordination, that determines the rhythm of a language. There are two basically different ways in which the chest-pulses and the stress-pulses can be combined, and these give rise to two main kinds of speech-rhythm. As far as is known, every language in the world is spoken with one kind of rhythm or with the other. In the one kind, known as a *syllable-timed* rhythm, the periodic recurrence of movement is supplied by the syllable-producing process: the chest-pulses, and hence the syllables, recur at equal intervals of time–they are *isochronous*. French, Telugu, Yoruba illustrate this mode of co-ordinating the two pulse systems: they are syllable-timed languages. In the other kind, known as a *stress-timed* rhythm, the periodic recurrence of movement is supplied by the stress-producing process: the stress-pulses, and hence the stressed syllables, are isochronous. English, Russian, Arabic illustrate this other mode: they are stress-timed languages.[7]

When one of the two series of pulses is in isochronous succession, the other will not be. Thus in a syllable-timed rhythm, the stress-pulses are unevenly spaced, and in a stress-timed rhythm the chest-pulses are unevenly spaced. It may not be immediately obvious why this should be the case. Consider, however, an utterance in English, a language with a stress-timed rhythm:

Which is the train for Crewe, please?

It contains four stressed syllables, *which, train, Crewe, please*, and their equal spacing in time can be made apparent (if it is not so at once) by tapping with a pencil on a hard surface simultaneously with these four syllables as the sentence is spoken. The resulting taps will be clearly isochronous. But if one taps on every syllable (there are seven in all), the taps will be unequally spaced, some of them coming more quickly than others. That this is bound to happen follows from the fact that the number of unstressed syllables which separate the stresses from each other is constantly varying, as is made evident if the stresses are marked off by vertical lines, thus:

|Which is the|train for|Crewe,|please?

We can see that *which* is separated from *train* by two unstressed syllables, *train* from *Crewe* by one, and *Crewe* from *please* by none; yet the interval of time separating them is the same in each case. The rate of syllable succession has thus to be continually adjusted, in order to fit varying numbers of syllables into the same time-interval. In other words, there is considerable variation in syllable-length in a language spoken with a stress-timed rhythm,[8] whereas in a language spoken with a syllable-timed rhythm the syllables tend to be equal in length.

On the other hand in French, a language with a syllable-timed rhythm, the constant rate of syllable-succession means that stresses separated by different numbers of unstressed syllables will be separated by different intervals of time. Thus if a sentence such as:

C'est ab*solume*nt ridi*cule*

is spoken (as it might be) with the italicized syllables stressed, *-ment* will necessarily be nearer in time to the stressed syllable preceding it than to the one following it, since one syllable intervenes in the former case, and two in the latter.

The rhythm of everyday speech is the foundation of verse, in most languages. Thus French verse is based on syllable-timed rhythm, and English verse on stress-timed rhythm.[9] Unless this close connexion between ordinary speech rhythm and verse rhythm is recognized, prosodic theory is likely to be unfruitful–as a great deal of it has been in the past. Since verse has its basis in natural speech rhythms, it is not necessary to learn to listen differently from the way one listens to conversation in order to appreciate verse–provided it is composed in one's mother tongue: the rhythm is intuitively experienced by 'phonetic empathy'. (If the verse is composed in a language which is not the mother tongue but has been acquired, and which has a different rhythmic basis, then learning to listen differently is unlikely to help to yield the direct intuitive appreciation one has for verse in the mother tongue. Thus English speakers find it difficult to feel French verse to be verse at all.) It is, however, necessary to learn to listen differently in order to be able to *analyse* speech rhythm, whether of one's mother tongue or another language, and to describe it in general phonetic terms. Few succeed in doing this without training.

5. *Tessitura and register*

Tessitura, the term for the next of the features of voice dynamics, is conveniently borrowed from the terminology of musicians. 'Voice', in its technical phonetic sense of sound resulting from phonation, is a musical tone which has a fundamental frequency, and therefore a recognizable pitch. The pitch of the voice is in continual fluctuation during speech (see section 6), but the fluctuations tend to take place round a central point: if we disregard the occasional extremes, a speaker has a characteristic range of notes, or compass, within which the pitch fluctuation of his voice falls during normal circumstances. This range or compass is the tessitura.[10] It can vary from person to person (we say someone has a 'low-pitched voice' or a 'high-pitched voice'), and it is possible that for everyone there is a tessitura which is best suited to the strength, size and condition of his vocal cords. However, even though there may be a tessitura which in this sense is natural to an individual, he is nevertheless free to change it considerably, and in special circumstances will do so. Tessitura is raised, for instance, when one has to speak to people further away than usual; and it is sometimes raised at close quarters also, as a result of loss of temper ('don't raise your voice to me' is ambiguous and could mean either 'don't speak to me louder than usual' or 'don't speak to me at a higher pitch than usual'–but as a matter of fact it usually means both simultaneously).

Tessitura, in some communities, is an institutionalized feature, copied from other people and therefore part of the characteristic way of speaking a language or dialect; thus native speakers of Tlingit (see p. 83) use a markedly lower tessitura than speakers of English.

The continual fluctuation of voice pitch which takes place within tessitura is of sufficient importance to merit a section to itself; but before we deal with it we must consider another contribution from the activity of the larynx to features of voice dynamics, namely *register*.

The term register, like tessitura, is borrowed from the terminology of musicians. One of its applications there is to a set of organ pipes having a certain tone-quality in common, but it is also used, in a somewhat analogous way, about voices in singing, and this is the source of our application of the term to the speaking voice. Registers of the singing voice are different qualities of sound arising from differences in the action of phonation; but there is considerable disagreement among musicians over the number of registers that should be distinguished (it varies from two to five), and also over appropriate names for them. 'Head' and 'chest' register are perhaps the two best-known terms, but 'thick' and 'thin', 'natural' and 'falsetto', 'upper', 'middle' and 'lower' are also used. As can be inferred from the last three terms, 'register', when used about the singing voice, implies a difference of pitch range as well as a difference of quality of sound. As the word is used here about the speaking voice, the meaning is extended somewhat from the musicians' sense, but not in a way that conflicts with it: here too registers are different qualities arising from differences in the action of phonation, but considerably more than five must be distinguished, and they are not tied to any particular pitch range.[11]

We have seen (p. 93) that a particular complex of adjustments of the various larynx muscles, affecting the mechanism of phonation, may provide, if it is a quasi-permanent feature of an individual's speech, an ingredient of the strand of voice quality. But most people, whatever the type of phonation that is their norm for ordinary talking, can produce several other modifications of phonation for use when the occasion demands them (the circumstances are different in different communities). Types of phonation which come into play for short periods in this way are better not considered a part of the strand of voice quality, since they are transitory; they should rather be looked on as features of voice dynamics. This is what the word 'register' is used for here; it is confined to types of phonation which the speaker varies at will. (In a similar way, a muscular adjustment of the articulators, if it is quasi-permanent, is taken to contribute to voice quality (see p. 93), but the same adjustment is considered a secondary articulation, contributing to the strand of segmental features, if it is short-lasting.)

The larynx is an extremely complex structure, and it would be out of place here to give a detailed account of the many modifications to the mechanism of phonation that adjustments of it can make. The more important adjustments have already been briefly mentioned above (p. 93). There may, for example, be variation in the length of the vocal cords, and in their thickness and their tension; the glottis may be entirely in vibration, or only in part, and the part that is not in vibration (usually the so-called cartilage glottis[12]) may be firmly closed, or may be sufficiently open to allow air to pass through at that point; two parts of the glottis may be in different modes of vibration simultaneously; the whole larynx may be raised or lowered in the throat; and the parts of the larynx above the glottis may or may not be constricted. For example, what was called above 'breathy phonation' is produced by part of the glottis being in vibration while the cartilage glottis is sufficiently open to allow air to pass freely through it; and what was called 'tight phonation' has the cartilage glottis firmly closed, the rest of the glottis in vibration, and constriction of the upper parts of the larynx. There is another kind of phonation known as 'creaky voice', in which the cartilage glottis is vibrating very slowly, while the rest of the glottis is in normal vibration (it is a characteristic of the accent of England known as 'Received Pronunciation' to use this register when the pitch of the voice falls below a certain point). The types of phonation produced in these ways are very different in sound from each other, and they are all different from the type mostly used by English speakers in which the whole glottis is in vibration at the one time. The differences, however, have to be demonstrated to be appreciated.

It can be seen that, with so many variables, a large number of different registers, in addition to the four just described, is possible. These different registers are not usually identified in terms of the different larynx adjustments explained above (the analysis of any given type of phonation in such terms is difficult and requires long practice), but rather by impressionistic labels, of which 'breathy', 'tight' and 'creaky' are good examples. J.C. Catford, however, has provided a basis for a more accurate and systematic nomenclature for phonation types, which it is hoped will be developed as their importance in linguistic analysis becomes more widely realized.[13]

Changes of register occur in many different circumstances. They may be used, for example, to express affective indices (see p. 9) – signs of emotional states and attitudes of the speaker; probably most communities do so, to at least some extent. Register used in this way is part of what is meant by 'tone of voice'. Speakers of many languages will typically change register in order to express tenderness, for instance, or irritability.[14] There is no good reason to suppose, however (as has sometimes been suggested), that the same registers carry the same affective indices in different cultures.

There are many languages in the world in which contrasts of register, in addition to providing affective indices, are used to provide language-bearing patterns as well. In Cambodian, for example, every syllable is spoken with one of two registers, which are mainly distinguished from each other by the position of the larynx in the throat. The same is true of Gujerati spoken in Surat, the difference here being between 'tight' and 'breathy' phonation. In Danish two such words as *hun* 'she' and *hund* 'dog' are pronounced alike except for a difference of register, the second having creaky voice. In various West African languages entire words are spoken with one of two registers: Nzema, for example, in Ghana (the mother-tongue of ex-president Nkrumah), and at least some of the varieties of Ijaw, in Nigeria. Register differences are found in some of the dialects of

Scots Gaelic. In many of these languages register differences are always accompanied by vowel-quality differences or pitch differences, or both together. It is to be expected that future research will disclose many more examples of the linguistic use of register.[15]

6. *Pitch fluctuation*

The pitch of the voice continually fluctuates while we are talking. It seldom rests on a held note for more than a fraction of a second, and most of the time it is in the process of either rising or falling. This fluctuation of voice-pitch is found in the speech of all communities. It is not a random fluctuation, but follows well-defined (though usually not generally acknowledged) melodic patterns which are common to the community and which are of considerable linguistic and social importance. Vibration of the vocal cords thus fills a dual role in speech: it provides in segments the voiced-voiceless distinction, and it also provides pitch fluctuation as one of the features of voice dynamics. Pitch is, of course, only really present during voiced segments, but we hear the melodic patterns of pitch-fluctuation as continuous, nevertheless; the tiny gaps which interrupt them, caused by the recurring presence in speech of voiceless sounds, pass unnoticed.

That languages, and even dialects, do not sound alike in the matter of pitch fluctuation is a matter of common knowledge; it does not take a trained ear to detect that differences exist. The accusation commonly made by one group of people about another that 'they sing when they talk' merely recognizes that they use different melodic patterns. Familiar patterns, those of the mother-tongue, go unremarked – they are not heard in terms of musical pitch as such, but simply as immediate indications of meaning and attitude. Unfamiliar patterns, however, since they do not convey these immediate indications, *are* heard as pitch fluctuation, and are therefore often said to sound like singing.

The existence of patterns of pitch fluctuation in human speech makes one wonder whether there can really be such a thing as 'tone deafness', that is to say a constitutional inability to hear pitch differences. People who claim to be tone deaf do not show the abnormality in speaking their mother-tongue which would be apparent if they got its patterns of pitch fluctuation wrong. Yet to get the patterns right, they must have been able, when they were learning them, to hear successfully the pitch differences on which the patterns depend. Many people, it is true, find it difficult to hear familiar patterns in terms of musical pitch, as 'tunes', and require special training before they can do so. The difficulty, however, does not lie in tone deafness, but rather in adopting an analytic attitude towards something which has become so familiar.

There may be another difficulty in learning to listen analytically to voice-pitch variation, which applies to both familiar and unfamiliar patterns: it arises from the fact that pitch levels and pitch movement have to be talked about in metaphors. We speak in English, for example, of 'high' notes and 'low' notes (and also of 'rising' and 'falling' pitch), using a metaphor drawn from the field of spatial (vertical) relations. Yet it is far from obvious that a metaphor taken from this field is appropriate to pitch, which is a non-spatial phenomenon. While most people do not seem to be worried by this, there seem to be some for whom the metaphor has no reality, and who therefore find it confusing to describe pitch, and to think about it analytically, in such terms. Certainly, all teachers of phonetics must have come across students who insist on describing what would usually be called a 'falling' pitch as a 'rising' one.

It is interesting to note that the spatial metaphor of 'high' and 'low' is not the only one which has been used for pitch relations in English, and in many languages it is not found at all. Latin bequeathed to English a now obsolete pair of terms 'acute' and 'grave' (curiously enough, these are not opposites in their non-figurative senses), which in turn were metaphors borrowed from Greek. 'Sharp', a near-synonym of 'acute', and 'flat', which makes a better opposite to it, still survive in English in their technical but restricted musical sense. Other languages use metaphors which could be translated as 'tight' and 'heavy' (another pair which are not opposites), 'small' and 'large', 'thin' and 'thick', according to reports of anthropologists and others. None of these metaphors are obviously and immediately intelligible, but all are perhaps more easily justifiable than 'high' and 'low'.[16] (There might be something to be said for the adoption of spatial metaphors in the horizontal instead of the vertical plane: 'right' and 'left', instead of 'high' and 'low', would at least correlate with the widely familiar arrangement of keyboard instruments.)

Fluctuation in the pitch of the voice is probably the most important of the features of voice dynamics. It owes its importance partly to its outstanding role as a bearer of affective indices. These indices, together with affective indices conveyed by register differences, make up what is meant by 'tone of voice', and the flow of conversation much depends on them. Voice-pitch fluctuation, in this function, is very similar to gesture, which it often accompanies. In fact this function of pitch fluctuation might be called *vocal gesture*, to use a term put forward by C.K. Ogden, after a suggestion by Leonard Bloomfield.[17]

But it owes its importance also to the fact that, as well as being a vehicle for indexical signs, it constantly carries language-bearing patterns, which operate simultaneously with, and interact with, the language-bearing patterns which the segmental features, and some of the other dynamic features, carry. Voice-pitch fluctuation thus has both an indexical and a linguistic function, and the latter is basic in the sense that the indexical signs are superimposed on the language-bearing patterns. Pitch fluctuation, in its linguistic function, may conveniently be called *speech melody*. Speech melody is part of the spoken form of a language, just as much as its segments are. It is advisable, in the analysis of voice-pitch fluctuation in a language, to keep, as far as possible, speech melody and vocal gesture distinct, though writers on the subject have often failed to do so. The former can be described in terms of structures and systems, but the latter is not susceptible of phonological treatment.

Speech melody is found in all languages, but there is the greatest diversity in the patterns which make it up, and in the nature of the linguistic functions it performs. Speech melody is not only part of a language, it is a highly distinctive part: languages differ at this point as much as they do at others. On the other hand it has been suggested that vocal gesture is instinctive and 'comes by nature', and therefore that all human beings use it in more or less the same way.[18] The same suggestion has at times been made about ordinary gesture, which is now more usually thought to be a kind of behaviour which is culturally determined.[19] It is at least possible that voice gesture too is learned, and not instinctive, behaviour.

The linguistic functions of speech melody are very varied, but of two fundamentally different kinds. In one case, the function of the speech melody patterns is to be part of the structure of sentences; in the other case, their function is to be part of the structure of words. In the former case, the patterns are called *intonation*, and in the latter case they are called *tone*. In every language the function of speech melody is predominantly either of one kind or the other, so that the languages of the world can be divided into two classes, intonation languages and tone languages. The speech melody in itself, of course, will not reveal into which category any language falls. The difference is not a difference of sound; it would probably not be possible, on hearing a language for the first time, to tell whether it was an intonation language or a tone language. It is only when analysis has established the linguistic function of speech melody in a language that it can be put in one category or the other. English is an example of an intonation language, and Chinese is perhaps the most famous of all tone languages (the expression 'Chinese language tones' was used as long ago as the seventeenth century).[20] To native English speakers, and other Europeans, tone languages are exotic and strange. Nevertheless a great number of tone languages exists, and in fact speakers of tone languages may be in the majority in the population of the world. They are certainly in the majority in Asia and Africa, and many tone languages are to be found, in addition, in North and Central America.

Tone is speech melody when it is a property of the word, while intonation is speech melody when it is a property of the sentence. This means that in a tone language a change of speech melody is likely to change the meaning of individual words, whereas in an intonation language a change of speech melody is likely to change the meaning of the sentence as a whole. For example, the two English utterances which could be written

'This is the place!'
'This is the place?'

are the same except for their pitch patterns, yet they have clearly a different meaning as sentences. It is a grammatical (more precisely a syntactical) difference in meaning, and not a lexical one.

If we consider the two English utterances

'Yes!'
'Yes?'

we find that they too are the same except for their pitch patterns, and they too have different meanings. They are not, however, different *words*. The difference between them is the same as that between the two utterances quoted in the last paragraph: they are different as sentences, even if they are one-word sentences. The difference, again, is a syntactical one. But if we take two comparable utterances in a tone language, say Mandarin Chinese, the difference in pitch pattern would make them into different words: for instance *ma* with one pitch pattern would mean 'mother', while with another it would mean 'horse'. The difference made here by a change in pitch pattern is lexical, not syntactical. In a tone language, a word is identified not only by its vowels and consonants, but also by its pitch characteristics. In an intonation language, a word is quite independent of any pitch characteristics, and it preserves its identity through any pitch changes it may undergo.

Tone languages must inevitably present special problems if they are used in circumstances which interfere with speech melody. When, for example, people are talking in a whisper, they are talking without phonation (see p. 28). There is therefore no fundamental, and no

8

pitch fluctuation. If a tone language is whispered, an essential part of the structure of its words will be removed. How, then, can a whispered tone language be understood? A number of experiments have been made in attempts to answer this question, but it is possible that the question does not really arise in many tone-language communities– whispering just does not seem to be used in them. The experiments have shown that some tone languages cannot be understood in a whisper except by skilful guessing from the context, though there are others which do seem to be comprehensible. However it is usually found that in these latter the pitch patterns are always accompanied either by rhythmic characteristics that are preserved in whisper, or by register differences that can be simulated, and these in themselves are sufficiently distinctive to provide intelligibility.[21]

Singing might seem to be another problem. Since a song imposes its own pitch pattern on the words that go with it, there is obviously the possibility of conflict if these words are words of a tone language. When songs are imported from other cultures into a tone-language community–translations of hymns introduced by Christian missionaries, for example–the tunes may lead the singers to express sentiments different from those intended. Indigenous song, however, seems always to be accommodated to speech melody patterns so that ambiguities do not result.[22]

But if tone languages seem to entail problems in communication from which intonation languages are free, they also have advantages which intonation languages do not possess. We saw from the case of whisper that, in a tone language, segments–vowels and consonants– without speech melody have little intelligibility. The converse, rather unexpectedly, is not the case. If the segments are removed, leaving only the speech melody, the words of a tone language preserve considerable intelligibility. But once the speech melody is divorced from the vowels and consonants, it no longer needs a human voice to convey it: any means of producing notes of varying pitch can do so, and there are many means which have more carrying power than the human voice. This is the secret of the talking drums in Africa. Drum signalling is not by means of a code: the signals are a direct transfer of linguistic pitch patterns and rhythm patterns to the drums. The advantages of this for long distance communication are obvious. Various other instruments are used in some tone-language communities for conveying the pitch patterns of words–flutes or horns, for instance.[23]

The speech melody of a tone language can also be transmitted by whistling, and in some parts of the world this is a regular practice. The best described instance of this method of communication is found in Mexico, among a people called the Mazateco, with whom it is highly developed.[24] It is only used by the males (boys learn it as soon as they learn to talk), though it is understood perfectly by the women and girls. It permits conversation to be carried on at a considerable distance – by travellers, for instance, who are out of sight of each other and beyond the range of normal speech. It also permits, in a group of people, two simultaneous conversations to be carried on without confusion, one in normal speech and one in whistled speech. (Other 'whistled languages' exist which are based on quite a different principle, that of modulating a labial whistle by the articulatory tongue movements of the segments of normal speech, thus producing patterns of pitch variation which are distinctive and recognizable, though they have no connexion with the speech melody of the language. The best described example of a whistled language of this sort is the one used on the island of La Gomera in the Canaries; another one, now dying out, has been found in the French Pyrenees.)[25]

In the phonological analysis and description of the patterns of speech melody of both tone and intonation languages, it is not *absolute* pitch that is of importance. Speech melody and musical melody have this in common. Not only are both based on patterns arising from pitch fluctuation, but in both it is the position of the points in the pattern *relative to each other* that counts, not their frequency in terms of number of vibrations per second. Speech melody and musical melody can both be 'transposed' without loss of identity. However, there is a crucial difference between them: the *intervals* between the points in the pattern are absolute and constant in the patterns of musical melody, but they are relative and variable in the patterns of speech melody. Thus a pattern in speech melody can be either compressed or expanded in the dimension of pitch and still remain the same pattern, although in one case the intervals are smaller and in the other larger. This could not happen with a pattern in musical melody: the pattern would either be 'out of tune', or else be a different pattern.

The intervals in musical melody are absolute because they are intervals between points which stand in simple mathematical ratios to each other.[26] The number of different points is limited, and they form a musical *scale*. In speech melody there is no scale behind the patterns; the voice may rest on any one of an infinite number of points (within its possible range); and the intervals between the points cannot be expressed as simple ratios. Thus speech melody can never literally be 'singing', in the sense that musical intervals and notes of a scale can be discerned in it.

The speech melody of intonation languages is inherently different from musical melody in another way. We have just seen that its patterns, like those of speech melody in tone languages, can be compressed or expanded in the pitch dimension. Its patterns can be compressed or expanded in the time dimension too. A pattern of speech melody in a tone language is part of a given word, is therefore co-extensive with that word, and is therefore as constant in its extent in time (tempo variation apart) as the word is. A pattern of speech melody in an intonation language, on the other hand, is independent of words and co-extensive with a sentence. But sentences vary greatly in the number of words they contain, and the same pattern can occur with a short sentence or a long one. Thus two utterances which could be written:

'Yes?'
'This is the place?'

could have the same pattern of speech melody, but occupying one syllable in the first and four syllables in the second. Clearly therefore in intonation languages speech melody patterns must be expansible and compressible in time in order to fit sentences of varying extent.[27]

(It should perhaps be said at this point that the terms 'word' and 'sentence' are purposely being used in very general senses in this section. Fortunately their imprecision when not strictly defined does not matter for the purpose of making the foregoing points, or those to be made later in the section; in fact it is an advantage. It is true that sometimes 'morpheme' or 'lexical item' might be thought preferable to 'word', and 'clause' or 'phrase' to 'sentence'; but their use would very considerably complicate the exposition for the sake of giving it a precision which is not appropriate in making the basic distinctions with which we are concerned.)

Within the broad division into tone languages and intonation languages, there are further differences to be found in both the function of the patterns of speech melody and their form. In some tone languages, for example, the patterns may serve to distinguish quite unrelated words which are otherwise alike, while in others the patterns may have a grammatical function, making the distinction between present and past tense in verbs, for example. In a large number of tone languages, the two functions are combined.[28] In intonation languages the speech melody pattern may determine sentence type, such as declarative or interrogative, command or request, dependent, or independent; or may indicate the principal point of information in the sentence (this function of intonation is often shown in writing (in English) by italics: compare the melodies of '*I* saw him' and 'I *saw* him').[29]

The lexical melody patterns in a tone language are not, of course, absolutely individual for each separate word. The contrasts of pitch on which they are based are limited, so that all the patterns can be analysed and described as arrangements of a small number of elements. Usually there is one tone element to each syllable. These elements may be different pitch *levels*, which contrast with each other as higher or lower (as in many tone languages in West Africa), or different pitch *movements*, which contrast as rises, falls, or more complex movements such as rise-falls (as in many tone languages in South-East Asia). Some tone languages must be analysed in terms of both types of contrast.

In intonation languages also, the patterns of speech melody must be analysed into small numbers of constituent elements, which will be either pitch levels or pitch movements, or a combination of both; though here there will not necessarily be one intonation element to each syllable – there may be more than one, or a single element may extend over several syllables. The intonation of French, for example, seems best analysed in terms of pitch-movement elements. The intonation of English can certainly be satisfactorily analysed in terms of pitch-level elements, though there is considerable disagreement as to whether this is the best way to do it.[30]

What has been said so far would make it appear that in a tone language the melody of an entire sentence is the sum of the melodic patterns of each individual word; and conversely, in an intonation language the melody of any individual word is a fragment of the melodic pattern of the whole sentence. This, though true, is not the whole truth, and some qualification and amplification are necessary.

First of all, both tone patterns and intonation patterns may be modified by the superimposition of vocal gesture. Tone patterns, moreover, are usually not constant, but subject to variation according to the other words next to which they are placed.[31] In addition to that, however, we sometimes find, in what is predominantly a tone language, a component of speech melody that has to be analysed as intonation, i.e. as part of the structure of sentences. This has been described in a number of languages, and there are various ways in which the intonation may be related to the tone patterns.[32] Similarly, we may find in what is predominantly an intonation language a component of speech melody that has to be analysed as tone, i.e. as part of the structure of words. This is a well-known feature of Swedish, Norwegian, and Slovenian, and it may be true of the Lewis dialect of

Scots Gaelic. It is theoretically possible that languages may exist in which speech melody is made up of tone and intonation in equal proportions.

The analysis of voice-pitch fluctuation in a language into the components of vocal gesture, tone and intonation can therefore be seen to be a very complex matter, and indeed it would probably be true to say that it has not yet been completed for any language in the world.[33]

7

Notation

1. *Phonetic symbols*

We have seen (ch. 3) how a full description of a segment can be abbreviated so as to provide a convenient and practical label for it, which is usually a three-term label such as 'close front rounded (vowel)', 'voiced dental fricative (consonant)', and so on. On occasions, however, we require something more compact than a label, however brief, in order to refer to a segment; we need, in other words, *symbols* which will stand for segments. A system of such symbols constitutes *phonetic notation*.

In many subjects notation is of the greatest importance, and phonetics is certainly one of these subjects. Historically, in fact, the notation came before the full development of the subject, and there is a long history of experiments, going back for centuries, in types of phonetic notation. It is probable that all conceivable notational devices and expedients have been given a trial at some time or other, and as a result the theory of phonetic notation is one of the strong points of the subject. Nevertheless it is, perhaps, rather unfortunate that in the public mind phonetics has to a great extent become identified with its notation; many people immediately think of 'funny letters' when the word 'phonetics' is mentioned. Although it is true that notation is of great importance to phonetics, yet it is not absolutely indispensable. In the last resort it is only an adjunct, however convenient, and it is possible to do without notation a lot of the time: thus in the present book it has been possible to write the first six chapters without making any use of phonetic symbols. However, it would not be convenient to go very much deeper into the subject without introducing them.

A very large number of phonetic notations have been invented from time to time, and they are of several different kinds. They fall broadly into two types, which can be characterized as *alphabetic* and *analphabetic* notations, respectively. Alphabetic notations are so called because they are based on the same principle as that which governs ordinary alphabetic writing, namely that of using one single simple symbol to represent each segment. *An*alphabetic notations (meaning notations which are *not* alphabetic) represent each segment by a composite symbol made up of a number of signs put together. The class of alphabetic notations is very considerably the larger, and must itself be further subdivided; but it will be convenient to deal with analphabetic notations first.

2. *Analphabetic notations*

The signs which make up a symbol for a segment in an analphabetic notation are, in effect, a descriptive label for the segment in abbreviated form. They resemble, in this way, the formulas of chemistry, which are also shortened descriptions. Thus

$$H_2O$$

is a chemical formula which stands for a molecule of water: the symbol informs us that the molecule is made up of two atoms of hydrogen, i.e. H_2, and one atom of oxygen, i.e. O. An analphabetic symbol for a segment is, in the same kind of way, an indication of the 'ingredients' of the segment, the ingredients being the activities of the organs of speech which are required to produce it. The symbol will show, in summary form, some or all of such factors as the active and passive articulators concerned, the nature of the stricture, the presence or absence of a velic closure, the state of the glottis, the air-stream mechanism, relevant secondary articulations, and so on.

Thus in an analphabetic notation a voiceless bilabial plosive could be represented by the symbol

$$\frac{1}{1}$$

There are three constituent signs in this symbol: there are two numerals, and there is the straight line which separates them, the whole being arranged so as to look like a vulgar fraction. The numerator, or upper numeral, of the fraction indicates the passive, or upper, articulator, and the denominator, or lower numeral, indicates the active, or lower, articulator (see p. 43). The fact that the numeral in this particular instance is 1 both above and below the line indicates that the passive articulator is the upper lip and the active articulator is the lower lip. The single straight line that separates the numerals is an indication that the stricture is one of complete closure. No other explicit information is provided by the symbol, but it does contain some implicit information: we could deduce from it that the segment must be voiceless, and also that there must be a velic closure, because if these two things were not so, express indications to the contrary would have been given by additional signs.

This is an example taken from an early, and rather simple, analphabetic notation which was invented by Thomas Wright Hill (1763–1851), a Birmingham schoolmaster (and father of Sir Rowland Hill, who was to become famous as the inventor of penny postage). T.W. Hill expounded his notation in a lecture entitled 'On the Articulation of Speech' which he gave in Birmingham in 1821, but which was not published until 1860, by which time it was posthumous.[1] Although it is deficient in certain respects, Hill's notation was well thought out and showed acute phonetic observation. It distinguished seven active articulators and seven passive articulators, and showed type of stricture by the spacing, shape and number of the lines separating numerator from denominator. Further signs could where necessary indicate voicing and nasalization. Hill was able, in his notation, to indicate the difference between the usual English alveolar nasal, and the dental nasal which, he pointed out, occurs in the English word *anthem*; and also to indicate the difference between the usual English bilabial nasal, and the labio-dental nasal which is sometimes heard in the word *pamphlet*. It was, clearly, a fairly flexible notation.

Hill was apparently unaware that he had a distinguished predecessor in this field who lived not very far away, in Lichfield. At any rate, he does not mention the fact that the principles on which one could base an analphabetic notation were quite clearly adumbrated, though not fully worked out, by Dr Erasmus Darwin (1731–1802), grandfather of Charles Darwin, and were published as early as 1803 in the notes to his long (and also posthumous) poem *The Temple of Nature*, where many other acute remarks on the subject of phonetics are to be found.[2]

Hill arranged the component signs of his analphabetic symbols vertically, which made them compact but awkward to print. In later schemes the signs are usually arranged horizontally, so as to form a more convenient sequence of signs. This is done in probably the best-known example of an analphabetic notation: the one devised by the Danish phonetician Otto Jespersen (1860–1943), who is also the originator of the term 'analphabetic' by which notations of this sort are known. He made his system public in 1889 in his book *The Articulations of Speech Sounds*. His analphabetic symbols give very detailed information about a segment, but they are much more complicated than they need be from a typographical point of view:

the notation makes use of roman letters, Greek letters, heavy type, italic, numerals, and subscript and superscript letters (sometimes both the latter simultaneously). A vowel of the quality found in the English word *all*, for example, would have the following analphabetic symbol or formula:

$$\alpha 7^b \beta g\gamma 7_k \delta 0_\epsilon 1$$

and the vowel in a Scottish pronunciation of the word *day* would be represented by:

$$\alpha 6^{bc} \beta e\gamma 5^g \delta 0_\epsilon 1$$

Each Greek letter in these symbols refers to an active organ of speech –lips, point of the tongue, upper surface of the tongue, velum, vocal cords; and the numbers and roman letters following the Greek letters indicate the posture or activity of the organs in the production of the particular segment. It is easy to see at a glance what two segments have in common and where they differ, but it may be questioned whether Jespersen chose the best way of presenting the information. At any rate, his scheme has been very little used by other writers.[3]

An analphabetic notation embodying a description of vocal sounds, in terms of the mechanics of their production, which is more complete than ever before has been worked out by K. L. Pike. It carries the analphabetic principle as far, probably, as it can be carried. An account of the notation concludes his book *Phonetics* (1943). It produces formulas of great length (a vowel requires a string of more than eighty separate characters, and a consonant such as a voiced bilabial implosive requires many more). It would be possible to abbreviate the formulas without loss of information at the cost of greater typographical complexity (Pike uses only the normal capital and lowercase letters of the alphabet in roman and italic form); but the formulas would still be impracticable. Pike, of course, did not intend his Functional Analphabetic Symbolism, as he called it, to be used as a practical notation; its purpose, which it fulfils very well, is to illustrate the thesis which Pike wishes to demonstrate in his book: that it is impossible to give a truly complete description of a segment, and that any attempt to approach completion involves far more factors than would at first be believed. An exhaustive analphabetic notation brings out the many assumptions that underlie abbreviated descriptions, such as three-term labels, of segments.

3. *Alphabetic notations: iconic*

Analphabetic notations, for the most part, are curiosities, and for all practical purposes it is alphabetic notations which are of most use.

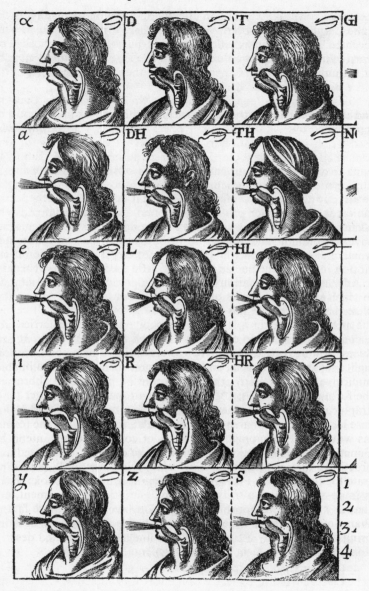

From John Wilkins, *An Essay towards a real character and a Philosophical Language*, 1668.

The most obvious basis for an alphabetic notation, probably, is the roman alphabet. However, quite a number of notations have been invented which are alphabetic in principle but which are not based on the roman or on any other existing alphabet, and something must be said about these, and the theories behind them, before coming to the more usual roman-based notations.

Non-roman notations are usually *iconic*, which means that the symbols are not arbitrary signs, but in some way resemble what they stand for. (A few are not iconic. Robert Robinson, for example, who used a non-roman notation in the early seventeenth century for long connected phonetic texts, preserved in manuscript, seemed simply to want to avoid the traditional associations of the roman alphabet.[4]) A phonetic symbol can be iconic in various ways. It cannot, of course, be directly like the *sound* of a segment, but it can portray the action of the vocal organs which produces the sound. No notations that can be taken seriously have tried direct representation of articulatory postures, though John Bulwer, in his book *Philocophus* (1648), suggested it would not only be possible, but desirable, to 'exhibit the motions of speech in the letters of the alphabet'; and somewhat later John Wilkins (1668) gave illustrations of a possible phonetic notation in which each symbol was a simplified picture (see p. 115), in profile, of the vocal organs in the head.[5]

Much more common, and more practicable, are notations which are iconic because they allot related shapes to related segments, and do not aim at being directly representational. A phonetic notation, intended to be used as a shorthand, in which 'all the simple characters are as analogous to each other as the sound they represent', was invented and published in 1766 by William Holdsworth and William Aldridge (see p. 117), two employees of the Bank of England. It does not appear to have had much success as a shorthand. However, the principle of using similar shapes for similar phonetic categories was applied to the construction of another, and much more successful, shorthand some seventy years later by Isaac Pitman, who spent his entire life experimenting with types of phonetic notation for different purposes.

Isaac Pitman published his *Stenographic Soundhand* in 1837. There were many later editions, and various alterations were made in the notation, but its iconic basis remained unchanged from the start. It would seem, at first sight, improbable that one of his symbols such as \ could be iconic. There is nevertheless a great deal of information to be derived from it, by virtue of the way it is related in shape to the other symbols of the notation. It is a straight line, and therefore the segment it represents must be a stop consonant; all stop consonants

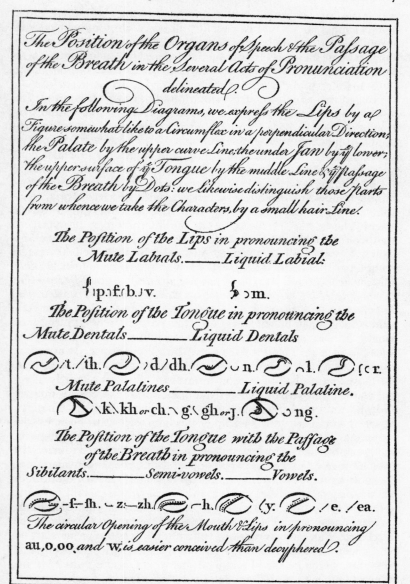

The Position of the Organs of Speech & the Passage of the Breath in the several Acts of Pronunciation delineated.

In the following Diagrams, we express the Lips by a Figure somewhat like to a Circumflex in a perpendicular Direction; the Palate by the upper curve Line; the under Jaw by ye lower; the upper surface of ye Tongue by the middle Line & ye passage of the Breath by Dots: we likewise distinguish those parts from whence we take the Characters, by a small hair Line.

The Position of the Lips in pronouncing the Mute Labials.——Liquid Labial.

p. f. b. v.   m.

The Position of the Tongue in pronouncing the Mute Dentals——Liquid Dentals

t. th. d. dh. n. l. r.

Mute Palatines——Liquid Palatine.

k. kh or ch. g. gh or j. ng.

The Position of the Tongue with the Passage of the Breath in pronouncing the Sibilants.——Semi-vowels.——Vowels.

f. sh. z. zh. h. y. e. ea.

The circular Opening of the Mouth & Lips in pronouncing au, o, oo, and w, is easier conceived than decyphered.

From W. Holdsworth and W. Aldridge, *Natural Short-hand*, 1766.

are shown by straight lines. It slopes backwards, and therefore the segment must be a labial consonant; all labial consonants have the same slope. It is a thin, rather than a thick, line, and therefore the segment must be voiceless rather than voiced; all pairs of symbols distinguished only by being thin or thick have this relation. Thus place, manner, and the state of the glottis can all be deduced from –provided the principles of the notation are known. It is, in fact, a compressed three-term label: voiceless labial stop. The symbols of Pitman's shorthand are iconic by analogy, and practically all shorthands invented since have followed suit.

Pitman's shorthand was a notation with a severely practical purpose, and its iconic basis had no very strong theoretical preconceptions behind it; it was simply of mnemonic value. Others have attributed much more theoretical importance to an iconic basis for a notation, and some have been convinced that it is the only possible scientific basis. Much more elaborate self-interpreting notations have been worked out in this belief. Probably the most famous is the one invented by an Edinburgh man, Alexander Melville Bell. He made his notation public in 1867 in a book with the revealing title *Visible Speech: the Science of Universal Alphabetics; or Self-interpreting Physiological Letters, for the Writing of all Languages in One Alphabet.* Bell claimed that 'the idea of representing the mechanism of speech-sounds in their alphabetic symbols' was 'entirely new', in which, of course, he was mistaken (and many inventors of iconic notations since his time have claimed the same thing). He attached very great importance to his invention, and had tried–vainly–to present it to the Government before the appearance of his book. Shortly after, when he had failed to get a Royal Commission established to pronounce on it, he emigrated to Canada, and eventually became an American citizen. He and his son, Alexander Graham Bell, who invented the telephone, used the notation widely in teaching the deaf to speak, and many books have been printed in it. The illustration on p. 119 gives an idea of its general appearance. The symbols provide about the same amount of information as do those of Pitman's shorthand, but since many more categories are involved–it is a general phonetic notation, not just one for English–they are of necessity more complex.

Henry Sweet shared Bell's conviction of the importance and value to science of an iconic notation, and he took over the principles and fundamental features of Bell's Visible Speech for his own Organic Alphabet, which he used in many of his works, and especially in his *Primer of Phonetics* (1890 and later editions). The Organic Alphabet, like Visible Speech, is not very difficult to learn, though it looks at first as if it was going to be (see illustration p. 120); some of Sweet's

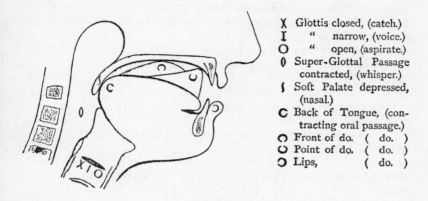

X Glottis closed, (catch.)
I   "   narrow, (voice.)
O   "   open, (aspirate.)
Ɵ Super-Glottal Passage
    contracted, (whisper.)
ʃ   Soft Palate depressed,
    (nasal.)
C Back of Tongue, (con-
    tracting oral passage.)
ᴑ Front of do. (do.)
ᴖ Point of do. (do.)
ᴐ Lips,   (do.)

Alexander Melville Bell's Visible Speech (from *English Visible
Speech in Twelve Lessons*, 1895, pp. vi and 38).

works, such as his essays on the pronunciation of Russian and of
Portuguese, have been unjustly neglected because people have been
disinclined to embark on it. Even when learnt, however, it is difficult
to read because many of the symbols are too much alike; it is difficult
to remember unless it is constantly used; and it sets difficult tasks for

The Organic Alphabet of Henry Sweet
(from *A Primer of Phonetics*, 3rd ed., 1906, p. 88; somewhat enlarged).

the printer and the proofreader. The advantages of an iconic notation
are largely illusory, and are outweighed by these drawbacks, which
seem to apply to all iconic notations that have so far been invented.
In any case, when such a notation has been learnt, the symbols lose
for the practised reader their iconic nature, and function just like any
other letters.

4. *Alphabetic notations: roman-based*

While imperfect legibility is a common shortcoming of iconic notations, they have another serious disadvantage. A symbol in an iconic
notation is likely to be tied to a particular theory of phonetic description–and this theory may turn out to be wrong or inadequate. An
analphabetic notation can be revised to accommodate changes in
theory; but, except within narrow limits, an iconic notation cannot
be. The very shape of an iconic symbol may impose an unwanted
theory on the person using it, and thereby constrain his thought.
Thus Sweet's Organic Alphabet commits us to his own classification
of vocoids, which is based on dubious criteria, is very complex, and
in general is unacceptable nowadays. A good notation must be
independent of particular theories of description. The roman alphabet
is highly legible; but it has an additional advantage in that its symbols
are completely arbitrary.

If, however, in a roman-based phonetic notation, we are to have a single separate symbol for every classifiable segment, it is clear that the roman alphabet will not provide enough, and that it will have, somehow, to be augmented. Before we examine the different expedients by which this can be done, we must first ascertain the alphabet's full resources: it can offer more, for the purposes of phonetic notation, than just the twenty-six letters of which, as we know it in this country, it consists. (It has not, of course, always had twenty-six letters; j, v, and w, for instance, are quite recent additions to it.)

First of all, many letters have more than one shape. For example, capital letters are not only usually bigger than 'lower-case' or small letters, but apart from their difference in size their design may be different. Italic letters also, apart from being sloped, may be of different design.[6] Thus we have

A	a	*a*
F	f	*f*
G	g	*g*
I	i	
R	r	
U	u	

and so on. Although we have here examples of different shapes of the *same* letter there is no reason why the different shapes should not be taken into a phonetic notation as *different* symbols, and many people have done this. Some systems of notation preserve capital and italic letters exactly as they are, with their existing size or slope respectively. Others make the notation more homogeneous in appearance by printing capitals in the form of small capitals, thus: G I R U; and making italic letters upright instead of sloped, without changing their basic design, thus: ɑ ʃ ɡ.

Then there are a number of other letters in the roman alphabet which are not used in writing modern English; some of these were once in use but are now obsolete, others are used in writing other languages. Examples of letters of this sort are: þ ð ʒ ſ (with an italic form *ʃ*) ø ç. Any of these will if needed make a phonetic symbol. Other signs, which are not letters of the alphabet, are often used in conjunction with it, such as the numerals, and £ @ & %. These are a possible source of phonetic symbols, but have seldom been impressed into service. Finally, in writing many languages letters with accents or *diacritics* added to them are used, such as á à â ą ä ã š ñ. Letters modified in this way are a further source of phonetic symbols.

9

By using the roman alphabet's full resources the symbols available for a phonetic notation can be considerably increased, but the alphabet still needs to be further extended before a really adequate stock of symbols is available. There are four expedients by which this can be done: by widening the use of diacritics, by borrowing symbols from other alphabets, by inventing new letters, and by using digraphs.

New diacritics are easy to devise. A good example of a new diacritic is a small circle under a letter (occasionally, if more convenient, over it): m̥ n̥ l̥ r̥ g̊ ḁ. Existing diacritics can be made more general in their application; for example the tilde, normally confined to ñ, can be placed over other letters: ã ũ ž; or it can be written through a letter: ɫ đ ƶ. (In most cases a diacritic is detached from–does not touch–the letter to which it is applied, though in the latter case this is clearly not so. But whether the diacritic is detached or not, for all practical purposes a letter plus a diacritic form a single unitary symbol.)

A good source from which letters can be borrowed is the Greek alphabet, and β γ ε θ φ χ, for example, have been made use of for centuries in roman-based phonetic notations. Borrowed Greek letters are sometimes redesigned so as to fit in with the general appearance of roman letters. The preceding six characters, for example, have for this reason been modified as follows: β ɣ ɛ θ ɸ χ. The Cyrillic alphabet can also offer possible new characters, such as ь ч, and the script form *ш*.

Entirely new letter-shapes can be obtained by outright invention, but the possibilities here are more limited than one would think–a brand-new letter usually looks too much like already existing ones to be distinctive. Still, a few satisfactory symbols can be obtained in this way, such as ƅ c ɬ. More profitable is the production of new letter-shapes by modifying existing ones. Letters turned upside-down, for example, often make good new symbols, such as ə ɔ ɾ ɟ ʌ ʎ ʮ ʞ. Another fruitful source is modification of the structure, in various ways, of existing letters, giving us for example ɓ ħ ɕ ʑ ɱ ʂ ƭ ɖ ŋ.

The use of digraphs is the least-favoured of expedients, since it can so easily lead to confusion. A digraph is two separate letters forming one single symbol, and digraphs such as sh, th, ch, ng are commonly used in the ordinary spelling of English, and they are also used in the spelling of many other European languages. (It is of interest that not only digraphs but all the other expedients mentioned above for producing phonetic symbols were called on when the roman alphabet was adapted to writing the European vernaculars.) A digraph may save the creation of a new letter, but it is only useful if there is no possibility of its being interpreted as two symbols instead of one.

A good general phonetic notation, or 'phonetic alphabet', should provide an adequate stock of symbols, with approximate general phonetic definitions, and with some general principles governing their use, so that the main categories of vocoids and contoids are covered; the symbols should be distinctive, simple to write, and should make good printing types; and means should be provided for extending the stock of symbols in any necessary direction as research and knowledge develop. The notation should not be biased in the direction of any particular language or group of languages, but should take into account the whole range of human speech-sounds, as far as it is known.

Innumerable phonetic alphabets have been invented on a roman basis; some have been widely used, some have been completely forgotten. Of those that have been widely-used, some rely mainly for their additional symbols on one of the above expedients, some on another. For example the so-called Standard Alphabet of K.R. Lepsius relies entirely on diacritics, there sometimes being as many as three attached to a single letter. J.A. Lundell's Swedish Dialect Alphabet (used for many more languages besides Swedish) relies almost entirely on the creation of new letters. Alexander J. Ellis's notation called Glossic (one of many he invented, often in collaboration with Isaac Pitman) relies almost entirely on digraphs.[7]

The alphabet of the International Phonetic Association (the IPA), which is used in this book, dates from the end of the nineteenth century. It is a notation which has been extensively used for a wide range of languages. Considerable care has been spent on its visual appearance. It is a compromise system, making use of every one of the above expedients for extending its stock of symbols. It is intended to be a genuine general phonetic alphabet, but capable at the same time of providing for any given language a notation in which each phoneme will have a plain single symbol, without diacritics, allophones of phonemes being either left to be accounted for by general rules, or else indicated by diacritics. Its stock of symbols is so organized, therefore, that every important segment type which is likely to be distinguished as a phoneme in a language is provided with a symbol. It could be described as a strongly 'phoneme-oriented' general phonetic alphabet.

The phonological bias of the alphabet is to be accounted for by the fact that, as Paul Passy, the Secretary of the Association, said in 1904, it was 'primarily designed as an aid to the teaching of the exact pronunciation of foreign languages'[8] (and also perhaps by the fact that the Association was from the beginning closely associated with spelling reform movements). The IPA has been, for most of its life, essentially an association of language teachers, and it came into existence to popularize 'reform' methods of language teaching, with their emphasis on the spoken language; the Association's periodical was originally *The Phonetic Teacher*, and it later became *Le Maître Phonétique*. The alphabet has done very well for these rather limited aims. Nowadays, however, phonetic notation is needed for a much greater variety of purposes, and deficiencies have become apparent in the IPA alphabet (and in all others) as a really general phonetic one, as we shall see later.

The IPA alphabet is fully set out and explained in *The Principles of the International Phonetic Association*, to which the reader is referred; many examples of its application to particular languages are given there. Only the main points of the alphabet will be explained here. The easiest way to exhibit the consonant symbols is by means of a 'consonant chart', as explained on p. 54; vowel symbols are discussed later, in chapter 10. The chart given here demonstrates some of the principal IPA consonant symbols; it is arranged with some of the categories of place (named by passive articulator, but including retroflex) down the left-hand side, and some of the categories of manner along the top (which is the contrary of most charts). The chart provides rough general phonetic definitions for the symbols shown on it. They appear in pairs, the first of a pair being the symbol for a voiceless segment, the second for a voiced one.

This chart gives the essential core of the consonant part of the IPA alphabet, but a number of comments on it are needed. First of all, it will be observed that seven of the 'pigeon-holes' contain no symbols. In four cases – retroflex trill, palatal trill, velar trill, uvular lateral – this is because in all probability such segments are not physiologically possible; in these cases the pigeon-hole is filled by a dash. The other three are left quite blank for the simple reason that satisfactory symbols have not so far been invented to fill them.

Two pairs of fricatives often appear in the same pigeon-hole. A more exact taxonomic specification would of course separate them; but we would then have an entire, otherwise empty, row for each pair, which is a disadvantage. They differ either in active articulator, in articulator shape, or in the exact point of the passive articulator involved. Of the two pairs of labial fricatives, the first is bilabial, the second labio-dental. Of the two pairs of alveolar fricatives, the first is grooved (p. 52), the second not. Of the two retroflex pairs, the first is more forward in the mouth, almost in the alveolar category, than the second. The area of the hard palate is large, and of the two pairs of palatal fricatives the first is almost alveolar, with some of the blade of the tongue being involved as active articulator, and the

SOME IPA CONSONANT SYMBOLS
(Pulmonic egressive air-stream)

	Plosive	Nasal	Trill	Fricative	Lateral
Labial	p b	m̥ m		ɸ β f v	
Dental	t̪ d̪	n̪̥ n̪	r̥ r	θ ð	l̪̥ l̪
Alveolar	t̲ d̲	n̥ n	r̥ r	s z ʃ ʒ	l̥ l
Retroflex	ʈ̥ ɖ	ɳ̥ ɳ	—	ɻ̝̊ ɻ̝ ʂ ʐ	ɭ̥ ɭ
Palatal	c ɟ	ɲ̥ ɲ	—	ç̝ ʝ̝ ç j	ʎ̥ ʎ
Velar	k g	ŋ̥ ŋ	—	x ɣ	
Uvular	q ɢ	ɴ̥ ɴ	ʀ̥ ʀ	χ ʁ	

second is further back, with the front of the tongue only as active articulator.

In several of the pairs of consonants, the voiceless member has the same symbol as the voiced one, with the diacritic ₒ added. This is the diacritic for voicelessness. More is said about diacritics below; this, however, is an important one, because it provides us with a symbol for a voiceless segment (whether contoid or vocoid) whenever needed by simply adding it to the symbol for the corresponding voiced sound. (It would be valuable if new symbols, not involving diacritics, could be devised for several of these.)

Diacritics also distinguish the symbols for dental consonants from alveolar ones. The diacritics can be omitted when it is not necessary to be specific. (Here too new symbols for at least the dental plosives would be valuable.)

There are, of course, more consonant symbols than appear on this chart. If all were included on it, the chart would become very much more complicated, and would have several entire rows and columns empty except for one or two symbols, which would detract from its synoptic value. There are five categories of manner not on it, most of which would be represented by only one symbol. They are: (i) *one-tap trill*, voiced alveolar ɾ; (ii) *flap*, voiced retroflex ɽ; (iii) *fricative-trill*, alveolar ř; (iv) *fricative-lateral*, alveolar ɬ ɮ (voiceless and voiced); (v) *approximant*, bilabial ɥ (clear), w (dark), labio-dental ʋ (there can be an approximant corresponding to every fricative, and often the same symbol is used for the former as for the latter, especially in the case of j ɣ ʁ. It would be useful to have a general diacritic which would convert a fricative symbol into one for an approximant when needed; ˌ has been suggested (e.g. ð̞), but is not officially accepted by the IPA). Two categories of place not on the chart are: (i) *pharyngal*, fricatives ħ and ʕ (voiceless and voiced); (ii) *glottal*, stop ʔ. (h, really a symbol for a voiceless vocoid, is often placed in this category, and so is ɦ, symbol for the so-called 'voiced h'; see p. 59.)

It will be observed that a slight manifestation of the iconic principle appears in some of the new letter-shapes, such as those for the nasals. Henry Sweet wrote in 1878 'new letters must be such as to show most clearly the relations of the sound they denote to those denoted by the old letter'.[9] This idea was adopted as one of the principles enunciated in 1888 as guiding the construction of the IPA alphabet: 'The new letters should be suggestive of the sounds they represent, by their resemblance to the old ones.'[10] One can see the effect of the principle in the symbols for retroflex consonants also.

Symbols for segments produced by other than a pulmonic egressive air-stream are also missing from the chart. The series of symbols for voiced implosives show the effect of the above principle: ɓ ɗ ʄ ɠ ʛ. Segments made with a glottalic egressive air-stream (ejectives) have the diacritic ' added after the symbol for the corresponding pulmonic egressive segment: p' t' c' k' q'. There are few symbols for velaric ingressive segments (clicks), the most important being ʇ (dental), ʗ (retroflex), ʖ (alveolar, laterally imploded).

There are two sorts of diacritics. One sort makes a symbol more specific: ˌ, meaning dental, is an example. More general are + and –, meaning advanced variety and retracted variety, respectively. The other sort shows the presence of a secondary articulation. The diacritic for palatalization is attached to the symbol: ţ ḑ ņ ḷ ŗ, and the one for velarization or pharyngalization passes through it : m̶ ɫ s̶ đ. The diacritic for labialization is ˎ, thus ḵ; and for nasalization is ˜, thus õ ũ ž̃.

Quantity is indicated by placing the 'length-mark' ː after the segment. (A double segment is indicated by writing the symbol twice. See p. 82.)

A syllabic contoid is shown by the diacritic ˌ placed below the symbol, thus m̩ ŗ.

Among the deficiencies of the IPA alphabet, as far as consonants are concerned, must be reckoned (i) the absence of general diacritics referring to air-streams; (ii) the fact that diacritics must be used to distinguish dental from alveolar consonants (ţ and t̠ are different phonemes in, for example, Temne, a language of Sierra Leone); (iii) lack of symbols for segments with double articulation (p. 64), which can only be represented by digraphs at present; (iv) lack of a general diacritic for approximants; (v) lack of symbols without diacritics for many voiceless contoids, particularly nasals.

The symbols for vowels are most easily explained in the chapter on Cardinal Vowels (p. 151).

5. *Transcription*

There are various ways in which phonetic notation is used. There is its 'label' use, when the symbol is used in isolation simply to identify either a segment type or a phonological item for purposes of discussion. An analphabetic notation is more or less limited to the label use. Phonetic notation is also used in the form of connected texts which record utterances or parts of utterances. It is then known as phonetic *transcription*.

The use of phonetic transcription is by no means confined to phoneticians; in fact it is apt to occur in anything written about language, from whatever point of view and for whatever purpose. The principles on which it is based are not always completely understood, and it is often misused in consequence. There are many different circumstances in which it can be needed, and several different, but equally correct, ways of transcribing any utterance are always possible. Some ways suit some circumstances better than others.

Strictly speaking, phonetic transcription records not an utterance but an analysis of an utterance, and the analysis may be of two basically different kinds: it may be in general phonetic terms, or it may be in phonological terms (see p. 70). There will therefore be two basically different types of transcription. If the analysis is in general phonetic terms, the transcriber will identify segments as the representatives of general phonetic taxonomic categories. If the analysis is in phonological terms, the transcriber will identify segments as the representatives of elements of structure and of items in systems.

The first type of transcription is called *impressionistic*, and the second *systematic*. The distinction is an important one. When making a systematic transcription, the transcriber knows in advance what all the possibilities are: segments exemplify a small and limited number of known units, for which symbols have been pre-selected. An almost infinite number of possibilities stretches before a transcriber making an impressionistic transcription. He must be ready for anything, and prepared to use symbols from the whole range offered by the notation. Impressionistic transcriptions are difficult to make; they require long training, continual practice, and familiarity with the whole of human phonetic capabilities. Systematic transcriptions are much easier to make, and are well within the powers of the beginner in phonetics.

An impressionistic transcription is sometimes used from necessity, sometimes from choice. It may be used from necessity in two sorts of situations. The first is when the patterns of system and structure of the language which is being transcribed are simply not known. This is the situation, for example, that faces a linguistic fieldworker when he is starting work on a hitherto undescribed language. He must get something down in writing in order to start analysing the language, and he will obviously wish to move towards a systematic transcription as soon as possible; but he has no choice at the outset but to use an impressionistic one.

The second situation is when one has to transcribe forms of speech which are so disorganized that it is not possible to find regularities of structure and system in them. If it is necessary to investigate, for example, the speech of very young children, of aphasics, of the very deaf, of sufferers from various nervous diseases, of drunken people, their utterances will have to be recorded in an impressionistic transcription.

A third reason for using an impressionistic transcription is not because one has to, but because the transcriber chooses to ignore the patterns of structure and system, even though they are known. This is necessary if non-phonological features are being investigated, such as speech defects, or indexical aspects of pronunciation. It might also be necessary when a dialect fieldworker is approaching a new variety of a language with which he is familiar, and does not wish to make assumptions about the phonology of the dialect which might turn out to be wrong.

The basis of a systematic transcription is the provision of a different symbol for each phoneme, though it is sometimes useful to indicate allophones by special extra symbols. The IPA alphabet is better designed to furnish systematic transcriptions than impressionistic ones. It should perhaps be noted here that (contrary to popular belief) the IPA does not have any 'official' styles of transcription for any language; this is inevitable, since it has no official analysis of the phonology of any language. All it does is to provide, apart from the repertoire of symbols, certain principles on which, given the phonological analysis, a transcription should be based.[11]

Systematic transcriptions are much more widely used than impressionistic ones. They have an important part to play in teaching the pronunciation of foreign languages, for example; they are found in almost all modern scientific descriptive grammars; and they are needed for pronouncing dictionaries of languages, such as English and French, which are erratically spelt.

Phonetic notation occurs most commonly, not in the form of long connected passages, but as short pieces of transcription, or as single 'labels', in the middle of ordinary printed matter. Whenever it occurs in these circumstances, it must be immediately recognizable as notation–it must be 'differentiated' from ordinary spelling. There are various ways of doing this; phonetic notation can be printed in italics, for example, as is done with Lundell's Swedish Dialect Alphabet. But much the most usual manner of differentiating phonetic notation is by placing the symbols within square brackets, thus:

the vowel [a]

There is no need, however, to differentiate phonetic symbols when they occur as a long connected phonetic text, where there could be no possibility of mistaking them for ordinary spelling.

Many different systematic transcriptions of English have been worked out, all based on IPA principles. They do not differ very much in the way the consonants are symbolized, and the following are symbols for the consonant system common to most of them:

```
p b m
      f v
      θ ð
t d n      l r
      s z
      ʃ ʒ
k g ŋ
```

There are in addition the three non-syllabic vocoids [h j w]. The values
of these symbols can be gathered roughly from the consonant chart
on p. 125; their exact value varies from accent to accent in different
parts of the English-speaking world.

It is in the symbols used for vowels that the main differences are
found between different types of transcription used for English; moreover it is in vowel-systems that the main differences between different
accents of English are found. The following symbols would do for
several kinds of English spoken in England (they would not do for
kinds spoken in Scotland or America):

i as in bead	ɜ as in bird
ɪ as in bid	ə as in *a*bout (first vowel)
ɛ as in bed	eɪ as in bade
a as in bad	oω as in bode
ɑ as in bard	aɪ as in bide
ɒ as in bog	aω as in loud
ɔ as in ball	ɒɪ as in Boyd
ω as in good	ɪə as in beard
u as in food	ɛə as in bared
ʌ as in bud	ωə as in gourd

6. *Non-segmental symbols*

Segmental features are much better provided for, in the way of notation, than are non-segmental features. There is less general agreement
on representation of the latter, and not as much thought has been
given to it, though there is growing interest in the subject. Nevertheless symbols for non-segmental features are not as often required as
they are for segmental ones. It is improbable that any sort of notational device could ever be needed for features of voice quality
(though some have been suggested); whatever it might be necessary
to record in this respect can simply be stated in words and prefaced
to a text.

An increasing amount of research, however, is nowadays being
devoted to the phonetics of conversation, and this inevitably involves attention to what have been called 'paralinguistic' phenomena,
that is to say features of voice dynamics such as continuity, variation
in loudness, in tempo, and in tessitura. If a record is to be provided
of a conversation in all its aspects as an interaction between people,
the segmental text will have to be augmented by indications of such
features as these. No settled practice has emerged as yet for dealing
with them, but clearly these features have to be represented in a
separate order, or orders, of symbols, distinct from those for segments, of which they must be independent. It is useful, in fact, to be
able to combine them with texts in ordinary spelling.[12]

The main reason, of course, why systematic transcriptions do not usually need to incorporate symbols for most of voice dynamics is that it does not enter into language-bearing patterns. In English, for example, only pitch variation and rhythm, but no other features of voice dynamics, would be relevant, and only when phonetic aspects of the sentence were being discussed (and even then their representation may often not be essential).

Less attention has been given to rhythm than to pitch variation. It is usual to mark stressed syllables by placing the 'stress-mark' ˈ at the beginning of the syllable, thus:

good 'after'noon

or, in segmental transcription:

[gɷd 'ɑftə'nun].

It is often more satisfactory in a connected text of a stress-timed language, as distinct from transcriptions of isolated words, to replace the stress-marks by vertical lines (see p. 98), which will divide it into isochronous periods which may be called *feet*. Thus:

good |after|noon

It is the notation of pitch variation that, among dynamic features, has had most attention paid to it. Here too we have nearly always a separate order of symbols, which can usefully, on occasion, accompany the ordinary spelling. Most notations for pitch variation are iconic, which is a simple matter for this dynamic feature, since it has variation in only one dimension. A mark which is higher than another in the line of writing represents a higher pitch. A continually varying line, for example (which disregards the momentary breaks in voicing), can be drawn either over or under the segmental symbols:

good afternoon

Of all iconic representations of pitch variation, the most effective consists of arranging the segmental symbols, or the letters of the ordinary spelling, so that they themselves form the iconic line of rise and fall in pitch:

good after^{n}o$_{\mathrm{o}_{\mathrm{n}}}$

Types of notation such as these are direct representations of the pitch fluctuation; they reveal no phonological analysis. It would not even be possible to distinguish a tone language from an intonation language from them. They are impressionistic, not systematic. A notation for speech melody proper must reflect an analysis. Different analyses are possible of speech melody patterns both of tone and of intonation languages, and these differences are naturally reflected in notation. There are many different analyses of the intonation of English, for example, some into pitch-level elements, some into pitch-movement elements. The elements can be represented either by conventional symbols or by iconic symbols. They can be given numbers, for example, which can be written over the syllables:

> 2   2   2 3-1
> good afternoon

The higher the number, the higher the pitch.[13] The same levels can be represented in a way which is more immediately iconic:

> good after<u>noon</u>

Or the same pattern shown in terms of pitch movement[14]:

> good ˌafterˈnoon

The same applies to tone languages. Here are two ways of showing the tones of four words, which all have the same segments, in Chinese:

> biau[1]   ¯biau
> biau[2]   ′biau
> biau[3]   ˌbiau
> biau[4]   ˋbiau

It is possible in some tone languages to show the tones by means of alphabetic symbols, incorporated into the symbols for segments, so that one order of symbols represents both. It is in fact very convenient to do this – for sending telegrams, for instance. This is possible in Chinese, and the above four words could be represented thus:

> biau
>
> byau
>
> beau
>
> biaw

where the changes in the alphabetic symbols imply a change of tone only, and no difference in the segments. The consonant and vowel systems of Chinese are such as to leave enough spare alphabetic symbols to make this possible.

8

Assimilation

The word 'assimilation' is often met with in works on language, but different writers have used it in a number of different ways. We can conveniently distinguish (following Daniel Jones[1]) three kinds of phenomena to which it has been applied:

(*a*) similitudes,
(*b*) historical assimilations,
(*c*) juxtapositional assimilations.

Similitudes have been dealt with briefly above, in Chapter 5, when the subject of the phoneme was discussed; we need not be concerned any further with them here. *Historical* assimilations are not, strictly speaking, the business of general phonetics, though it will nevertheless be useful to explain here briefly what they are; this is best deferred, however, until after discussion of *juxtapositional* assimilations, which are the most important for our present purposes of the above three kinds of phenomena to which the word is applied. Whenever the word 'assimilation' is used here without further qualification, it should be taken to mean *juxtapositional* assimilation.

Juxtapositional assimilations are changes[2] in pronunciation which take place under certain circumstances at the ends and the beginnings of words (changes at word 'boundaries', that is to say) when these words occur in connected speech, or in compounds. What this means can best be made clear by starting with an example. The word *is* is usually pronounced [ɪz], and the word *she* is pronounced [ʃi]; but when these two words come together in the phrase *is she*, they are often pronounced [ɪʒ ʃi] rather than [ɪz ʃi].

There are two things to notice about the use of [ʒ] instead of [z] as the final segment of *is* in this way of pronouncing the phrase. First, it is a direct consequence of the juxtaposition of the two words, or more exactly of the resulting contact of the final segment of the first word

with the initial segment of the second word; second, the points of
contact of the words have been *assimilated*–the final segment of the
first and the initial segment of the second have become *similar* in
certain respects in which before they were different.

They are similar in so far as the sequence [-ʒ ʃ-] is made by one and
the same articulatory posture, whereas the sequence [-z ʃ-] requires a
succession of two different articulatory postures. Such an assimilation, or making similar, of the points of contact of words can take
two forms: either the final segment of the first word is changed, or the
initial segment of the second word is changed. The two forms can
be expressed briefly by means of formulae, in which the symbol F is
used to mean 'final segment of a word', I to mean 'initial segment of a
word', and A to mean 'assimilated segment', i.e. a segment which
owes part of its characteristics to a segment of another word with
which it is in contact. Thus an assimilation is either of the type

    (i)   ——F+I—— = ——AI——

or of the type

    (ii)   ——F+I—— = ——FA——

In (i), a word which in most circumstances ends in the segment F
is immediately followed, in a phrase or compound word, by a word
which in most circumstances begins with the segment I. When the
two words are juxtaposed in utterance in this way, the segment F may
be replaced by the 'assimilated' segment, A, under the influence of
the segment I, which remains unchanged. In this case the 'assimilating
influence' moves backwards, as shown by the arrow:

$$\overset{\longleftarrow}{——F+I——},$$

and for this reason an assimilation of this type is called a *regressive*
assimilation (or by some people an 'anticipatory' assimilation).

In (ii), just as in the previous instance, a word which in most
circumstances ends in the segment F is immediately followed in an
utterance by a word which in most circumstances begins with the
segment I. In this conjunction of words, however, it is the segment I
which is replaced by another segment (here also indicated by A)
under the influence of the segment F, which remains unchanged. In
this case the assimilating influence moves forwards, as shown by the
arrow:

$$\overset{\longrightarrow}{——F+I——}$$

This is called *progressive* assimilation.

The example [ɪʒ ʃi] which was given above is an example of regressive assimilation, for it is the segment at the end of the first word which is altered, under the influence of the segment at the beginning of the second, i.e.

F = [z]
I = [ʃ]
A = [ʒ]

An example of progressive assimilation would be the pronunciation of *did* [dɪd] and *you* [ju] in sequence as [dɪdʒu]: the segment at the beginning of the *second* word is altered, under the influence of the segment at the end of the first, i.e.

F = [d]
I = [j]
A = [ʒ]

Assimilations are not 'compulsory' in many languages, including English: that is to say a speaker may, if he chooses, avoid making them. When they are made, however, they have the effect, whether they are progressive or regressive, of producing some *economy of effort* in the utterance of a sequence of words. The result of the assimilation is to reduce the number, or the extent, of the movements and adjustments which the speech-producing organs have to perform in the transition from one word to the next. Assimilations save effort by means of three different sorts of changes in the sequence of speech-producing movements:

(1) those involving the state of the glottis;
(2) those involving velic action;
(3) those involving movement of the articulators.

Each of these three will be considered in turn. It should be remembered that an instance of assimilation may economize effort in more than one of these ways at once.

(1) *Assimilations involving the state of the glottis.* The result of making an assimilation of this type is that two successive different states of the glottis are replaced by a single state which is maintained unchanged. For instance, two words might be brought next to each other in an utterance, one with a voiced segment and one with a voiceless segment at the point of contact; an adjustment in the state of the glottis would therefore be necessary in the transition from the one to the other, if they remain as they are. However, the speaker may make an assimilation by which the adjustment becomes unnecessary,

either because both segments become voiced, or because both become voiceless, the former being known as *assimilation of voice* and the latter as *assimilation of voicelessness* (or sometimes as assimilation of breath).

Regressive assimilations of voice may be found very commonly, though not universally, among speakers of educated Scots. Thus the word *with*, which under most circumstances ends in a voiceless consonant in Scottish English, may be pronounced with a voiced one in *with them* by assimilation to the voiced consonant at the beginning of *them*. Similarly in the compounds *blackboard* or *birthday* the words *black* and *birth*, which normally end in voiceless consonants, may be pronounced with voiced ones. Such regressive assimilations of voice appear to be found in no other kind of English, though they are the regular thing in French, Dutch, and several other languages.

Assimilations of voicelessness are common in all types of English. Many people make a regressive assimilation of voicelessness when they pronounce the phrases *of course* or *have to* with the voiceless consonant [f] (instead of the voiced [v]). Another frequently heard example is the pronunciation of *news* with the voiceless segment [s] (instead of the voiced [z]) in the compound *newspaper*. A progressive assimilation of voicelessness occurs when the word *is* is pronounced [s] in *what's*, *it's*.

(2) *Assimilations involving velic action.* An assimilation of this type effects an economy by eliminating a movement of the velum. When a nasal (or nasalized) segment at the boundary of one word and an oral segment at the boundary of another are brought next to each other in an utterance, the movement of the velum required in the transition between them will be eliminated if both become nasal, or both lose their nasality. Such assimilations are rare (or non-existent) in English, but they may be found in other languages. In French, for instance, the phrase *une langue moderne* may be pronounced [yn lɑ̃ŋ mɔdɛrn], where [ŋ] replaces, by a regressive assimilation of nasality, the [g] that would be used when the word is said in isolation.

(3) *Assimilations involving movements of the articulators.* In an assimilation of this kind, successive movements of two different articulators are replaced by a movement of one articulator only. This is much the most frequent type of assimilation in English, and a wide variety of examples can be found. The more familiar and the more rapid the style of speech, the more frequent such assimilations are likely to be. In the majority of cases they are regressive. The pronunciation of *is she* as [ɪʒ ʃi] comes under this heading; other examples are: [tɛm mɪnɪts] for *ten minutes*, [aɪŋ goʊɪŋ] for *I'm going*.

Such assimilations are liable to be described by purists as 'careless speech' when attention is drawn to them, though most of the time they pass unnoticed.

Assimilations of this third type may often be combined with assimilations involving the state of the glottis. Thus [ɪʃ ʃi] may be heard for *is she*, as well as [ɪʒ ʃi], the voiceless [ʃ] taking the place of the voiced [ʒ] or [z].

All the preceding examples may be characterised as *complete* assimilations. It is useful to distinguish complete assimilations from incomplete or *partial* assimilations; these latter also entail an economy of effort in the movements of the organs of speech, but to a lesser degree. An assimilation of type (1) above, for example, is *complete* if it results in there being only one state of the glottis at the boundaries of the two words where there were two states before; but it is *partial* when there still remains a succession of two different states after the assimilation, though these states have been accommodated to each other to the extent that their succession involves less effort than before. For example, when a voiced segment and a voiceless segment at the boundaries of two words are brought next to each other in an utterance, a partial assimilation may be made by which the former becomes *whispered* (in the technical phonetic sense: see p. 28 – the vocal cords are closely approximated, but do not vibrate); or by which it becomes voiced for part of its duration and voiceless or whispered for the rest. In both cases it is convenient to call the segment 'partially devoiced'.

Partial assimilations involving adjustments of the state of the glottis are particularly common in English, and they may be either progressive or regressive. The examples given above of complete regressive assimilation of voicelessness (as in *of course*, *have to*, or *newspaper*) concern a succession of words which form a frequently recurring phrase or a compound. When the words are not closely linked by custom in this way, assimilations are usually partial. For example, the word *his* in the phrase *his daughter* ends in a voiced segment [z], but in the phrase *his son* the final segment of *his* may, by a partial assimilation, be whispered, or voiced at the start of the segment but whispered or voiceless at its end. The segment is not, that is to say, a fully voiceless [s], as a comparison with *this son* (in which a really fully voiceless [s] is found at the end of *this*) will clearly demonstrate. (It should be noted that in phonetic transcription the final segment of *his*, in a case like this, would normally be represented by [z], even though it is not fully voiced: the partial assimilation is implied by the juxtaposition of the symbol [z] and the symbol for the voiceless consonant which begins the next word.) In such regressive

partial assimilations of voicelessness in English, the assimilated segment is always a plosive or a fricative.

A comparable replacement of a fully voiced segment by a partly
voiced one is found in English in utterance-final position, before a
pause. This is really a kind of assimilation, the assimilating factor in
this case being silence, and the consequent relaxed state of the vocal
cords (which is similar to their state for a voiceless segment). This
is usually referred to as 'final devoicing'. It is particularly noticeable
when the word ends in a consonant cluster, as in *fields, sands, sings,
graves*.

Historical assimilations are changes which have taken place, over a
period of time, *within* a word; they are the business of historians of
languages, and they find no place in the description of a language as
it actually is at any one given time. Historical assimilations, like
juxtapositional assimilations, may be either regressive or progressive,
and they too can be shown to result in economy of effort by effecting
a saving in either the number, or the extent, of movements and adjustments either of the state of the glottis, the velum, or the articulators.
An example of a historical assimilation which is regressive and con-
cerns movements of the articulators is the development of the Italian
word *fatto* from the Latin *factum*: the single movement of the point
of the tongue required for -*tt*- has been substituted for the successive
movements of back of the tongue and point of the tongue required
for -*ct*-. The history of every language offers numerous examples of
such changes.

Historical assimilations are sometimes reflected in the spelling, and
sometimes they are not. An assimilation once took place in the middle
of the English word *orchard*, which was originally a compound word
ort + yard (the element *ort* probably deriving from the Latin *hortus*[3]).
The sequence [-tj-] was replaced, by a progressive assimilation, by
[-tʃ-]. Since this happened a long time ago, the spelling shows it. An
exactly similar progressive assimilation, yielding the same sound in
the middle of the word, took place more recently (perhaps three or
four centuries ago) in the word *nature*, now pronounced [neɪtʃə], but
in this case the spelling has been left unchanged.

Historical assimilations which are not reflected in the spelling pass
unnoticed most of the time. When they are noticed, however, they
are often strongly reprobated by educational authorities, even when
they have 300 or more years of tradition behind them. Many people
who are not entirely self-confident in their speech, when they have
been made aware that they use a 'concealed' assimilation of this sort,
feel that they are guilty of (literally) an illiteracy, and they proceed to

modify their pronunciation in a direction which accords better with the spelling. Innovations in pronunciation of this sort are known as 'spelling pronunciations', and a very large number of them have established themselves in the language since the rapid spread of literacy in the nineteenth century. Thus *immediate* was once usually pronounced with [-dʒ-] in the middle of it, though now it is perhaps more common to hear [-dj-]. There are good reasons for thinking words like *clean* and *glove* were once widely pronounced with [tl-] and [dl-] respectively at the beginning, as a result of a regressive assimilation; though [kl-] and [gl-] are now what most people would say, the unassimilated forms having been restored under the influence of the spelling.[4]

9

Stop Consonants

1. *Three phases of a stop*

In the taxonomy of consonants (or more strictly speaking of contoids; see ch. 5), a stop, like all other contoid classes except a flap, is classified as a *posture*, a positioning of the articulators producing a stricture of complete closure (see ch. 4). This is perfectly adequate for classificatory purposes; but for understanding its function in connected speech, it will not do to look on a stop simply as a posture –it is much too static a view. A stop involves not only a posture; it involves a movement to that posture and a movement away from it, and the manner in which this posture is taken up, and subsequently relinquished, are additional factors which have to be taken into account.[1] In order to discuss the function of a stop in connected speech, therefore, we must distinguish three phases in its production:

> phase i, the shutting phase, leading to
> phase ii, the closure phase, followed by
> phase iii, the opening phase.

The three phases are clearly visible if we pronounce, say, a voiced bilabial plosive with an open unrounded vowel such as [a] before and after it, i.e. [aba]. The lips can be observed to come together, to stay together for a moment, and then to part. We can represent this movement of the articulators by the following diagram:

FIGURE 1.

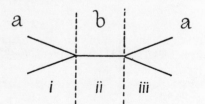

The two converging lines and the two separating lines represent the articulators coming together (phase i) and opening again (phase iii) respectively, and the single straight line which is between represents phase ii, with the articulators in contact making a stricture of complete closure.

A plosive entails a momentary but complete interruption of the air-stream (because there is a velic closure as well as the articulatory stricture of complete closure) which starts as soon as phase i is completed, and continues until the barrier to the air-stream is removed with phase iii. Each phase is, of course, very brief in duration—a fraction of a second only: the speed at which articulator movements are carried out is very great. Even so, there is enough time during phase ii, when the air-stream is interrupted, for the air pressure behind the closure to be altered by the action of the air-stream mechanism: if the air-stream is egressive, the pressure will be raised, i.e. the air will be compressed, and if the air-stream is ingressive, the pressure will be lowered, i.e. the air will be rarefied. Consequently phase iii will be accompanied by equalization of the pressure behind the stricture with that of the outside air. In the former case, as the articulators separate, the compressed air explodes outwards. The technical term for this release of pressure is *plosion*. In the latter case, as the articulators separate, air implodes inwards. The technical term for this is *implosion*.

It will simplify matters if, for the rest of this chapter, the problems of stops are discussed and illustrated mainly in terms of a pulmonic egressive air-stream, though most of what will be said applies (*mutatis mutandis*) to stops made with all air-streams. Stops may be made to seem here rather complicated segments. However, although the difficulties which arise from treating a segment as a static posture are more obvious in the case of stops than other contoids, they are not more complicated as movements. It is the complete interruption of the air-stream that makes them appear so.

Phase ii of a stop is the least conspicuous, auditorily, of the three phases; during it there is either a low murmur, if the stop is voiced, or complete silence if it is not (complete silence, of course, since it has duration, is perfectly perceptible when other sounds surround it). Phase i is not very conspicuous either, and if the stop is in utterance-initial position, it is imperceptible. Phase iii, however, usually has more noise than the other two phases associated with it, because of the sudden explosive release of air pressure built up during phase ii (in special circumstances, to be described below, this release of air pressure does not take place).

Though it is auditorily inconspicuous, phase ii of a stop is present in the same form under all circumstances (which gives it its taxonomic importance, and makes it the posture on the basis of which stops are classified). Phases i and iii, however, may be modified in various ways, or may even be absent altogether. How this happens is what we must now consider.

2. *Stops and velic action*

The opening movement which constitutes phase iii of a stop may be transferred from the articulators to the velum. This occurs, for example, with the plosive consonant [b] in the English word *submarine*. The articulators remain in position at the conclusion of phase ii, but the velum is lowered so that the velic closure is removed; the compressed air thus escapes through the nose instead of through the mouth. The plosion is then *nasal plosion* instead of oral plosion, as it otherwise would be.

Nasal plosion only takes place when a stop is immediately followed by a *homorganic* nasal (that is, a nasal made by the same articulators as the stop is). It is easy to observe, at the transition from the [b] of *submarine* to the [m], that no movement of the two lips, the articulators, takes place; the three phases of a stop are, however, still present, as can be shown by an augmented version of Fig. 1 above, in which velic action as well as articulator action is represented. As in Fig. 1, a complete closure (velic or articulatory) is shown by a single straight line; converging lines and separating lines represent vocal organs coming together and opening again respectively. The upper half of the diagram represents articulatory action, opening or closing the passage through the mouth, and the lower half represents velic action, opening or closing the passage through the nose. Oral plosion can then be shown as in Fig. 2; a single straight line appears for the nose passage since a velic closure is maintained throughout:

FIGURE 2.

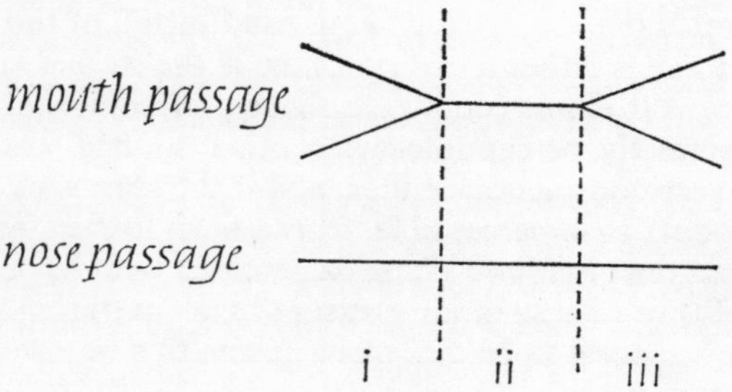

How this compares with nasal plosion can be seen from the way phase iii appears in Fig. 3:

FIGURE 3.

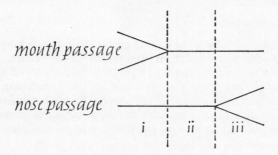

Nasal plosion is common in English, both within words and at word junctions, as in *submarine, topmost, ape man, Sydney, Totnes, that night*. With many (perhaps most) speakers it is found before a syllabic [n̩], as in *suddenly, eaten, bidden*. Others, however, avoid it in this position, using oral plosion instead, though they would use nasal plosion under other circumstances. One may occasionally hear oral plosion instead of nasal plosion at word junctions, in for example *that night*, in a rhetorical style of delivery; but this is usually considered to be affected.

All the instances of nasal plosion which occur in English involve abutting consonants: the plosive ends one syllable, and the nasal begins the next, whether within a word or at word boundaries. Nasal plosion involving a consonant cluster, that is to say within a syllable, does not occur in English either in releasing or arresting position, though such clusters can be found in other languages – in releasing position, for example, in some of the aboriginal languages of Australia, and in arresting position in Icelandic. (It is possible that nasal plosion in a releasing cluster once occurred in English in a word like *know*, which early phoneticians sometimes transcribe phonetically [tno].)

Nasal plosion is the transference of phase iii to velic action from articulator action. Phase i may also be transferred from articulator to velic action, giving so to speak the 'converse' of nasal plosion. This is found in all languages when a nasal is followed by a homorganic stop, as in English *under, hunger, sombre, sinker, hand, lump*. This is shown diagrammatically at the top of page 144:

FIGURE 4.

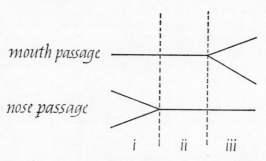

Here phase i is represented by the raising of the velum to make a velic closure; the articulators are already in the posture required for the stop. There is no name for this phenomenon, and probably none is needed. As can be seen from the above examples, it is not confined in English to abutting consonants, but occurs commonly in arresting clusters. It does not occur in English in releasing clusters, however, though it does in other languages in many parts of the world (for example, Kikuyu, Sinhalese, Xhosa, Guaraní). In many African languages, however, a nasal and a following homorganic stop at the beginning of a word do not form a cluster: the nasal is syllabic, as in the Ghanaian name *Nkrumah*, for example.

Both phase i and phase iii of a stop may be transferred from articulator to velic movement, as in the English *Saint Nicholas*, *stamp machine*, where we have stops preceded and followed by homorganic nasals: [ntn], [mpm]. A diagram illustrating this would now appear as the reverse of Fig. 2, with a single straight line appearing at the top instead of at the bottom:

FIGURE 5.

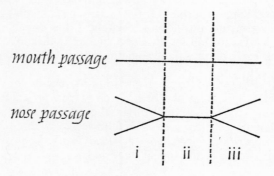

3. *Lateral plosion*

We have seen that plosion may be oral or nasal. Oral plosion may be central, as in all the examples given so far, or it may be lateral. If the plosion is central, there is central passage in the vocal tract (see p. 45) of the air released after its compression behind the closure; lateral plosion results when contact of the articulators is maintained in the centre of the vocal tract, allowing only lateral passage of the air compressed behind the closure. Lateral plosion is found when a plosive is followed by a homorganic lateral. In English lateral plosion of [t] and [d] is common; lateral plosion of [k] and [g] is found only in certain accents or as an individual peculiarity (a velar lateral is a rare sound); lateral plosion of [p] and [b] is unknown (and has not been reported from any other language).

Lateral plosion of [t] and [d] is found in English both within words and at word junctions. It is usually at syllable boundaries: the stop and the lateral are abutting consonants, and do not form a cluster. Examples: *at last*, *badly*, and (for many English speakers) *middle*, *little*. In these cases, phase iii is confined to the sides of the tongue; the point does not leave the alveolar ridge, as it does for central plosion, and the escape of air takes place round the sides of the tongue (or on one side only, with many speakers).

It should be noted that the last two of the above examples are not valid for all speakers of English. If there is lateral plosion in these words, the [l] must necessarily be syllabic. Some speakers, however, though using lateral plosion in other circumstances, always avoid it if it would result in syllabic [l]; they use central plosion instead, that is to say the point of the tongue is removed during phase iii of the stop, and then returned for the [l].

Lateral plosion within a consonant cluster is not common in English, though there are a number of speakers, as we have seen (p. 77) who say, for example, *A.tlantic*, with [tl] as a releasing cluster, rather than as two abutting consonants. Lateral plosion in a releasing cluster at the beginning of a word is more unusual, but many speakers in England replace word-initial releasing [kl] and [gl] by [tl] and [dl], as in the example [tlinˈdlʌvz] for [klin glʌvz] quoted above in ch. 8 (p. 139). The same substitution is also found within a word, as [ɪntlaɪn] for [ɪnklaɪn] *incline*. The two pairs of clusters are, in fact, auditorily very similar, and, as already pointed out, [tl] and [dl] may once have been very much more common in English than now, the modern [kl] and [gl] being 'spelling pronunciations'. Lateral plosion in releasing clusters is found in many other languages, however; for example in Welsh. In an arresting cluster lateral plosion is not found in English, but this too is found in other languages, for example in Icelandic. The lateral consonant in clusters involving lateral plosion is often a lateral fricative; and the whole cluster is sometimes ejective, as for example in Zulu, and in several American Indian languages.

4. *Incomplete stops*

Plosion, as well as being oral (either lateral or central), or nasal, may be suppressed; phase iii, though still present as an articulatory movement, is not accompanied by release of compressed air. This results in an 'unexploded' stop, which is one sort of 'incomplete' stop. In English incomplete stops are found whenever two stops occur in succession, either within words or at word boundaries, as in *apt, up to*. Both stops here are incomplete (auditorily, not articulatorily), though in different respects: [p] lacks an audible phase iii, [t] lacks an audible phase i. What happens is as follows: phase i of the second stop, [t], takes place during phase ii, the closure phase, of the first stop [p]; so that when phase iii of [p] comes there can be no burst of escaping air, with its accompanying noise, since the stricture for [t] prevents this. There may be 'a little faintish smack' as the lips separate, as Abraham Tucker pointed out in 1773,[2] but for practical purposes the stop is incomplete auditorily, and may be more specifically referred to as unexploded. The [t] also is incomplete, in the sense that phase i, which takes place behind closed lips, produces no auditory effect. A diagram of how the phases of the two stops overlap may make this clearer:

FIGURE 6.

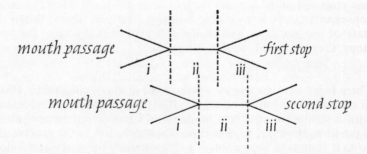

Other examples are: *actor, big dog, exactly* (in which phase iii of the second stop, [t], has lateral plosion), *egg beater, Atkins*.

In English one may have a sequence of three stops, and when this happens the middle one is doubly incomplete–it lacks an audible phase i and an audible phase iii; e.g. *locked cupboard, apt pupil.* When the middle stop is voiceless, as in these examples, it is quite inaudible in itself, being represented merely by a period of silence.

A phonological rule in English is that any two consecutive stops are both incomplete, in the manner described. In French, by contrast, incomplete stops do not occur in these conditions. Thus in French *apte*, as distinct from English *apt*, phase i of [t] comes after phase ii of [p] is completed and phase iii has started; there is no overlapping of the closure phases. The following diagram should be compared with Fig. 6:

FIGURE 7.

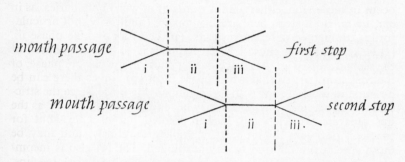

When two consecutive stops in English have the same articulation, as in *egg cup, scrap book, that time, bookcase*, the rule also applies, though here the stops really are incomplete, in all senses—there are no articulatory movements at all corresponding to phase iii in the first stop and phase i in the second. Such stops are always abutting consonants: there is a syllable boundary between them. When the state of the glottis as well as the articulation is the same for both stops, they are called 'double' (see p. 82).

5. *Affrication*

There is yet another way in which phase iii may be modified. Phase iii normally takes place so rapidly that the noise which is associated with it results entirely from the burst of escaping compressed air. It is possible, however, to slow down the separation of the articulators so that they take long enough to pass through a stricture of close approximation for the resulting friction to be audible, even though it is brief. This is known as affrication, and the plosion is then said to be *affricated*; phase iii could now be represented as follows on the diagram at the top of page 148:

FIGURE 8.

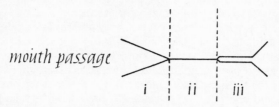

mouth passage

      i   ii   iii

Stops with affricated plosion, or 'affricated stops', are heard in many types of English; they are for the most part disliked by those who do not use them, and thought to be dialectal. They are accepted standard forms of stops in many other languages (Danish, e.g.).

When the friction following the stop is sufficiently marked to be considered a separate segment, the cluster of stop and homorganic fricative is usually known as an *affricate* (to be distinguished from an affricated stop). Examples are the beginning of the English words *cheese, jam*, or of the German word *zeit*. The term is only used when it is convenient to treat the cluster as a single phonological unit. (There is a difference of opinion about whether [tʃ] and [dʒ] should be so considered in English. The initial clusters in *tray* and *dray* are not often called affricates, though phonetically they are exactly comparable, because they are never considered to be single phonological units.)

6. *Aspiration*

Finally, we must consider the co-ordination of states of the glottis with the different phases of a stop. If the glottis is open during phase ii, the stop is called voiceless; but we still have to take into account what happens during phase iii. If voicing does not set in until after phase iii is completed, the plosion itself will be voiceless, and the stop is said to be voiceless *aspirated*. If, however, voicing starts simultaneously with the beginning of phase iii, then the plosion is voiced, and the stop is termed voiceless *unaspirated*. Aspiration, in other words, is a period of voicelessness that follows the voiceless closure phase of a stop. The diagram on page 149 will make these relationships of stops with glottal states clearer; the lower line represents the state of the glottis. It is wavy if the glottis is in vibration, straight if it is not.

A voiced stop, a voiceless unaspirated stop and a voiceless aspirated stop differ, then, according to the point at which voicing sets in during the course of the successive phases of the stop. There can, of course, be many intermediate points, in addition to these, at which voicing sets in: from 'fully voiced' to 'voiceless fully aspirated' is a

FIGURE 9.

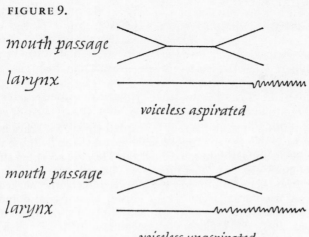

voiceless aspirated

voiceless unaspirated

continuum. The term 'aspirated' is also used in conjunction with the term 'voiced stop', but it then has a fairly different sense, there being no question in this case of a period of voicelessness after the plosion. Many languages of India (and some in other parts of the world) possess 'voiced aspirated stops', and their characteristic is that they are followed by a vowel pronounced with 'breathy voice' (see p. 93), i.e. with a different register. Such stops are not part of the continuum referred to above, and it adds nothing to speak of a voiced *unaspirated* stop, which would be the same as a voiced stop.

7. *Notation*

In phonetic transcription, it is not normally necessary to give specific indication of nasal and lateral plosion: they are left unmarked, and taken to be an implication of the juxtaposition of a symbol for a stop and a symbol for the homorganic nasal or lateral, as the case may be. It follows therefore that the *absence* of nasal or lateral plosion must be specifically indicated, by the insertion of the appropriate vowel symbol, as in [bɪdən] *bidden*, [itən] *eaten*, [lɪtəl] *little*; or if there is no voice between the plosive and the nasal, by [ʰ] representing a non-syllabic voiceless vocoid, as in [ðatʰnaɪt] *that night*. On the rare occasions when it is found necessary to give a specific indication of nasal or lateral plosion, the signs [ᴺ] and [ᴸ], respectively, can be placed after the symbol for the stop, as [tᴺ, tᴸ, bᴺ, gᴸ], and so on. (These are not official IPA symbols.)

The difference between the usual English pronunciation of *apt* and the usual French pronunciation of *apte* would normally not appear in phonetic transcription. Whether the stop is unexploded or not would be stated once and for all for each language. If it should be found necessary to distinguish the two in notation, they can be shown as [ap°t] and [apʰt] respectively (the former not being an official IPA symbol).

Affricated stops can be indicated by placing a raised small symbol for the homorganic fricative after the symbol for the stop, as [tˢ, dᶻ]. When a stop, followed by a homorganic fricative which is a full segment, is treated as a single phonological unit or affricate, it may be represented by a ligature, as [t͡ʃ] for [tʃ], [d͡ʒ] for [dʒ], [ts] for [ts], etc.

Aspirated stops may be shown thus: [pʰ, tʰ, kʰ], etc., or if the aspiration is strong [ph, th, kh] may be used.

10

Cardinal Vowels

1. *Theory*

We saw in chapter 4 that vowels can be classified in articulatory terms on the basis of three 'dimensions' of classification (highest point of the tongue on the vertical axis, highest point of the tongue on the horizontal axis, posture of the lips), and that they can be approximately identified by the three-term labels which these dimensions provide. The identification is no more than approximate, however, and this method of description, although it does very well for a number of practical purposes, is certainly not capable of specifying a vowel segment exactly. There are twenty-four three-term labels for vowels (see p. 58), and each one of them could be applied to several easily discriminable qualities of sound. Another method of identifying vowel segments is therefore needed for occasions when it is necessary to specify vowels with high precision. Such a method is provided by the system of Cardinal Vowels.[1]

Identification by three-term articulatory labels depends on the principle of fitting the vowel which is to be described into a number of categories, one for each of the dimensions of classification, and so progressively narrowing down the area in which the vowel is to be found. The method of identifying vowel segments by Cardinal Vowels has quite a different sort of basis. A Cardinal Vowel is a fixed and unchanging reference point, established within the total range of vowel quality, to which any other vowel sound can be directly related. A number of such reference points constitutes a *system* of Cardinal Vowels, and any vowel in any language can be identified by being 'placed' within the system.

The idea of a system of reference points of this sort was originally put forward by A. J. Ellis in 1844, and the word 'cardinal' itself was first used in connexion with such a system (on the analogy, of course, of the way the word is used about points of the compass) by A. M.

Bell in 1867. The notion, therefore, is a fairly old one.[2] It was quite a long time, however, before it was put into practice, and a fully worked-out system did not become generally available until Daniel Jones developed one in connexion with his teaching at University College, London, and made it public about the time of the first World War.[3] Jones's system has since been widely adopted, and it is the one that will be explained here. There is, indeed, no other system of cardinal vowels which has ever been brought into general use (though the term 'cardinal vowel' is occasionally used in the literature without reference to Jones's or, apparently, any other system.[4])

Eight cardinal vowels form the core of the Daniel Jones system (there are a number of 'secondary' cardinal vowels whose function will be explained later; the eight cardinal vowels are sometimes called 'primary' in contrast to these). They are arbitrarily selected, that is to say they are not based on the vowels of any existing language (though they are sometimes mistakenly alleged to be based on the vowels of French). The system is a *general phonetic* one.

It will be remembered (see p. 56) that when a vowel is pronounced the main body of the tongue, although it can assume many different shapes, always has a convex upper surface: it is always in the shape of a 'hump'. There are limits in the mouth within which the highest point of this hump, whatever the vowel may be, must always lie. These limits derive from two sorts of constraint: first, it is not physically possible for the tongue to assume shapes which would bring its highest point further than a certain distance from the centre of the mouth in a forwards or a downwards direction; and second, if the highest point is further than a certain distance in an upwards or a backwards direction, the stricture so formed will be one of close and not open approximation (p. 45); hence the resulting sound will contain audible friction, and the segment will have to be classified as a fricative and not a vowel.

The space inside these limits is the *vowel area* of the mouth, bounded by its *periphery* on which lies the highest point of the tongue at its furthest extreme, in any direction, from the centre of the mouth. Cardinal vowels should be selected, if they are to form an adequate system, in such a way that they provide points of reference as convenient as possible in relation to the vowel area as a whole. The eight cardinal vowels selected to form Daniel Jones's system are all vowels pronounced with the highest point of the tongue lying on the periphery, for Jones believes that *peripheral* vowels, as they are called, provide the most convenient points of reference.

The selecting of the eight points on the periphery to serve as cardinal vowels is carried out in three stages. The first stage is to establish a vowel at each of the two most widely separated points of the periphery. These two vowels will be (*a*) the vowel made with the tongue as *high* and as far *front* in the mouth as possible; (*b*) the vowel made with the tongue as *low* and as far *back* in the mouth as possible. Any further movement of the tongue in either direction would produce a fricative: in the former case it would be a fricative with stricture between the front of the tongue and the hard palate (a palatal fricative), and in the latter case one with stricture between the root of the tongue and the back wall of the pharynx (a pharyngal fricative). These two cardinal vowels, therefore, have limiting positions which are defined in clear articulatory terms: they are qualities of sound that result from exactly specified tongue postures. They are probably the only vowel articulations that *can* be exactly specified in such terms. The remaining cardinal vowels 'hinge' on these two (the word *cardinal* derives from Latin *cardo*, a hinge), and they are established not in articulatory but primarily in auditory terms. This is done in the second and third stages.

It should be remembered that the total human range of vowel quality forms a *continuum*, with no breaks or sudden changes in it. The second stage is to insert three more cardinal vowels in that part of the continuum of vowel quality which lies on the forward part, nearest the lips, of the periphery between the two 'hinge' vowels. These three cardinal vowels are chosen in such a way that, together with the two 'hinge' vowels, they form a series of five *auditorily equidistant steps* of vowel quality: each one of the three new vowels has a quality which is half-way between the cardinal vowel above it and the cardinal vowel below it.

The most convenient way of identifying cardinal vowels is by giving a number to each one. Those that have been established so far are numbered One to Five; Number One is the most forward 'hinge' vowel, Number Five is the furthest back 'hinge' vowel, and Two, Three and Four come on the front of the periphery between them. It should be noted that these five steps of vowel quality all result from different postures of the tongue only; the posture of the lips is unrounded for all of them.

The third stage continues this series of five vowels separated by auditorily equidistant steps by adding, at the same intervals of sound quality, three more cardinal vowels, ascending upwards from Number Five, along the back of the periphery. These cardinal vowels are numbered Six, Seven and Eight respectively. They are all rounded vowels: the auditorily equidistant steps are brought about by changes in tongue and lip posture simultaneously. Number Six is the least rounded, Number Seven is more rounded, and Number Eight is more

11

rounded still (see p. 58). The eight cardinal vowels, therefore, are eight equally-spaced auditory points forming a kind of *scale* of vowel quality.

The cardinal vowels may be described in the (somewhat rough-and-ready) terms of the categories of vowel classification explained in Chapter 4 as follows (it will be convenient, from now on, to refer to any cardinal vowel by the abbreviation 'C.V.' followed by its number):

	front	*back*
close	C.V.One	C.V.Eight
half-close	C.V.Two	C.V.Seven
half-open	C.V.Three	C.V.Six
open	C.V.Four	C.V.Five

C.V.s One to Five are unrounded; C.V.s Six to Eight are rounded.

The symbols of the IPA alphabet which have been allotted to the cardinal vowels are as follows:

C.V.One: i
C.V.Two: e
C.V.Three: ε
C.V.Four: a
C.V.Five: ɑ
C.V.Six: ɔ
C.V.Seven: o
C.V.Eight: u

The most important points concerning the cardinal vowels of Daniel Jones's system may be summarized as follows:

(i) they are arbitrarily selected; a cardinal vowel is a descriptive device, not something that occurs in a language;
(ii) they are of exactly determined and invariable quality;
(iii) they are peripheral vowels: the highest point of the tongue for each of them lies on the extreme outside limits of the vowel area;
(iv) they are auditorily equidistant;
(v) they are eight in number.

The first two of these five points are *necessary* features of any system of cardinal vowels. The remaining three points are merely *convenient*, and it would be perfectly possible to work out a different system of cardinal vowels to which they did not apply. Points (iii) and (iv) are probably a help in learning the cardinal vowels, and in remembering them when learnt; certainly any cardinal vowel system which is to be of practical use must have the vowels well spaced out at strategic points over the whole vowel area or continuum. As far as point (v) is concerned, it is not easy to judge whether eight cardinal vowels is the ideal number for a system, but one can say that a system with less than seven or more than ten vowels would probably be difficult to work with: if the cardinal vowels were less than seven, they would be too sparsely distributed over the vowel area, and if they were more than ten, they would be difficult to hold in the memory.

2. *Application*

The specialist phonetician has first to learn to pronounce the cardinal vowels with infallible precision (as far as such a thing is humanly possible), and when that is done he must acquire the technique by which they are put to practical use in the description of vowels of actual languages. These skills should not be expected of the beginning student in phonetics: it is enough that he should be familiar with the theory of cardinal vowels, and be aware, more or less, of what they sound like. It would not be reasonable to expect full command over their production without long training, and their successful application as a descriptive device comes only after considerable experience and practice. One should not forget that for many practical purposes the method of describing and classifying vowels set out in Chapter 4 is perfectly adequate.

As Daniel Jones has frequently insisted, the cardinal vowels cannot be learnt from written descriptions. Some idea of the auditory quality of cardinal vowels can be given by key-words taken from actual languages, but these can only be very rough indications of their quality, and are quite useless for learning to pronounce them. Recordings, of course, can convey the exact quality of the cardinal vowels, but most people would not be able to learn to pronounce them simply from hearing them, although exceptionally gifted individuals might perhaps manage it. Most people need explicit instruction, and the great majority of phoneticians who are able to use the cardinal vowel technique have learnt to pronounce the vowels under the direct supervision of a competent teacher.

Once the pronunciation of the cardinal vowels has been learnt, mastery of their application can follow. It should be noted, in passing, that it is one thing to learn to pronounce the cardinal vowels in regular order, one after the other, as a *system* in which each vowel is consistently related in quality to its neighbours; it is another, and much more difficult, thing to acquire the ability to produce any one of them at will, immediately, without reference to the others. Without this ability, however, it is hardly possible to use them as a descriptive technique.

As we have seen, description by means of the cardinal vowels is

different from most other techniques of phonetic description, in that
it does not depend on *classification* by means of general categories.
Rather, each vowel quality to be described is identified by its unique
relation to the cardinal vowels. The relation is spatial: the cardinal
vowels are situated on the periphery of a space, the vowel area; and
the vowel to be described is placed by reference to them either on the
periphery of the area or within it. The location of any given vowel
relative to the cardinal vowels is its description.

'Location relative to the cardinal vowels' is perhaps a rather ellipti-
cal expression, and to be more precise we ought to say 'location of
the *highest point of the tongue* relative to that of the cardinal vowels'.
In other words the cardinal vowel technique of description is an
articulatory technique. This needs further explanation, since at first
sight it seems to involve a contradiction. As we have seen, only two
cardinal vowels–C.V.One and C.V.Five–are established in articulatory terms: the others are established by reference to these two, but
in auditory terms. Yet all are used in description as *articulatory* reference points.

However, it is necessary to keep quite distinct the process by which
the cardinal vowels are established from the process by which they
are used for description. The fact is that they all have both an
articulatory and an auditory aspect. C.V.One and C.V.Five are defined articulatorily, by tongue posture; from these two postures, two
sound qualities result; on the basis of these sound qualities C.V.s
Two, Three, Four, Six, Seven and Eight are auditorily established,
there being initially no articulatory requirement concerning them
except that they should be peripheral vowels; finally, once these six
are established as sound qualities, attention can then be directed to
the tongue postures responsible for the qualities.

The eight cardinal vowels, therefore, in whatever way they were
established, are used as articulatory postures for descriptive purposes.
No doubt there are differences among phoneticians in the way they
apply the technique, but it seems bound to entail the following steps.
The investigator first obtains from an informant (who may of course
be the investigator himself, if it is his mother-tongue that is being
examined) an authoritative version of the vowel to be described, and
then learns to pronounce the vowel himself (if he cannot already do
so) to the informant's complete satisfaction. He then compares the
tongue posture of the vowel with that of the nearest cardinal vowel
(or vowels) by passing repeatedly from one to the other, in doing so
becoming kinesthetically aware of the place of the vowel in the vowel
area, in other words of where the highest point of the tongue lies
relative to the highest point of the tongue for the cardinal vowels.

With experience, the process of placing vowels in relation to the cardinal vowels becomes very much less laborious than it is at first, and than this description makes it sound.

A tacit assumption must be made explicit at this point: lip posture – both of the vowel to be described, and of the cardinal vowels – is disregarded in placing a vowel within the vowel area; it is only tongue posture that is involved. But once the tongue posture for a vowel has been established and a description of it given, information about the state of the lips must, of course, be added. This is not a difficult matter: the lip posture is perfectly obvious to inspection. However it is, for this reason, extremely difficult to apply the cardinal vowel technique of description to recorded versions of vowels (however high the quality of the recordings might be). The investigator needs to be able to *see* the informant: he judges the contribution of the tongue posture to the vowel quality that he hears in the light of what he can see of the lip posture. If he has no information about lip posture, and has only the sound to go on, he may be seriously misled concerning tongue posture.

How is this placing of a vowel relative to the cardinal vowels, which constitutes its description, to be made public? There are various ways of doing this. One could simply say, for instance, 'the vowel in question is a peripheral one half-way between C.V.s Two and Three'. Although this is sometimes convenient, an explanation in words would often be fairly complicated. Much the most convenient way of making the description public is by means of a diagram, or map, of the vowel area, on which the locations of the cardinal vowels and of the vowel to be described are marked. Thus the spatial relation between that vowel and the cardinal vowels is immediately clear to view. The vowel area has roughly the following shape; the two 'hinge' vowels are marked on it by crosses:

FIGURE 1.

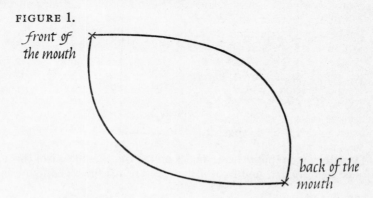

front of the mouth

back of the mouth

This figure, which is based on x-ray photographs of peripheral vowels, is a difficult shape to draw, however, and even more difficult to reproduce from memory; and a conventional stylized version of the figure, bounded by straight lines, was introduced by Daniel Jones from the start for the purpose of demonstrating 'placings' of vowels. The figure is of course distorted by straightening the lines in the same way as a map projection is; however, the distortion is small, and easily allowed for by the phonetician who is used to working with the figure. This stylized 'trapezoid' figure looks like this:

FIGURE 2.

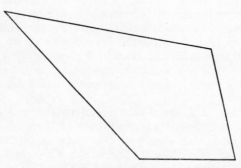

Even this figure is a little too irregular to be easily reproduced (none of its angles are right angles), and a still more conventionalized version is widely used by many. This figure is the more regular shape known as a 'trapezium':

FIGURE 3.

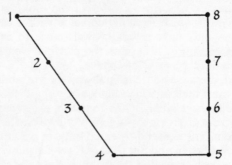

It will be seen that the two angles on the right-hand side of this figure are right angles, and two of its sides are parallel. The figure is still easier to remember and reproduce because of the simple proportions of three of the lines: the bottom line, the right-hand vertical line, and the top line are in the proportions 2 : 3 : 4 respectively. The locations of the eight cardinal vowels are shown on the figure by dots.

Although even more distortion is introduced by this stylized representation of the vowel area, it is probably, nevertheless, the most convenient figure to work with. The figure is made easier to use by the addition of lines within it which divide it up into notional areas, as follows:

FIGURE 4.

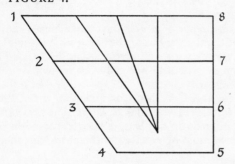

It is this form of the diagram that is usually known as the 'cardinal vowel figure'. All that need be done to make clear the location of any given vowel, in relation to the cardinal vowels, is to place a dot on the figure at the appropriate place. When this is done by a phonetician well-trained in the technique, another phonetician equally well-trained is able to reproduce the vowel with great accuracy (provided the lip posture has been adequately described), simply from looking at the diagram. A vowel may, of course, actually coincide with a cardinal vowel. Some languages may have several vowels close to cardinal vowels, some may have none. This, since the cardinal vowels are arbitrarily chosen, is purely a matter of chance.

It is often assumed, because the cardinal vowels are auditorily equidistant, that they must therefore be articulatorily equidistant too, that is to say that the highest point of the tongue must descend by equal steps in passing from C.V.One through C.V.s Two and Three to C.V.Four; and must similarly descend by equal steps in passing from C.V.Eight through C.V.s Seven and Six to C.V.Five. Certainly, most phoneticians who have been trained in the technique usually say they feel these steps to be equal. However, the feeling appears to be an illusion and the assumption to be wrong: x-ray photographs of the cardinal vowels, such as have been made, do not bear them out,[5] and seem to show, for instance, that the step from C.V.One to C.V.Two is smaller than the step from C.V.Two to C.V.Three, while the step from C.V.Eight to C.V.Seven is greater than the step from C.V.Seven to C.V.Six. The fact that auditorily equal steps do not correspond to articulatorily equal steps is in any case probably, on theoretical grounds, to be expected. Nevertheless, all the steps between C.V.s One to Four, and all the steps between C.V.s Eight to Five, are shown as equidistant on the cardinal vowel trapezium, and this, therefore, is another distortion, in addition to the distortion which results from straightening the curved lines of the periphery, which the cardinal vowel figure in this form entails.

This additional distortion has of course the convenience that it preserves the regularity of the figure; but at the same time it might seem likely to reduce the accuracy with which vowels can be located on it. However the distortion is probably not only convenient but necessary. The number of auditorily discriminable points lying on the periphery between C.V.One and C.V.Two, for instance, is the same as the number lying between C.V.Two and C.V.Three. The same amount of space, therefore, neither more nor less, is needed for noting these points: auditory distance must be equated with spatial distance.

3. *Secondary cardinals*

The cardinal vowel technique is based on the eight 'primary' cardinal vowels, which are in themselves sufficient for descriptive purposes. A number of secondary cardinal vowels, however, have been established which are associated with them and which, like the primary cardinal vowels, are of fixed and unvarying quality. Unlike the primary cardinals, they are not all peripheral vowels. There are fourteen of them, of which ten are peripheral and four are not.

The first eight of the secondary cardinals are directly derived from the primary ones. They have exactly the same tongue positions, but have different lip postures: where the primary cardinals are rounded, the corresponding secondary cardinals are not rounded, and vice versa. Thus the first five secondary cardinals are rounded vowels, and the next three are unrounded vowels. The degree of rounding of the rounded secondary cardinals is correlated with the amount of jaw opening, as is the case with the primary cardinals (see pp. 153, 58). The two most open secondary cardinals, with tongue positions corresponding to C.V.Four and C.V.Five, have the least amount of rounding, less than for any primary cardinal; while those with tongue positions corresponding to C.V.s Three, Two and One have the same degree of rounding as C.V.s Six, Seven and Eight respectively.

These eight secondary cardinals have been given numbers which
continue the numbering of the primary cardinals, i.e. they are numbered from Nine to Sixteen, starting with the highest front vowel;
and they have been given symbols as follows:[6]

C.V.Nine:	y	C.V.Thirteen:	ɒ
C.V.Ten:	ø	C.V.Fourteen:	ʌ
C.V.Eleven	œ	C.V.Fifteen:	ɤ
C.V.Twelve:	Œ	C.V.Sixteen:	ɯ

Many find that these numbers are not particularly easy to remember
(the secondary cardinals are less often referred to than the primary),
and in practice phoneticians often prefer to say, 'C.V.One rounded'
instead of C.V.Nine; and 'C.V.Eight unrounded', instead of C.V.
Sixteen; and so on.

There are six more secondary cardinals.[7] They consist of three pairs
of vowels, the vowels in each pair having the same tongue posture
but one being unrounded and the other rounded. All are central
vowels, and two pairs are not peripheral. The first pair lies on the
periphery half-way between C.V.One and C.V.Eight; they are numbered C.V.Seventeen (unrounded) and C.V.Eighteen (rounded). The
next pair lies half-way between C.V.Two and C.V.Seven, and they are
numbered C.V.Nineteen (unrounded) and C.V.Twenty (rounded);
and the vowels of the remaining pair lie half-way between C.V.Three
and C.V.Six, and are numbered C.V.Twenty-one and C.V.Twenty-
two. The symbols of these six secondary cardinals are as follows:

C.V.Seventeen:	ɨ	C.V.Eighteen:	ʉ
C.V.Nineteen:	ə	C.V.Twenty:	ɵ
C.V.Twenty-one:	ɜ	C.V.Twenty-two:	ɞ

The fourteen secondary cardinals have the following places on the
cardinal vowel figure:

FIGURE 5.

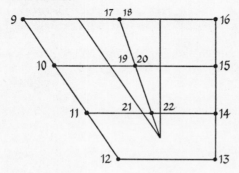

It should be noted that the IPA alphabet provides a series of 'spare' vowel symbols which have no cardinal definitions but which are often useful in transcribing languages with large vowel systems. They are: (front vowels) ɪ ʏ æ, (central vowels) ə ɐ, (back vowel) ɔ.

NOTES

WORKS CONSULTED

INDEX

Notes

Notes to Chapter One

1   M. A. K. Halliday, 'Categories of the theory of grammar'.
2   There is, however, room for a subject of this sort, one that would bear the same relation to the written medium as phonetics does to the spoken. A first step towards its establishment has been taken by I. J. Gelb in *A Study of Writing*, where he proposes the name 'grammatology' for it. Other names which have been suggested for the new subject are 'graphiology' (by L. Hjelmslev, *Studia Linguistica*, Vol. 1, p. 69, 1948), 'graphonomy' (by C. F. Hockett, *Language*, Vol. 27, p. 445, 1951), and 'graphology' (by several writers). The last term, however, has the disadvantage that it is already in use for the study of one special aspect of the medium; see p. 6.
3   Norbert Wiener, *The Human Use of Human Beings* (1950), p. 201; 2nd ed. revised (1956), p. 168.
4   See *The Psychology of the Movements of Handwriting*, translated and arranged by L. K. Given-Wilson from the works of J. Crépieux-Jamin (1926). Cf. also G. G. Neill Wright, *The Writing of Arabic Numerals* (1952), p. 11: 'Every written symbol is the automatic record of one aspect of a bodily movement.'
5   The terms 'index' and 'indexical' are borrowed from C. S. Peirce (1839–1914). See *The Philosophy of Peirce: Selected Writings*, ed. J. Buchler (1940).
6   Judges, xii. 5–6. The quotation is from the 1611 translation. The word *shibboleth* in Hebrew meant, among other things, 'river'.
7   See Klara G. Roman, *Handwriting: A Key to Personality* (1952).
8   Edward Sapir (1884–1939) has written in various places on linguistic indices; see for instance 'Speech as a personality trait' (1927). The works of T. H. Pear may also be consulted, particularly *Voice and Personality* (1931); *The Psychology of Effective Speaking* (1933); *Personality, Appearance and Speech* (1957).
9   Samuel Z. Klausner, 'Phonetics, personality and status in Israel' (1955), pp. 209–16.
10 Nicolete Gray, *Lettering on Buildings* (1960), pp. 19 f. See also Sapir, *Selected Writings*, p. 382: 'Writing at all times has constituted a plastic as well as a symbolic problem. The conveyance of thought has been only one of its uses; the delineation of pleasing contours, now severe and statuesque, now flowing in graceful meanderings, has always been something more than a by-product.' Cf. Gelb, *A Study of Writing*, pp. 229 ff.
11 Fluctuations in tamber give us the succession of vowels and consonants in speech (sheer noise also entering into the consonants). (The spelling *tamber* instead of *timbre*, which is the French form of the

word, was put forward as a suitable anglicization by Robert Bridges in 1920 (Society for Pure English, *Tract No. III*, Oxford), and it has since been adopted by a number of writers.)

12 Ida C. Ward, *The Phonetics of English*, Ch. 1.

13 F. de Saussure, *Cours de linguistique générale*, p. 100: 'le signe linguistique est arbitraire.'

14 W. Bedell Stanford, *Greek Metaphor* (1936), p. 43. Cf. also pp. 63–9. See also June E. Downey, *Creative Imagination* (1929), Ch. IX.

15 The Latin is by one Nicolas Rowley, and it was quoted in a letter written by the Bishop of Winchester in 1542 to John Cheke, professor of Greek in Cambridge, in the course of an argument on the pronunciation of Greek. It is reproduced in John Strype's *Life of the Learned Sir John Cheke, Kt.* (1705). The English version is by R. Nares, *Elements of Orthoepy* (1784), p. 27.

16 O. Jespersen, 'Symbolic value of the vowel *I*' (1922); E. Sapir, 'A study in phonetic symbolism' (1929); J. Orr, 'On some sound values in English' (1944).

17 *Didascalocophus or the Deaf and Dumb Man's Tutor* (1680), p. 21.

18 See L. Bloomfield, *An Introduction to the Study of Language* (1914), p. 79; *Language* (1935), p. 245; I. A. Richards, *The Philosophy of Rhetoric* (1936), p. 59.

19 J. R. Firth, *Speech* (1930), Ch. VI; 'The use and distribution of certain English sounds' (1935); 'Modes of meaning' (1951).

20 PAT stands for Parametric Artificial Talking device, and it was designed by Walter Lawrence of the Ministry of Aviation. Other synthetic speech machines are at the Haskins Laboratories in New York, at the Massachusetts Institute of Technology, and at the Royal Institute of Technology, Stockholm.

21 For the best statement of why the view is unacceptable, see H. Bradley, 'On the relations between Spoken and Written Language with special reference to English' (1913). Many American linguists, however, hold the view today, and it has been most forcibly expressed by L. Bloomfield. See, for instance, his *Linguistic Aspects of Science* (1939): 'For all linguistic study it is of primary importance to know that writing is not the same thing as language' (p. 6).

22 See D. Abercrombie, *Problems and Principles in Language Study* (1956), Ch. IV; and T. Hill, 'Institutional linguistics' (1958).

23 Sir Philip Hartog, *On the Relation of Poetry to Verse* (1926).

Notes to Chapter Two

1 Edward Sapir, *Language* (1921), Ch. I.

2 See, for instance, C. D. Darlington, 'The genetic component of language', (1947); Darlington and K. Mather, *The Elements of Genetics* (1949), Ch. XVI.

3 K. Bühler, *The Mental Development of the Child* (1930), Ch. II.

4 L. E. Travis, *Speech Pathology* (1931), Ch. I.

5   Sir Victor Negus, *The Mechanism of the Larynx* (1929); *The Compara-tive Anatomy and Physiology of the Larynx* (1949).

6   L. E. Travis, *Speech Pathology*, Ch. I, particularly p. 7.

7   The dumb can, however, be taught to talk, even though they cannot hear, by special techniques. See K.W. Hodgson, *The Deaf and their Problems* (1953); I.R. Ewing and A.W.G. Ewing, *Speech and the Deaf Child* (1954).

8   'It is possible to exaggerate the importance of the ear in speech. There is also a visual-kinesthetic stimulus, and once the speech-habit is established, the sixth sense becomes all-important. From certain ob-served facts it would seem that the listener refers what he hears to how he would say it. Thus he translates exteroceptor into proprioceptor sensations, the kinesthetic memory serving as stimulus.'–Stephen Jones, 'The accent in French–what is accent?' (1932).
Cf. also 'The ear is not enough', by P.E. Vernon (1929): 'Many also hear or think of music muscularly. They raise their heads or contract some other muscle when the music rises, or they perceive it in terms of their hands at the pianoforte or other instruments.'

9   '[The] chief characteristic [of speech] and the one that gives it the greatest value is that it is subconscious or automatic. Robbed of this characteristic . . . it fails . . . to perform its chief function, namely to convey thought, because it monopolizes thought in its own production.'
'–H. Crichton-Miller, 'A note on the psychic factor in stammering' (1936). Cf. also Sir Charles Sherrington, *Man on his Nature*, Ch. VI.

10   For a good short account, with plentiful diagrams, see Ch. II of R.-M.S. Heffner, *General Phonetics* (1949). See also R. Curry, *The Mechanism of the Human Voice* (1940).
More specialized studies are Negus, op. cit.; G.N. Jenkins, *The Physio-logy of the Mouth* (contains a somewhat disappointing chapter on speech); and, on hearing, H. Fletcher, *Speech and Hearing in Com-munication*. An earlier though still interesting book is G. H. von Meyer, *The Organs of Speech* (1883).

11   The term *air-stream mechanism* was introduced by K.L. Pike in his *Phonetics* (1943). See Ch. VI, where the mechanisms are very fully described. The terms *pulmonic, glottalic, velaric* are taken from D.M. Beach, *The Phonetics of the Hottentot Language* (1938); they were first given general application by J.C. Catford, 'On the classification of stop consonants' (1939).

12   Ingressive pulmonic speech is used for this purpose in the island of Mindoro in the Philippines; see H.C. Conklin in the *American Anthropologist*, Vol. 51, p. 268 (1949). A similar use has been re-ported from other parts of the world.

13   High-speed films of the vocal cords of phonetic interest have been made by Bell Telephones Laboratories, New Jersey; by Mrs E.T. Uldall, Edinburgh University; and by Paul Moore and Hans Von Leden of Northwestern University, U.S.A.

14 The details of the manner of vibration of the vocal cords are to some extent still a matter of dispute.

15 Terms which have been used for *voiced* include vocal, sonorous, vibrant, sonant, intonated; and for *voiceless* include (in addition to breathed) spiral, aspirate, mute, spirate, surd.

16 *Velum* is short for *velum palati* or 'veil of the palate'. It was so named by Fallopius in the sixteenth century (R.S. Stevenson and D. Guthrie, *A History of Oto-Laryngology*).

Notes to Chapter Three

1 'A word is not a united compound of a definite number of independent sounds, of which each can be expressed by an alphabetical sign; but it is essentially a continuous series of infinitely numerous sounds.'– *Principles of the History of Language*, by Hermann Paul, translated by H.A. Strong (1891), p. 39.

2 Daniel Jones, *Outline of English Phonetics*, 8th ed., 1956, p. 245.

3 P.-J. Rousselot, *Principes de phonétique expérimentale* (1924), p. 307: 'le malade conserve très bien la notion de la syllabe; il fait, quand il essaye de parler, autant d'efforts expiratoires qu'il y a de syllabes dans le mot.'

4 See 'Syllables and stress', by P. Ladefoged, M.H. Draper and D. Whitteridge (1958); 'Respiratory Muscles in Speech', by M.H. Draper, P. Ladefoged and D. Whitteridge (1959).

5 Stetson's two most important publications are *Motor Phonetics, a study of speech movements in action* and *Bases of Phonology*. Stetson (1872–1950) was Professor of Psychology at Oberlin University, Ohio, from 1909 to 1939.

6 See H. Pedersen, *Linguistic Science in the Nineteenth Century*, translated by J.W. Spargo, Ch. VI; I.J. Gelb, *A Study of Writing*.

Although the word 'alphabet' is semitic in origin, semitic writing systems are not alphabetic; they are syllabic systems of a somewhat unusual kind.

Notes to Chapter Four

1 This very necessary term was coined by Henry Sweet, and was first used by him in his *Handbook of Phonetics* (1877).

2 The term is adapted from K.L. Pike (see *Phonetics*, 1943).

3 A ballistic movement of a limb or other organ (such as the eye) takes place when 'a brief and predetermined force is exerted' on it, and it 'moves for a time, often greatly exceeding the duration of muscular contraction' (E.G. Walsh, *Physiology of the Nervous System*, 1957). See R.H. Stetson, 'Mechanism of the different types of movement' (1923).

4 The term *flap* was used, somewhat vaguely, by A.M. Bell and A.J. Ellis, but Henry Sweet gave it the more exact sense in which it is used here (*A History of English Sounds*, 2nd ed., 1888, p. 12).

5 See D. Westermann and I.C. Ward, *Practical Phonetics for Students of African Languages*, p. 76.

6 The term *dorsal* is ambiguous: it is also commonly used to mean 'made with the back of the tongue'. *Apical* and *laminal* are respectively from Latin apex 'point', and lamina 'blade'.

7 Cf. P. Ladefoged, 'The Classification of Vowels' (1956), especially p. 123.

8 The terms *high*, *mid-high*, *mid-low*, *low*, referring to the distance of the tongue from the floor of the mouth, are used by some writers instead of *close*, *half-close*, *half-open*, *open* respectively.

9 See, for this view, the various works of Henry Sweet. Many other investigators have followed him in attributing importance to muscular tension of the tongue.

10 It is stated by P. Passy, in his *Petite Phonétique comparée* (1906), pp. 62 and 114, that under the circumstances described here these vowels are whispered. This does not appear, however, to be the normal usage of French speakers.

11 Cf. D. Jones, *The Pronunciation of English* (4th ed., 1956), p. 115. That *h* is equivalent to a voiceless vowel has often been pointed out in the past; see for instance J. Brodie, *The Alphabet Explained* (1840), p. 27: 'H . . . . has no particular seat or place of formation, being, in fact, merely a hard breathing before or after a vowel, while the mouth is in the position which the vowel requires.'

12 They occur in Nzema, a language of Ghana (I.K. Chinebuah, unpublished thesis).

13 Abraham Tucker (1705–1774) published his book on phonetics, *Vocal Sounds*, in 1773 under the name of Edward Search. He was described as a 'prolix but pleasing philosopher' by Winston H.F. Barnes, *The Philosophical Predicament*, p. 47.

14 Cf. K.L. Pike, *Phonetics* (1943), p. 152: 'no phonetic description, no matter how detailed, is complete.' Some of the factors which are often neglected in phonetic description are described by Pike, *loc. cit.*

15 *Elements of Speech* (1669), p. 19.

Notes to Chapter Five

1 *The Conditions of Knowing* (1951).

2 The word *phonology* has been used in many different senses; the sense in which it is used in this book is one of its earliest. Peter S. Duponceau, for example, read a paper to the American Philosophical Society in 1817 which was entitled 'English phonology; or An Essay towards an Analysis and Description of the component sounds of the English Language'. It is also worth quoting from a collection of posthumously published papers (1895) by H.D. Darbishire, entitled *Relliquiae Philologicae*, p. 186: 'The study of the spoken sounds of any language (as distinct from other languages) is called phonology, which also embraces the study of the changes in those sounds during the history of the

language. The system of spoken sounds possessed by any language is called its phonological system or more briefly its phonology.'

The use of the word exclusively for the study of sound changes during the history of a language was common in Britain during the early part of this century, but is now almost obsolete.

3 The terms *syntagmatic* and *paradigmatic* were introduced by Louis Hjelmslev (see, for example, his *Prolegomena to a Theory of Language*).

4 The use of the words *system* and *structure* in this way is due to J.R. Firth and his colleagues at the School of Oriental and African Studies.

5 André Martinet, *Phonology as Functional Phonetics* (1949).

6 Robert F. Spencer, 'The phonemes of Keresan' (1946).

7 In a famous article, 'Linguistics as an exact science' (1940).

8 Hans Vogt, 'Phoneme classes and phoneme classification' (1964).

9 The terms *abutting consonants* and *consonant cluster*, distinguished as in this book, were put forward by R.H. Stetson, *Motor Phonetics* (1928).

10 See J.R. Firth, Papers in Linguistics, p. 123.

11 Eli Fischer-Jørgensen, 'On the definition of phoneme categories on a distributional basis' (1952), p. 18.

12 Cf. Daniel Jones, *Outline of English Phonetics* (8th ed., 1956), pp. 327–30.

13 For other examples see A.E. Sharp, 'Stress and Juncture in English' (1961). *Tawdry* derives from the phrase *St. Audrey's lace*; see *OED*.

14 L. Bloomfield, *Language*, p. 102.

15 Herbert D. Darbishire, *Relliquiae Philologicae* (1895), pp. 194 ff., introduces the term *adsonant*. F. de Saussure, *Cours de linguistique générale* (1916), writes: 'Les termes de voyelles et consonnes désignent des espèces différentes; sonantes et consonantes désignent au contraire des fonctions dans la syllabe. Cette double terminologie permet d'éviter une confusion qui a longtemps régné' (p. 90; see p. 87 of later editions, and p. 57 of the English translation by Wade Baskin). Bloomfield, in his *Language*, p. 130, divides *sonants* into *consonantoids* and *vocaloids*, in a somewhat complicated classification.

16 See pp. 78, 143 of *Phonetics*.

17 Their rigorous definition is their great advantage; without it their usefulness is destroyed. It is a pity that, since Pike introduced them, the precision of the terms has been blunted by other writers who have taken them over; see, for example, C.F. Hockett, *A Manual of Phonology* (1955), p. 30.

18 For details about segment length in English, see E.A. Meyer, *Englische Lautdauer* (1903); also Otto Jespersen, *A Modern English Grammar. Part I: Sounds and Spellings* (1909), pp. 448–52, and Daniel Jones, *The Phoneme* (1950), Ch. XXIII.

19 Lorna F. Gibson, 'Pame (Otomi) Phonemics and Morphophonemics' (1956).

20 J.C. Catford, 'The Kabardian language' (1942).

21 Paul L. Garvin, 'Wichita I: phonemics' (1950).

22 *Speech* (1930), p. 24.
23 The term *conversion* is taken from Martin Joos, *Acoustic Phonetics*, p. 63.
24 The term *allophone* was coined by B. L. Whorf, and introduced by him in 1943 in his 'Phonemic analysis of the English of Eastern Massachusetts'.
25 See especially W. F. Twaddell, *On Defining the Phoneme* (1935); K. L. Pike, *Phonemics* (1947); Daniel Jones, *The Phoneme: its Nature and Use* (1950).
26 The term *similitude*, to be distinguished from *assimilation*, was put forward by Daniel Jones in the 3rd ed. of *An Outline of English Phonetics* (1932), p. 203.

Notes to Chapter Six

1 The distinguishing of these three strands in the medium derives from Edward Sapir, 'Speech as a personality trait' (1927). A great deal of the present chapter is owed to this article.
2 Considerable research is being undertaken in different places at the present time on the factors concerned in 'speaker recognition'.
3 For a very full and clear account of adjustments of this sort, and how they characterize particular languages, see 'Articulatory settings', by Beatrice Honikman (1964).
4 Different larynx adjustments during phonation are described in 'Phonation types: the classification of some laryngeal components of speech production', by J. C. Catford (1964).
5 Henry Sweet referred very briefly to some of the factors concerned in voice quality in his *Handbook of Phonetics* (1877), pp. 97 ff., and *Primer of Phonetics* (3rd ed., 1906, p. 72). Terminological suggestions have been made by K. L. Pike, *The Intonation of American English* (1946) pp. 99 ff., and G. L. Trager, 'Paralanguage: a first approximation' (1958). See also C. F. Lindsley, 'The psycho-physical determinants of voice quality' (1934).
6 See 'Hesitation, information, and levels of speech production' by Frieda Goldman-Eisler. Dr Goldman-Eisler has shown that 'pausing is as much part of the act of speaking as the vocal utterance of words itself', and has pointed out that 'an average of about 40–50 per cent of utterance time is occupied by pauses.' See also H. Maclay and C. E. Osgood, 'Hesitation Phenomena in Spontaneous English Speech' (1959).
7 The existence of the two basically different kinds of speech rhythm was pointed out by Arthur Lloyd James in *Speech Signals in Telephony* (1940), p. 25: he called them 'machine-gun rhythm' and 'morse-code rhythm'. The more apt terms 'syllable-timed' and 'stress-timed' were coined by K. L. Pike and first used by him in *The Intonation of American English*, p. 35. Many writers since the eighteenth century have pointed out that in English stressed syllables tend to be isochronous.

8   For a discussion of the factors governing lengths of syllables in English, see David Abercrombie, 'Syllable quantity and enclitics in English' (1964).

9   See David Abercrombie, 'A phonetician's view of verse structure' (1964), for an account of the basis of English verse.

10   Part of the definition of the term in *A New Dictionary of Music*, by A. Jacobs (1958), reads: 'the compass of notes to which a particular singer's voice naturally inclines. . . .'

11   A.J. Ellis, in *Speech in Song* (1878), p. 16, discusses 'speaking registers' very briefly, but does not given them any linguistic significance, though he indicates that a speaker has a choice of register. The word was first used as a technical term in phonetics by Eugénie J.A. Henderson, 'The main features of Cambodian pronunciation' (1952).

12   For a simple account of the anatomy of the larynx, see the article 'Voice' (by Sir Victor Negus and Stephen Jones) in the current edition of the *Encyclopedia Britannica*.

13   See J.C. Catford, *op. cit.* Henry Sweet in his *Handbook of Phonetics* (1877) mentioned (p. 3) that phonation could take place in different ways, and enlarged somewhat on this in his *Primer of Phonetics* (3rd ed., 1906, pp. 10, 13). Not much advance on this was made by phoneticians until K.L. Pike, *Phonetics* (1943), pp. 126 ff., and *Phonemics* (1947), pp. 21, 22.

14   The importance of 'tone of voice' is well brought out in *The First Five Minutes: A Sample of Microscopic Interview Analysis*, by Robert E. Pittenger, C.F. Hockett and J.J. Danehy, New York, 1960.

15   The linguistic use of register is discussed (not under that name) in Daniel Jones, *The Phoneme*, p. 82, and in J.C. Catford, *op. cit.* p. 36. For registers in Cambodian, see Eugénie J.A. Henderson, *op. cit.*; in Gujerati, see J.R. Firth, 'Phonological features of some Indian languages' (1936); in Danish, see H.J. Uldall, *A Danish Phonetic Reader* (1933), p. ix (where the creaky phonation is described as 'a glottal roll'); in Nzema, see J. Berry, 'Some notes on the phonology of the Nzema and Ahanta dialects' (1955); in Ijaw, see E.C. Rowlands 'Tone and intonation systems in Brass-Nembe Ijaw' (1960).

16   'Acute' and 'grave' are only very recently obsolete; they are found, for example, in William Pole, *The Philosophy of Music*, London, 1879: 'The word *pitch*, in its general sense, refers to the position of any sound in the musical scale of acuteness and gravity' (p. 29).

Note also, for the older use of 'sharp' and flat', Edwin Guest, *A History of English Rhythms*, Vol. I, 1838 (speaking of vibration of the vocal cords): 'we can at pleasure regulate the sharpness and the loudness of the sound produced' (p. 5). 'Sharp' and 'flat' are nowadays used as musical terms only of small differences in pitch.

William Pole writes of the terms 'high' and 'low' (*op. cit.* p. 29): 'there is no imaginable connection between any number of vibrations per second, and any degree of elevation above the earth's surface. They (the terms) were, however, also used in very early times; and when musical notation first arose by the use of the relative *position* of marks or points, the idea was seized on to guide such positions (the paper being supposed to be placed vertically), and thus the connection between "high" notes and quick vibrations has become firmly implanted in our minds.'

Metaphors for pitch are discussed in W. Bedell Stanford, *Greek Metaphor*, 1936, p. 49; further information may be found in G. Herzog, 'Drum signalling in a West African tribe' (1945), and M.M. Cowan and M.E. Davis, *Hymn Writing in Aboriginal Languages* (1955), p. 1.

17　See C.K. Ogden, 'Sound, Sense, and Intelligibility' (1935), p. 28; and L. Bloomfield, *Language* (1933), p. 114. This function of voice-pitch fluctuation has been the subject of experiments by Elizabeth T. Uldall; see 'Dimensions of meaning in intonation' (1964). Compare also Nien-Chuang T. Chang, 'Tones and Intonation in the Chengtu Dialect' (1958).

18　It is, for example, said by D. L. Bolinger to be connected with 'instinctive reactions' ('Intonation and analysis', p. 249), and to be 'partly prelinguistic in that it directly reflects certain bodily states' ('The melody of language', p. 28).

19　See David Abercrombie, *Problems and Principles in Language Study*, 1956, Ch. vi, 'Gesture'.

20　By Robert Hooke, recording discussions among Royal Society Fellows in 1679 at Garaway's coffee house. See *The Diary of Robert Hooke 1672–80*, ed. H.W. Robinson and W. Adams (1935), p. 412. (The earliest quotation in the *OED*. for 'tone' in this sense is nearly 100 years later.)

21　'Musical accent and whisper', by Banarsi Das Jain and Stephen Jones; 'Recognition of word tones in whispered speech', by Martin Kloster Jensen; 'Word tone recognition in Vietnamese whispered speech', by J.D. Miller.

22　Y.R. Chao, 'Singing in Chinese'; J.H.K. Nketia, *African Music in Ghana*, p. 47; M.M. Cowan and M.E. Davis, *op. cit.* pp. 15 ff.

23　J.F. Carrington, *Talking Drums of Africa;* L.W. Doob, *Communication in Africa*.

24　George M. Cowan, 'Mazateco whistle speech'. Whistle speech is also reported to be found among other tribes, such as the Zapoteco and the Chinanteco, living, like the Mazateco, in the State of Oaxaca in Mexico.

25　A. Classe, 'Phonetics of the Silbo Gomero' (1957), pp. 44–61; R.G. Busnel, A. Moles and B. Vallancien, 'Sur l'aspect phonétique d'une langue sifflée des Pyrénées françaises' (1962).

26　See C.L.T. Griffith, 'The "isolation" of the ratios of musical intervals' (1933).

27　For a clear exposition of this point, and of many others connected with intonation, see F. Daneš, 'Sentence intonation from a functional point of view' (1960). Daneš speaks of the 'segmental base' of the intonation patterns; the latter 'extend and contract like an accordion according to their segmental base'.

28 See D. Westermann and I. C. Ward, *Practical Phonetics for Students of African Languages*, pp. 134 ff.

29 The functions of speech melody in English are well described in M. A. K. Halliday, 'Intonation in English grammar' (1964). See also M. Schubiger, *The Role of Intonation in Spoken English* (1935); L. S. Hultzén, 'Information points in intonation' (1959).

30 For French, see H. N. Coustenoble and L. E. Armstrong, *Studies in French Intonation* (1934). For English, H. E. Palmer put forward a pitch-movement analysis in his *English Intonation with Systematic Exercises* (1922). A pitch-level analysis was first put forward (for American English) by R. S. Wells, 'The pitch phonemes of English' (1945). See also D. L. Bolinger, 'Intonation: levels versus configurations' (1951).

31 For an interesting discussion of this point see A. E. Sharp, 'A tonal analysis of the disyllabic noun in the Machame dialect of Chaga' (1954).

32 See, for example, Daniel Jones, *The Tones of Sechuana Nouns* (1928). A very clear account of intonation in tone languages has been given by H. A. Gleason Jr. in a review in *Language*, Vol. XXXVII, 1961, pp. 294–308. Gleason believes that all tone languages have some sort of intonation system. See also N.-C. T. Chang, *op. cit.*

33 The task is not made any easier by the existence of widespread inconsistencies in terminology among research workers on the subject. Particularly confusing are the ambiguities of the key terms *tone* and *intonation*, which in the present chapter have been confined strictly to the meanings 'lexical melodic pattern' and 'syntactic melodic pattern' respectively.

Intonation, for instance, is used by many writers to refer to the whole of voice-pitch fluctuation, i.e. the sum total of vocal gesture and speech melody. By others it is used to refer to speech melody only, but without differentiating syntactic and lexical functions. Yet a third use is to refer to complex syntactic patterns made up not only of pitch fluctuation but with components of stress and quantity added. (The word has as well, of course, a quite distinct meaning as a technical term in music.)

Tone, on the whole, is a less ambiguous term, but it has a number of popular senses which can add to the confusion, and there is also a technical sense which is different from the one given it here: some writers use it to mean an element into which intonation (in our sense) is analysed.

Notes to Chapter Seven

1 *Selections from the Papers of the late Thomas Wright Hill* (1860).
2 For his life, see *Dr Darwin*, by Hesketh Pearson (1930).
3 The analphabetic notation, with some modifications, was made use of by F. de Saussure; see his *Cours de linguistique générale*.

4 Robert Robinson's phonetic texts are available in *The Phonetic Writings of Robert Robinson*, edited by E.J. Dobson. Unfortunately they are not given in their original form, which makes it difficult to judge Robinson's system.

5 In his *Essay towards a Real Character, and a Philosophical Language*. He gives examples there of two other phonetic notations.

6 Cf. Eric Gill, *An Essay on Typography*, Chapter 3.

7 Specimens of many different phonetic notations can be found in M. Heepe, *Lautzeichen und ihre Anwendung in verschiedenen Sprachgebieten* (1928).

8 See *Aim and Principles of the International Phonetic Association*, p. 20.

9 See his *Collected Papers*, p. 120.

10 See *The Principles of the International Phonetic Association* (1949).

11 The different types of systematic transcription that are possible for English are discussed in D. Abercrombie, *English Phonetic Texts*.

12 For examples, see G.L. Trager, 'Paralanguage: a first approximation' (1958); R.E. Pittenger, C.F. Hockett, J.J. Danehy, *The First Five Minutes* (1960); W.M. Austin, 'Some social aspects of paralanguage' (1965).

13 There are many examples of the use of numbers for pitch levels. Three levels were distinguished, as here, by W. Ripman in *Good Speech* (1922), p. 68; and as many as nine by H.O. Coleman in 'Intonation and emphasis' (1914). Most writers nowadays distinguish four.

14 A very widely used and convenient notation of this sort has been devised by Roger Kingdon; see, for example, *The Groundwork of English Intonation* (1958).

Notes to Chapter Eight

1 See D. Jones, *An Outline of English Phonetics*, Ch. xxvi. In the 8th ed. (1956) the term *juxtapositional assimilation* is replaced by *contextual assimilation*, but we preserve the older term here.

  See also D. Jones, *The Pronunciation of English*, Ch. ix; I.C. Ward, *The Phonetics of English*, Ch. xvi; L.E. Armstrong, *The Phonetics of French*, Ch. xxi; D. Westermann and I.C. Ward, *Practical Phonetics for Students of African Languages*, Ch. xxiii.

2 It is convenient for purposes of exposition to use the word 'change' in this connexion, even though its use seems to attribute priority to one of the forms concerned. Assimilation does not involve departure from a norm, and it is not intended to give the impression here that it does.

3 See *OED*, s.v. 'orchard'.

4 See, for instance, Thomas Carpenter, *The Scholar's Orthographical and Orthoëpical Assistant*, 1803, p. 23: '*G* before *l* at the beginning of words, is pronounced like *d* by the generality of speakers.' Other earlier writers on English drew attention to this; and Claude Mauger, in his *French Grammar*, 1656, complained that 'the English do pronounce *gloire d'loire*'.

Notes to Chapter Nine

1 This chapter owes a great deal to Daniel Jones's treatment of the same topic in his *Outline of English Phonetics*. See also his *Pronunciation of English*, 3rd and subsequent editions; Ida Ward, *The Phonetics of English*; P.A.D. MacCarthy, *English Pronunciation*. My treatment differs from these writers in certain respects, and particularly in regarding nasal plosion and lateral plosion as taking place only in the case of homorganic sequences.

2 *Vocal Sounds*, p. 44.

Notes to Chapter Ten

1 If we accept the useful distinction made by K.L. Pike between *vowel* and *vocoid* (see Ch. 5), then we ought really to say that the present chapter is concerned with cardinal *vocoids* rather than vowels. The word 'vowel' is so firmly established in this collocation, however, and causes so little misunderstanding, that it is thought best to retain it here. Cardinal *vowel*, using the latter word as a phonological term, would strictly speaking be a meaningless phrase, though an apparent misunderstanding of the intended function of cardinal vowels in C.F. Hockett's *Manual of Phonology* (p. 193) may perhaps be due to trying to take the word 'vowel' in this sense. (It is not clear from the wording of this passage, curiously enough, whether Hockett himself has misunderstood the purpose of cardinal vowels, or whether he thinks other people have.)

2 A.J. Ellis wrote in *The Alphabet of Nature* (1844), p. 52: 'The list of vowels, just given, form a circle, and, consequently, every other vowel sound must have a place in this circle between some of the principal vowels there given. We may, therefore, take these seven principal vowels as fixed points in the circle of vocal sound from which to measure the others.' A.M. Bell, in *Visible Speech* (1867), p. 16, spoke of nine 'fixed points' of tongue position which furnish 'the means of noting, as by lines of latitude and longitude, the precise *place* of any vowel in the mouth'; the nine points are obtained by combining three 'cardinal degrees' of aperture between tongue and palate with three 'cardinal degrees' of tongue position from front to back. Henry Sweet also adopted the idea, writing in his *Handbook of Phonetics* (1877), p. 11: 'As each new position of the tongue produces a new vowel, and as the positions are infinite, it follows that the number of possible vowel sounds is infinite. It becomes necessary, therefore, to select certain definite positions as fixed points whence to measure the intermediate positions', and these fixed points he called 'cardinal vowel positions'. (The number of possible vowel sounds is not, of course, infinite, only very large – getting on for three figures in fact.)

3 Cardinal Vowels are used for identifying the vowels of English in the first edition of Daniel Jones's *English Pronouncing Dictionary* (1917), and those of Sinhalese in H.S. Pereira and D. Jones, *A Colloquial*

Sinhalese Reader (1919). They were made use of in the 2nd ed. (1922) of Daniel Jones's *Outline of English Phonetics*, but not in the 1st (mostly in print by 1914, though not published till 1918). They figure in a very large number of publications by various authors which have appeared since. Gramophone records of the cardinal vowels, spoken by Daniel Jones, have been made commercially available by the HMV Gramophone Co. in 1917 (B 804), and the Linguaphone Co. in 1943 (DAJO 1–2) and in 1955 (ENG 252–3 and 254–5). Descriptions of the system appear, among many other places, in Daniel Jones, *The Pronunciation of English*, Ch. IV; Daniel Jones, *An Outline of English Phonetics*, Ch. VIII; Ida Ward, *The Phonetics of English*, Ch. IX; *Principles of the International Phonetic Association*, pp. 4–7.

4   For example J. van den Berg speaks of 'eleven cardinal vowels of the IPA', though the vowels he is discussing are all in fact Dutch.

5   See Stephen Jones, 'Radiography and pronunciation' (1929). P. Ladefoged has discussed this discrepancy, and other problems of the cardinal vowels, in 'The classification of vowels' (1956), 'The nature of vowel quality' (1960), 'The value of phonetic statements' (1960). See also J.D.M.H. Laver, 'Variability in vowel perception' (1965).

6   Although the symbol for C.V. 12 is in fairly general use, it has not yet been officially accepted by the IPA.

7   Not all these six secondary cardinals are acknowledged by Daniel Jones.

List of Works Consulted

This list includes all works referred to in the text. Different editions of books are mentioned only when they involve substantial differences. The following abbreviations of titles of periodicals are used:

BSOS = *Bulletin of the School of Oriental Studies*
BSOAS = *Bulletin of the School of Oriental and African Studies*
IJAL = *International Journal of American Linguistics*
JASA = *Journal of the Acoustical Society of America*
mf = lə meːtrə fɔnetik (*Le Maître Phonétique*)
Proc. 2nd/4th Int. Congr. Ph. Sc. = *Proceedings of the Second/Fourth International Congress of Phonetic Sciences*
SIL = *Studies in Linguistics*
TPS = *Transactions of the Philological Society*

ABERCROMBIE, D. *Problems and Principles in Language Study*, London, 1956
– 'Syllable quantity and enclitics in English' in *In Honour of Daniel Jones*, London, 1964. Reprinted in *Studies in Phonetics and Linguistics*
– 'A phonetician's view of verse structure' in *Linguistics*, No. 6 (1964) 5–13. Reprinted in *Studies in Phonetics and Linguistics*
– *English Phonetic Texts*, London, 1964
– *Studies in Phonetics and Linguistics*, London, 1965
–, FRY, D. B. *et al.* (eds.) *In Honour of Daniel Jones*, London, 1964
ALLEN, W. S. *Phonetics in Ancient India*, London, 1953
ARMSTRONG, L. E. *The Phonetics of French*, London, 1932
– and WARD, I. C. *Handbook of English Intonation* (2nd ed.) Cambridge and Leipzig, 1931
AUSTIN, W. M. 'Some social aspects of paralanguage' in *Canadian Journal of Linguistics*, 11 (1965) 31–9
BARNES, W. H. F. *The Philosophical Predicament*, London, 1950
BAUDOUIN DE COURTENAY, J. *Versuch einer Theorie phonetischer Alternationen*, Strasburg, 1895
BAZELL, C. E. *Linguistic Form*, Istanbul, 1953
BEACH, D. M. *The Phonetics of the Hottentot Language*, Cambridge, 1938
BEATTY, R. T. *Hearing in Man and Animals*, London, 1932
BELL, A. G. *Lectures upon the Mechanism of Speech*, New York, 1906
BELL, A. M. *Visible Speech: the Science of Universal Alphabetics*, London, 1867

BELL, A. M. *Sounds and their Relations*, London, 1882
– *English Visible Speech in Twelve Lessons*, Washington, 1895. 2nd ed.
  1899; 3rd ed. 1907; 4th ed. 1932
BERG, J. VAN DEN 'Transmission of the vocal cavities' in *J A S A*, 27
  (1955) 161–8
BERRY, J. 'Some notes on the phonology of the Nzema and Ahanta
  dialects' in *B S O A S*, 17 (1955) 160–5
BLOOMFIELD, L. *An Introduction to the Study of Language*, London and
  New York, 1914
– *Language*, New York, 1933; London, 1935
– *Linguistic Aspects of Science* (International Encyclopedia of Unified
  Science), Chicago, 1939
BOLINGER, D. L. 'Intonation and analysis' in *Word*, 5 (1949) 248–54
– 'Intonation: levels versus configurations' in *Word*, 7 (1951) 199–210
– 'The melody of language' in *Modern Language Forum*, 40 (1955) 19–30
– *Generality, Gradience, and the All-or-None*, The Hague, 1961
BRADLEY, H. 'On the relations between Spoken and Written Language
  with special reference to English' in *Proceedings of the British
  Academy*, 6 (1913). Reprinted as a separate pamphlet, Oxford, 1919
BRIDGES, R. Editorial notes to L. P. Smith, *A Few Practical Suggestions*
  (Society for Pure English Tract No. III), Oxford, 1920
BRODIE, J. *The Alphabet Explained*, Edinburgh, 1840
BRÜCKE, E. *Grundzüge der Physiologie und Systematik der Sprachlaute
  für Linguisten und Taubstummenlehrer* (2nd ed.) Vienna, 1876
BÜHLER, K. *The Mental Development of the Child* (translated by Oscar
  Oeser from the fifth German edition), London, 1930
– *Sprachtheorie*, Jena, 1934
BULWER, J. *Philocophus: or the Deafe and Dumbe Mans Friend*, London,
  1648
BUSNEL, R. G., MOLES, A. and VALLANCIEN, B. 'Sur l'aspect
  phonétique d'une langue sifflée des Pyrénées françaises' in *Proc. 4th.
  Int. Congr. Ph. Sc.* (1962) 533–46
CARPENTER, T. *The Scholar's Orthographical and Orthoëpical Assistant*,
  London, 1803
CARRINGTON, J. F. *Talking Drums of Africa*, London, 1949
CARRUTHERS, S. W. *A Contribution to the Mechanism of Articulate
  Speech*, Edinburgh, 1900
CATFORD, J. C. 'On the classification of stop consonants' in *mf* 1939 2–5
– 'The Kabardian language' in *mf* 1942 15–18
– 'Phonation types: the classification of some laryngeal components of
  speech production' in *In Honour of Daniel Jones*, London, 1964
CHANG, NIEN-CHUANG T. 'Tones and intonation in the Chengtu
  dialect' in *Phonetica*, 2 (1958) 59–85
CHAO, Y. R. 'Singing in Chinese' in *mf* 1924 9–10
– 'The non-uniqueness of phonemic solutions of phonetic systems' in
  *Bulletin of the National Research Institute of History and Philology of
  the Academia Sinica*, 4 (1933) 363–97

CHAVES, MERCEDES V. A. P. DE *Problemas de fonetica experimental*, La Plata, 1948

CHIBA, T. *A Study of Accent*, Tokyo, 1935

– and KAJIYAMA, M. *The Vowel: its Nature and Structure*, Tokyo, 1941

CHINEBUAH, I. K. *A Phonetic and Phonological Study of the Nominal Piece in Nzema*. (Unpublished M.A. thesis, London University) 1962

CLASSE, A. *The Rhythm of English Prose*, Oxford, 1939

– *Handbook of French Pronunciation*, London, 1942

– 'Phonetics of the silbo Gomero' in *Archivum Linguisticum*, 9 (1957) 44–61

COLEMAN, H. O. 'Intonation and emphasis' in *Miscellanea Phonetica*, 1 (1914) Bourg-la-Reine and London

CONKLIN, H. C. 'Preliminary report on field work on the islands of Mindoro and Palawan, Philippines' in *American Anthropologist*, 51 (1949) 268–73

COSERIU, E. *Forma y sustancia en los sonidos del lenguaje*, Montevideo, 1954

COUSTENOBLE, H. N. *La phonétique du Provençal moderne*, Hertford, 1945

– and ARMSTRONG, L. E. *Studies in French Intonation*, Cambridge, 1934

COWAN, G. M. 'Mazateco whistle speech' in *Language*, 24 (1948) 280–6

COWAN, M. M. and DAVIS, M. E. *Hymn Writing in Aboriginal Languages*, Summer Institute of Linguistics, 1955

CRÉPIEUX-JAMIN, J. *The Psychology of the Movements of Handwriting* (Translated and arranged by L. K. Given-Wilson) London, 1926

CRICHTON-MILLER, H. 'A note on the psychic factor in stammering' in *Speech*, 1 (1936) 42–4

CURRY, R. *The Mechanism of the Human Voice*, London, 1940

DALGARNO, G. *Didascalocophus: or the Deaf and Dumb Man's Tutor*, Oxford, 1680. Reprinted in *The Works of George Dalgarno*

– *The Works of George Dalgarno of Aberdeen*, Edinburgh, 1834

DANEŠ, F. 'Sentence intonation from a functional point of view' in *Word*, 16 (1960) 34–54

DARBISHIRE, H. D. *Relliquiae Philologicae* (ed. R. S. Conway) Cambridge, 1895

DARLINGTON, C. D. 'The genetic component of language' in *Heredity*, 1 (1947) 269–86

– and MATHER, K. *The Elements of Genetics*, London, 1949

DENES, P. B. and PINSON, E. N. *The Speech Chain*, Baltimore, 1963

DOKE, C. M. *A Comparative Study in Shona Phonetics*, Johannesburg, 1931

DOOB, L. W. *Communication in Africa*, New Haven and London, 1961

DOWNEY, JUNE E. *Creative Imagination*, London, 1929

DRAPER, M. H., LADEFOGED, P. and WHITTERIDGE, D. 'Respiratory muscles in speech' in *Journal of Speech and Hearing Research*, 2 (1959) 16–27

DUMVILLE, B. *The Science of Speech*, London, 1909 (2nd ed. 1926)

DUPONCEAU, P. S. 'English phonology; or an essay towards an analysis and description of the component sounds of the English language' in *Transactions of the American Philosophical Society*, 1 (New Series) (1818) 228–46

EDMONDS, G. *The Philosophic Alphabet*, London, 1832

ELLIS, A. J. *The Alphabet of Nature*, Bath, 1845

– *The Essentials of Phonetics*, London, 1848

– *Pronunciation for Singers*, London, 1877

– *Speech in Song*, London and New York, 1878

EWING, I. R. *Lipreading and Hearing Aids*, Manchester, 1944

EWING, I. R. and EWING, A. W. G. *Speech and the Deaf Child*, Manchester, 1954

FANT, G. *Acoustic Theory of Speech Production*, The Hague, 1960

FAURE, G. *Recherches sur les caractères et le rôle des éléments musicaux dans la prononciation anglaise*, Paris, 1962

FIRTH, J. R. *Speech*, London, 1930. Reprinted in *The Tongues of Men and Speech*, 1964

– 'The use and distribution of certain English sounds' in *English Studies*, 17 (1935) 2–12. Reprinted in *Papers in Linguistics*

– *The Tongues of Men*, London, 1937. Reprinted in *The Tongues of Men and Speech*, 1964

– 'Phonological features of some Indian languages' in *Proc. 2nd Int. Congr. Ph. Sc.* (1936). Reprinted in *Papers in Linguistics*

– 'Modes of Meaning' in *Essays and Studies 1951* (The English Association) 118–49. Reprinted in *Papers in Linguistics*

– *Papers in Linguistics 1934–51*, London, 1957

– *The Tongues of Men and Speech*, London, 1964

FISCHER-JØRGENSEN, E. 'On the definition of phoneme categories on a distributional basis' in *Acta Linguistica*, 7 (1952) 8–39

FLETCHER, H. *Speech and Hearing in Communication*, New York, 1953

FORCHHAMMER, J. *Die Grundlage der Phonetik*, Heidelberg, 1924

– *Allgemeine Sprechkunde*, Heidelberg, 1951

FOUCHÉ, P. *Etudes de phonétique générale*, Paris, 1927

FUHRKEN, G. E. *Standard English Speech*, Cambridge, 1932

FU, YI-CHIN *The Phonemic Structure of English Words*, Taipei, Taiwan, 1963

GARVIN, P. L. 'Wichita I: phonemics' in *IJAL*, 16 (1950) 179–84

GELB, I. J. *A Study of Writing*, London, 1952. 2nd (revised) ed. University of Chicago Press, 1963

GIBSON, LORNA F. 'Pame (Otomi) Phonemics and Morphophonemics' in *IJAL*, 22 (1956) 242–65

GILL, ERIC *An Essay on Typography* (2nd ed.) London, 1936

GIMSON, A. C. *An Introduction to the Pronunciation of English*, London, 1962

GLEASON, H. A., Jr *An Introduction to Descriptive Linguistics*, New York, 1955 (2nd ed. 1961)

– Book review in *Language*, 37 (1961) 294–308

GOLDMAN-EISLER, FRIEDA 'Hesitation, information, and levels of speech production' in Reuck and O'Connor (eds) *Disorders of Language*, London, 1964

GRAMMONT, M. *Traité de phonétique*, Paris, 1933

GRANDGENT, C. H. *German and English Sounds*, Boston, 1892

GRAY, G. W. and WISE, C. M. *The Bases of Speech*, New York, 1934

GREEN, P. S. *Consonant-Vowel Transitions*, Lund, 1959

GRIFFITH, C. L. T. 'The "isolation" of the ratios of musical intervals' in *Psyche*, 13 (1933) 25–7

GUEST, E. *A History of English Rhythms* (in 2 vols) London, 1838. 2nd ed., ed. W. W. Skeat, London, 1882

GRAY, NICOLETE *Lettering on Buildings*, London, 1960

HADDING-KOCH, K. *Acoustico-Phonetic Studies in the Intonation of Southern Swedish*, Lund, 1961

HADEN, E. F. *The Physiology of French Consonant Changes*, Baltimore, 1938

HALLIDAY, M. A. K. 'Categories of the theory of grammar' in *Word*, 17 (1961) 241–92

– 'The tones of English' in *Archivum Linguisticum*, 15 (1963) 1–28

– 'Intonation in English grammar' in *TPS 1963* (1964) 143–69

– McINTOSH, A. and STREVENS, P. *The Linguistic Sciences and Language Teaching*, London, 1964

HAMP, E. P. *A Glossary of American Technical Linguistic Usage 1925–1950*, Utrecht and Antwerp, 1957

HARRIS, Z. S. *Structural Linguistics*, 1951. (Originally entitled *Methods in Structural Linguistics*)

HARTOG, Sir P. *On the Relation of Poetry to Verse* (English Association Pamphlet No. 64) London, 1926

HAUGEN, E. 'The syllable in linguistic description' in *For Roman Jakobson* (1956) 213–21

HEEPE, M. *Lautzeichen und ihre Anwendung in verschiedenen Sprachgebieten*, Berlin, 1928

HEFFNER, R.-M. S. *General Phonetics*, University of Wisconsin Press, 1949

HELMHOLTZ, H. L. F. *On the Sensations of Tone* (translated by A. J. Ellis) (2nd ed.) 1885; reprinted, New York, 1954

HENDERSON, EUGÉNIE J. A. 'The main features of Cambodian pronunciation' in *BSOAS*, 14 (1952) 149–74

HERZOG, G. 'Drum signalling in a West African tribe' in *Word*, 1 (1945) 217–38

HILL, T. 'Institutional Linguistics' in *Orbis*, 7 (1958) 441–55

HJELMSLEV, L. 'Structural analysis of language' in *Studia Linguistica*, 1 (1947) 69–78

– *Prolegomena to a Theory of Language* (translated by Francis J. Whitfield) Baltimore, 1953. 2nd ed., Madison, Wisconsin, 1961

– *Essais linguistiques*, Copenhagen, 1959

HOCKETT, C. F. Review of J. de Francis, *Nationalism and Language Reform in China* in *Language*, 27 (1951) 439–45

HOCKETT, C. F. *A Manual of Phonology*, Baltimore, 1955
– *A Course in Modern Linguistics*, New York, 1958
HODGSON, K. W. *The Deaf and their Problems*, London, 1953
HOLDER, W. *Elements of Speech*, London, 1669
HOLDSWORTH, W. and ALDRIDGE, W. *Natural Short-hand*, London, 1766
HONIKMAN, BEATRICE 'Articulatory Settings' in *In Honour of Daniel Jones*, London, 1964
HULTZÉN, L. S. 'Information points in intonation' in *Phonetica*, 4 (1959) 107–20
INTERNATIONAL PHONETIC ASSOCIATION. *Exposé des principes de l'Association Phonétique Internationale*, Bourg-la-Reine, 1900
– *Aim and Principles of the International Phonetic Association*, Bourg-la-Reine, 1904
– *The Principles of the International Phonetic Association*, Bourg-la-Reine and London, 1912. 2nd ed., London, 1949
– *L'Ecriture phonétique internationale*, Liéfra and London, 1921
JACOBS, A. *A New Dictionary of Music*, Harmondsworth, 1958
JAIN, B. D. and JONES, S. 'Musical accent and whisper' in *BSOS*, 4 (1926–8) 213–15
JAKOBSON, R., FANT, C. G. M. and HALLE, M. *Preliminaries to Speech Analysis*, Cambridge, Mass., 1952
JAKOBSON, R. and HALLE, M. *Fundamentals of Language*, The Hague, 1956
JASSEM, W. *Intonation of Conversational English*, Wroclaw, 1952
JENKINS, G. N. *The Physiology of the Mouth*, Oxford, 1954
JENSEN, M. K. 'Recognition of word tones in whispered speech' in *Word* 14 (1958) 187–96
JESPERSEN, O. *The Articulations of Speech Sounds*, Marburg, 1889
– *Phonetische Grundfragen*, Leipzig and Berlin, 1904
– *A Modern English Grammar*. Part I: *Sounds and Spellings*, Heidelberg, 1909
– 'Symbolic value of the vowel I' in *Philologica* 1 (1922). Reprinted in *Linguistica*
– *Lehrbuch der Phonetik*, Leipzig and Berlin, 1913
– *Linguistica: selected papers in English, French and German*, Copenhagen and London, 1933
JONES, D. *The Pronunciation of English*, Cambridge, 1909. 3rd ed. 1950; 4th ed. 1956
– *An English Pronouncing Dictionary*, London, 1917. 4th ed. 1937; 11th ed. 1956
– *Outline of English Phonetics*, Leipzig and Berlin, 1918. 2nd ed. 1922; 3rd ed., Cambridge, 1932; 8th ed. 1956
– *The Tones of Sechuana Nouns*, London, 1928
– *The Phoneme: its Nature and Use*, Cambridge, 1950
– and CAMILLI, A. *Fondamenti di Grafia Fonetica*, Liéfra and London, 1933
– and DAHL, I. *Fundamentos de Escritura Fonética*, London, 1944

184 *List of Works Consulted*

JONES, S. 'Radiography and pronunciation' in *British Journal of Radiology*, 2 (New Series) (1929) 149, 150
- 'The accent in French – what is accent?' in *Le Maître Phonétique* (1932) 74, 75
JOOS, M. *Acoustic Phonetics*, Baltimore, 1948
KAISER, L. (ed.) *Manual of Phonetics*, Amsterdam, 1957
KANTNER, C. E. and WEST, R. *Phonetics*, New York, 1933
KINGDON, R. *The Groundwork of English Intonation*, London, 1958
KLAUSNER, S. Z. 'Phonetics, personality and status in Israel' in *Word*, 11 (1955) 209–16
KRUISINGA, E. *The Phonetic Structure of English Words*, Bern, 1943
LADEFOGED, P. 'The classification of vowels' in *Lingua*, 5 (1956) 113–28
- 'The nature of vowel quality' in *Revista do Laboratório de Fonetica Experimental, Coimbra*, 5 (1960) 73–162
- 'The value of phonetic statements' in *Language*, 36 (1960) 387–96
- *Elements of Acoustic Phonetics*, Edinburgh, 1962
- *A Phonetic Study of West African Languages*, Cambridge, 1964
- DRAPER, M. H. and WHITTERIDGE, D. 'Syllables and stress' in *Miscellanea Phonetica*, III London, 1958
LAVER, J. D. M. H. 'Variability in vowel perception' in *Language and Speech*, 8 (1965) 95–121
LINDSLEY, C. F. 'The psycho-physical determinants of voice quality' in *Speech Monographs* 1 (1934) 79–116
LLOYD JAMES, A. *Speech Signals in Telephony*, London, 1940
- *Historical Introduction to French Phonetics*, London, 1929
- *The Broadcast Word*, London, 1935
LLOYD, R. J. *Northern English*, Leipzig, 1899
LUNDELL, J. A. 'The Swedish dialect alphabet' in *Studia Neophilologica* 1 (1928) 1–17
MACDONALD, MARGARET 'C. S. Peirce on language' in *Psyche*, 15 (1935) 108–28
MACLAY, H. and OSGOOD, C. E. 'Hesitation phenomena in spontaneous English speech' in *Word*, 15 (1959) 19–44
MALMBERG, B. *La phonétique*, Paris, 1962. (English translation, *Phonetics*, New York, 1963)
MARTINET, A. *Phonology as Functional Phonetics*, London, 1949
MENZERATH, P. *Der Diphthong*, Bonn and Berlin, 1941
- and LACERDA, A. DE *Koartikulation, Steuerung und Lautabgrenzung*, Berlin and Bonn, 1933
MERKEL, C. L. *Physiologie der menschlichen Sprache (physiologische Laletik)*, Leipzig, 1866
MEYER, E. A. *Englische Lautdauer*, Uppsala, 1903
VON MEYER, G. H. *The Organs of Speech and their application in the Formation of Articulate Sounds*, London, 1883
MILLER, J. D. 'Word tone recognition in Vietnamese whispered speech' in *Word* 17 (1961) 11–15
MOL, H. *Fundamentals of Phonetics*, The Hague, 1963

MOTT, F. W. *The Brain and the Voice in Speech and Song*, London and New York, 1910

NAISH, C. M. *A Syntactic Study of Tlingit*. (Unpublished M.A. thesis, London University) 1966

NARES, R. *Elements of Orthoepy*, London, 1784

NEGUS, Sir VICTOR E. *The Mechanism of the Larynx*, London, 1929
– *The Comparative Anatomy and Physiology of the Larynx*, London, 1949
– and JONES, S. 'Voice' in *Encyclopedia Britannica* (14th and subsequent editions) 1929

NKETIA, J. H. K. *African Music in Ghana*, Accra, 1962

NOËL-ARMFIELD, G. *General Phonetics*, Cambridge, 1915. 3rd ed. 1924; 4th ed. 1931

OGDEN, C. K. 'Sound, sense, and intelligibility' in *Psyche*, 15 (1935) 19–76

O'GRADY, H. *Class-room Phonetics*, London, 1915.

ORR, J. 'On some sound values in English' in *British Journal of Psychology*, 25 (1944) 1–8. (Reprinted in *Words and Sounds in English and French*)
– *Words and Sounds in English and French*, Oxford, 1953

PAGET, Sir RICHARD. *Human Speech*, London, 1930

PALMER, H. E. *English Intonation with Systematic Exercises*, Cambridge, 1922
– *Concerning Pronunciation*, Tokyo, 1928

PANCONCELLI-CALZIA, G. *Einführung in die angewandte Phonetik*, Berlin, 1914
– *Die experimentelle Phonetik in ihre Anwendung auf die Sprachwissenschaft*, (2nd ed.) Berlin, 1924
– *Das AlsOb in der Phonetik*, Hamburg, 1947
– *Phonetik als Naturwissenschaft*, Berlin, 1948

PASSY, P. *Etude sur les changements phonétiques*, Paris, 1890
– *Petite phonétique comparée*, Leipzig, 1906

PAUL, H. *Principles of the History of Language*, London, 1891 (translated by H. A. Strong)

PEAR, T. H. *Voice and Personality*, London, 1931
– *The Psychology of Effective Speaking*, London, 1933
– *Personality, Appearance and Speech*, London, 1957

PEARSON, H. *Dr. Darwin*, London, 1930

PEDERSEN, H. *Linguistic Science in the Nineteenth Century*, Harvard University Press, 1931 (translated by J. W. Spargo. Re-issued under the title *The Discovery of Language*, Bloomington, Indiana, 1962.)

PEIRCE, C. S. *The Philosophy of Peirce: Selected Writings* (ed. J. Buchler) London, 1940

PEREIRA, H. S. and JONES, D. *A Colloquial Sinhalese Reader*, Manchester, 1919

PERRETT, W. *Some Questions of Phonetic Theory*, Part I, Chs. I–IV, London, 1916; Ch. V, Cambridge, 1919; Ch. VI, Cambridge, 1923; Ch. VIA, Cambridge, 1924

PICKETT, J. M. 'Tactual communication of speech sounds to the deaf: comparison with lip-reading' in *Journal of Speech and Hearing Disorders*, 28 (1963) 315–30

– and PICKETT, B. H. 'Communication of speech sounds by a tactual vocoder' in *Journal of Speech and Hearing Research*, 6 (1963) 207–22

PIKE, K. L. *Phonetics: a critical analysis of phonetic theory and a technic for the practical description of sounds*, Ann Arbor, 1943

– *The Intonation of American English*, Ann Arbor, 1946

– *Phonemics*, Ann Arbor, 1947

– *Tone Languages*, Ann Arbor, 1948

– *Language in Relation to a Unified Theory of the Structure of Human Behavior*, Glendale, California, Part I, 1954; Part II, 1955; Part III, 1960

PITTENGER, R. E., HOCKETT, C. F. and DANEHY, J. J. *The First Five Minutes: A Sample of Miscroscopic Interview Analysis*, New York, 1960

POLE, W. *The Philosophy of Music*, London, 1879

POTTER, R. K., KOPP, G. A. and GREEN, H. C. *Visible Speech*, York, 1947

Proceedings of the International Congress of Phonetic Sciences, The Hague, 1933

Proceedings of the Second International Congress of Phonetic Sciences, Cambridge, 1936

Proceedings of the Third International Congress of Phonetic Sciences, Ghent, 1939

Proceedings of the Fourth International Congress of Phonetic Sciences, The Hague, 1962

RAUDNITZKY, H. *Die Bell-Sweetsche Schule*, Marburg, 1911

PULGRAM, E. *Introduction to the Spectrography of Speech*, The Hague, 1959

REUCK, A. V. S. DE and O'CONNOR, MAEVE (eds.) *Disorders of Language*, London, 1964

RICHARDS, I. A. *The Philosophy of Rhetoric*, New York and London, 1936

RIPMAN, W. *Good Speech*, London, 1922

ROBINSON, R. *The Art of Pronunciation*, London, 1617

– *The Phonetic Writings of Robert Robinson* (ed. E. J. Dobson) London, 1957

ROBINSON, H. W. and ADAMS, W. *The Diary of Robert Hooke 1672–1680*, London, 1935

ROMAN, K. G. *Handwriting: A Key to Personality*, New York, 1952

ROUSSELOT, P.-J. *Principes de phonétique expérimentale*, Paris, 1901–8. (New ed., Paris, 1924–5)

ROWLANDS, E. C. 'Tone and intonation systems in Brass-Nembe Ijaw' in *African Language Studies*, 1 (1960) 137–54

RUSSELL, G. O. *The Vowel*, Columbus, Ohio, 1928

– *Speech and Voice*, New York, 1931

SAPIR, E. *Language: an Introduction to the Study of Speech*, New York, 1921

– 'Speech as a personality trait' in *American Journal of Sociology* 32 (1927) 892–905. Reprinted in *Selected Writings*

– 'A study in phonetic symbolism' in *Journal of Experimental Psychology* 12 (1929) 225–39. Reprinted in *Selected Writings*

– *Selected Writings of Edward Sapir in Language, Culture, and Personality* (ed. D. G. Mandelbaum) Berkeley and Los Angeles, 1949

– *Culture, Language and Personality*. Selected essays (ed. D. G. Mandelbaum) Berkeley and Los Angeles, 1956. Revised edition 1960

SAUSSURE, F. DE *Cours de linguistique générale*, Paris, 1916. 2nd ed. 1922

– *Course in General Linguistics*, New York, 1959. Translated by Wade Baskin

SCHUBIGER, M. *The Role of Intonation in Spoken English*, St. Gall, 1935

SHARP, A. E. 'A tonal analysis of the disyllabic noun in the Machame dialect of Chaga' in *BSOAS* 16 (1954) 157–69

– 'Stress and juncture in English' in *TPS 1960* (1961) 104–35

SHERRINGTON, Sir CHARLES. *Man on His Nature*, Cambridge University Press (2nd ed.) 1951

SIEVERS, E. *Grundzüge der Lautphysiologie*, Leipzig, 1876. (Later editions entitled *Grundzüge der Phonetik*)

SINCLAIR, A. *The Conditions of Knowing*, London, 1951

SPENCER, R. F. 'The phonemes of Keresan' in *IJAL*, 12 (1946) 229–36

STANFORD, W. BEDELL. *Greek Metaphor*, Oxford, 1936

STETSON, R. H. 'Mechanism of the different types of movement' in *Psychological Monographs* 32 (1923) 18–40

– *Motor Phonetics* (vol. III of Archives neérlandaises de phonétique expérimentale) The Hague, 1928. 2nd ed. Amsterdam, 1951

– *Bases of Phonology*, Oberlin, Ohio, 1945

STEVENSON, R. S. and GUTHRIE, D. *A History of Oto-Laryngology*, Edinburgh, 1949

STORY, G. L. *A Morphological Study of Tlingit*. (Unpublished M.A. thesis, London University) 1966

STRYPE, J. *Life of the Learned Sir John Cheke, Kt.*, 1705

SWEET, H. *A History of English Sounds*, London, 1874. 2nd ed. Oxford, 1888

– *Primer of Phonetics*, Oxford, 1890. 2nd ed. 1902; 3rd ed. 1906

– *Handbook of Phonetics*, Oxford, 1877

– *Collected Papers of Henry Sweet* (arranged by H. C. Wyld), Oxford, 1913

TECHMER, F. *Phonetik*, Leipzig, 1880

THAUSING, M. *Das natürliche Lautsystem der menschlichen Sprache*, Leipzig, 1863

TRAGER, G. L. 'Paralanguage: a first approximation' in *Studies in Linguistics*, 13 (1958) 1–12

TRAVIS, L. E. *Speech Pathology*, New York, 1931

13*

TRUBETZKOY, N. S. *Grundzüge der Phonologie,* Prague, 1939. (Translated by J. Cantineau, *Principes de phonologie,* Paris, 1949)

TRUBY, H. M. *Acoustico-cineradiographic Analysis Considerations,* Stockholm, 1959

TUCKER, ABRAHAM (Edward Search). *Vocal Sounds,* London, 1773

TWADDELL, W. F. *On Defining the Phoneme,* Baltimore, 1935

ULDALL, E. T. 'Dimensions of meaning in intonation' in *In Honour of Daniel Jones,* London, 1964

ULDALL, H. J. *A Danish Phonetic Reader,* London, 1933

VACHEK, J. *Dictionnaire de linguistique de l'école de Prague,* Utrecht and Antwerp, 1960

VERNON, P. E. 'The ear is not enough' in *Pleasures of Music* (ed. Jacques Barzun) London, 1952

VIËTOR, W. *Elemente der Phonetik,* Leipzig, 1884

– *Elements of Phonetics* (translated and adapted by W. Ripman) London, 1905

VOGT, HANS. 'Phoneme classes and phoneme classification' in *Word,* 10 (1964) 28–34

WALSH, E. G. *Physiology of the Nervous System,* London, 1957

WARD, IDA C. *The Phonetics of English,* Cambridge, 1929. 3rd (revised) ed. 1939

– *Defects of Speech: their Nature and their Cure,* London, 1923

WELLS, R. S. 'The pitch phonemes of English' in *Language* 21 (1945) 27–39

WESTERMANN, D. and WARD, IDA C. *Practical Phonetics for Students of African Languages,* London, 1933. 2nd ed. 1949

WHORF, B. L. 'Linguistics as an exact science' in *The Technology Review* 43 (1940) 61–3, 80–3. Reprinted frequently, for example in Whorf, *Four Articles on Metalinguistics,* Washington, 1950; *Collected Papers on Metalinguistics,* Washington, 1952; *Language, Thought, and Reality,* London, 1956

– 'Phonemic analysis of the English of Eastern Massachusetts' in *SIL,* 2 (1943) 21–40

WIENER, N. *The Human Use of Human Beings,* Boston, 1950. 2nd (revised) ed. New York, 1956

WILKINS, J. *An Essay towards a Real Character and a Philosophical Language,* London, 1668

WITTING, C. *Physical and Functional Aspects of Speech Sounds,* Uppsala and Wiesbaden, 1959

WRIGHT, G. G. NEILL. *The Writing of Arabic Numerals,* London, 1952

YASUI, MINORU. *Consonant Patterning in English,* Tokyo, n.d.

ZWIRNER, E. and ZWIRNER, K. *Grundfragen der Phonometrie,* Berlin, 1936

Index

Numbers refer to pages, except that numbers preceded by the letter 'n' refer to the Notes. Thus '36n2' is to be read 'page 36, note 2'. The reader can then turn to page 36, to find the subject matter being dealt with, or to the Notes (pp. 165-77) where, under the appropriate heading ('Notes to pp. 26-49'), will be found the note itself.

Where several page numbers are given, the more important references are printed in bold type.